A Birdwatcher's Guide to Japan

Mark Brazil

KODANSHA INTERNATIONAL
in cooperation with
THE WILD BIRD SOCIETY OF JAPAN

Cover illustrations by Takashi Taniguchi
Maps by Yasunori Yoshida

Distributed in the United States by Kodansha International/USA Ltd.,
through Harper & Row, Publishers, Inc., 10 East 53rd Street, New
York, New York 10022. Published by Kodansha International Ltd., 2-
2, Otowa 1-chome, Bunkyo-ku, Tokyo 112 and Kodansha Interna-
tional/USA Ltd., 10 East 53rd Street, New York, New York 10022, in
cooperation with the Wild Bird Society of Japan, Aoyama Flower
Building, 1-1-4, Shibuya, Shibuya-ku, Tokyo 150.
LC 87-81675
ISBN 0-87011-849-8 (U.S.)
ISBN 4-7700-1349-3 (Japan)
First edition, 1987

CONTENTS

PREFACE

My first introduction to Japan took place in early 1980, when I spent more than a month traveling in Hokkaido and northern Honshu doing research into the behavior and ecology of the Whooper Swan. During that visit I became increasingly fascinated by the people, the culture, and the birds of Japan. I returned again in early 1982, and since I intended to stay only a short time, I traveled extensively, seeing as much as I could of the birds and the country.

When I first arrived in Japan, not only was there no proper English-language field guide, but there was no information about where to find the birds I hoped to see. The experience I gleaned in the field while traveling the length and breadth of Japan to study birds during a stay that lengthened from months into more than five years has been all the more memorable for the effort I expended.

As my interest in the Japanese avifauna began to focus on several little-known and rare species, I decided I had to move either to the extreme north or the extreme south. I had made several visits to Hokkaido in 1982, and finally decided to move there. As a result, I was able to spend much of the next three years studying sea eagles and fish owls, with regular sorties south to Okinawa for studies of the Okinawa Rail, and elsewhere in search of the breeding birds of Japan.

Travel, from Soya Misaki, the northernmost cape of Hokkaido, to Nakanokamishima, a tiny island in the southern Nansei Shoto, and from sea level to the top of Fuji-san, at 3,776 m Japan's highest peak, and personal contact with other researchers led to many marvellous opportunities that stand out in my memory: finding Masked Booby, Red-tailed Tropicbird, and Bulwer's Petrel chicks on Nakanokamishima; chasing Rhinoceros Auklet in the dark with nets on poles to catch and ring them, while listening to the calls of Leach's Petrel on Moyururijima, off southeast Hokkaido; standing in deep snow on the creaking ice of a frozen river to study fish owls; hiking in the Japanese Alps to watch ptarmigan; spending weeks at the ice-bound mouth of the Sashiruigawa on Shiretoko Hanto, with Steller's Sea Eagle all around, then afterwards soaking in an outdoor hot spring; mapping the distribution of Okinawa Rail in the subtropical forests of Okinawa at night with fruit bats circling my recorder; standing at the rail of the northbound ferry with albatrosses, dolphins, and fur seals off the bows; encountering Brown Bear and Wild Boar, Racoon Dog and Japanese Serow; watching eagles and foxes fighting over fish among a dancing flock of Japanese Crane; the huge flocks of geese at dawn at Izu-numa; the cranes in Kyushu; and the phenomenal falls of migrants on Hegurajima.

As a resident birdwatcher and research ornithologist in Japan, I have received a steady flow of requests for information about animals and birds. In attempting to answer these I first wrote fact sheets about various areas. Then in 1983, with the publication of *Finding Birds in Japan: The Tokyo Area*, I started to describe all the best places I had visited and how to find the Japanese birds that visiting birdwatchers most wanted to see. This was followed in 1985 by *Finding Birds in Japan: Honshu*, and finally here is a guide to the whole of Japan.

My aim in writing this book has been to provide the basic information that I wish had been available when I first arrived. I hope that by using it to visit a few of my favorite places the reader will experience some of the immense pleasure and satisfaction I have gained from the birds and wildlife of Japan.

Acknowledgments

I am greatly indebted to the Oba family of Zushi who looked after me so kindly when I first came to Japan, and to the many Japanese bird-watchers I have met during my travels who have generously provided hints on where to go and what to see and, on occasion, have provided food, transport, accommodation, and even all three. Of those with whom I have enjoyed sharing time in the field or who have kindly answered correspondence and supplied information, I thank: Donald Bradshaw, Chris Cook, Hideo Doi, Masayuki Egawa, Yoshiaki Ijima, Dr. Ryozo Kakizawa, Masahiko Kaneshiro, Peter Kennerley, Hiroyoshi Kohno, Nobumichi Kurosawa, Osamu Kurosawa, Dr. Hiroyuki Masatomi, David Melville, John and Misa Nedderman, Akiko Oba, Nariko Oka, Mariko Otsu, Kiyoaki Ozaki, Michael Poulsen, Tadashi Shimada, the late Shinji Takano, Mamoru Tsuneda, Dr. Keisuke Ueda, Dr. David Waugh, John Williams, Dr. Masashi Yoshii, Masayuki Yabuuchi, and Noboru Yoshizato. For their enthusiasm, kindness, and many long hours spent discussing Japanese birds, I thank Dr. Hiroyoshi Higuchi, Hiroshi Ikenaga, Ichiro Kikuta, Masayuki Kurechi, Dr. Hiroyuki Morioka, Tsutomu Suzuki, Masaru Takada, and Sumio Yamamoto. In writing various sections of this book I have drawn on their knowledge and experience, and on the knowledge of others, both in Japan and further afield. I am extremely grateful to: Dr. Dennis Brazil, Chris Cook, Paul Hale, Susanne Holschuh, and Koichiro Sonobe, who all read and helped to improve the manuscript; Mark Beaman, who gave useful comments on the introduction; Douglas McWhirter and Hiroshi Ikenaga for checking the Kyushu and Okinawa sections; Dr. Yuzo Fujimaki, Marie-Jo Ikawa, Tsuneo Hayashida, Momoki Kawabe, and Hideaki Anzai for advice on the Hokkaido section; Masayuki Kurechi for help with sites in Tohoku; and Phoebe Snetsinger for advice on the checklist. Their aid has been invaluable and has speeded completion of this book. My thanks also to Jules Young and Nobuhiro Katakura of Kodansha International, and to Takashi Taniguchi for the paintings on the cover.

The Wild Bird Society of Japan has been extremely kind and helpful, and in particular I would like to thank Shinichi Hanawa, Noritaka Ichida, Koichiro Sonobe, and Yuzo Tsukamoto for finding the time to answer my many requests for information. Last but certainly not least, I thank my friend Masaru Takada for teaching me so much about the fascinating natural history of his homeland and, with his wife, for making me so welcome on so many occasions in their home in east Hokkaido, my favorite part of Japan.

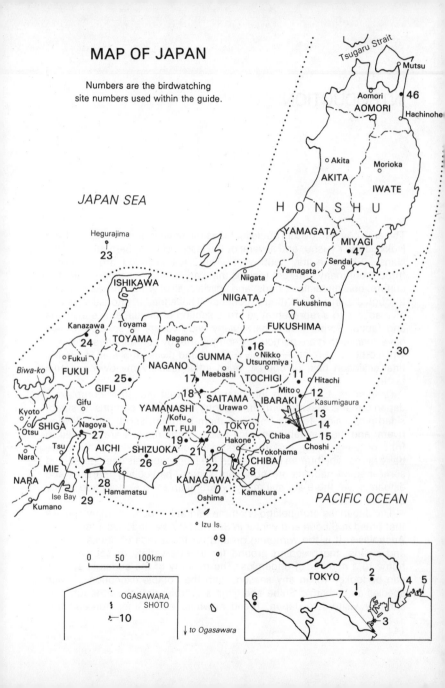

MAP OF JAPAN

Numbers are the birdwatching
site numbers used within the guide.

Tsugaru Strait

Mutsu

Aomori • 46
AOMORI Hachinohe

JAPAN SEA

○ Akita Morioka ○
AKITA **IWATE**

H O N S H U

YAMAGATA
MIYAGI
• 47
Sendai ○
Hegurajima
23

Niigata ○ Yamagata ○

ISHIKAWA **NIIGATA**
Fukushima ○
FUKUSHIMA

Kanazawa Toyama ○ Nagano ○
24 **TOYAMA**
○ Fukui **NAGANO** **GUNMA** • 16
Nikko **30**
FUKUI Utsunomiya ○
Biwa-ko **25** Maebashi ○ 11
GIFU **17** **TOCHIGI** • Hitachi
Kyoto ○ Gifu ○ **18** Mito ○ 12
Otsu ○ **YAMANASHI** **SAITAMA** **IBARAKI** Kasumigaura
SHIGA Nagoya ○ Kofu ○ Urawa ○ 13
Nara ○ **27** **MT. FUJI** **20** **TOKYO** 14
AICHI **19** Chiba ○ 15
MIE **SHIZUOKA** **21** Hakone Choshi
NARA **26** **22** Yokohama
28 **KANAGAWA** **CHIBA**
Ise Bay Hamamatsu **8**
Kumano **29** Kamakura
Oshima *PACIFIC OCEAN*

○ Izu Is.

9

○

0   50   100km

**OGASAWARA
SHOTO**

10

↓ *to Ogasawara*

TOKYO • 2
• 4 • 5
• 1 • 3
• 6 • 7

INTRODUCTION

The area covered by this guide includes the main islands of Japan, from Hokkaido to Kyushu, and several of the lesser islands, particularly in the Nansei Shoto in the southwest. The sites included are scattered throughout many different regions that vary greatly in scenery, climate, culture, cuisine, dialect, birds, and animals, all of which makes traveling through Japan a fascinating experience. I have tried to choose sites that give access to a representative cross-section of the Japanese avifauna and fauna. Some have a particularly wide variety of species; others have species that are particularly sought after by non-Japanese visitors; while others are relatively easily reached and pleasant places to go. My final selection has, of course, been influenced by my own personal taste.

Despite its 120 million inhabitants and vast industrial complexes, Japan remains essentially a rural country, its scenery comprising steep-sided mountains, forests (many of them planted), short, swift-flowing rivers, and the inevitable tiny rice fields. Some regions are devoted to fruit- or tea-growing, and in others, particularly in Hokkaido, there are dairy farms. The human influence on the landscape has been great, and some natural habitats are now very scarce, particularly marshes and estuaries, yet there are still many beautiful areas to explore and plenty of birds to see.

The Japanese archipelago is on the migration route of many species that breed in Siberia and winter in Southeast Asia, Indonesia, and even Australasia. It is the wintering ground for thousands of ducks, geese, and swans, the breeding ground for a wide variety of species, and home to a number of endemics. The majority of the endemic species can be looked for in any season, with the notable exception of such species as Latham's Snipe and Ijima's Warbler, which, although only summer visitors to Japan, breed nowhere else. Other non-endemic

Japanese specialities such as the cranes and eagles are restricted both in range and season. Japan is an extremely challenging country for bird-watchers, who can see more than 300 species a year here—I once saw 330—making it roughly comparable to the British Isles.

The long string of islands of which Japan consists is conducive to the evolution not only of endemic species but also of distinct subspecies. The variety is fascinating: chestnut-headed Eurasian Jay and white-headed Long-tailed Tit in Hokkaido, large chestnut-cheeked Varied Tit in the Izu Islands, gray Great Tit and small Jungle Crow in the Nansei Shoto, and so on, making even familiar Palearctic species interesting. And if one tires of land birds, numerous commercial ferries along both the Japan Sea and Pacific coasts, connecting the various islands, put pelagic birds in easy reach.

Japan has six well-defined seasons, but because of the length of the archipelago and because many of the islands are far apart, wide variations in weather occur in different regions at the same season, with obvious consequences for the fauna and avifauna, and for the contents of a birdwatcher's luggage.

It is impossible to see everything in any single season and without considerable outlay, for the distances to be covered are great; it is more than 3,500 km from the southwestern extremity of the Nansei Shoto to the northern tip of Hokkaido, and to see a good cross-section of Japanese birds it is necessary to travel almost the whole distance during both winter and summer. The migration seasons are perhaps rather too prolonged to plan a visit around, although certain sites for observing the autumn raptor migration and the small islands in the Japan Sea where many interesting passerines occur are extremely interesting and still relatively poorly known, providing a good opportunity for adding rarities to the Japanese list. For the resident birder islands such as Yonagunijima, Tsushima, Hegurajima, and Awashima exert a compelling attraction, and there are great opportunities to search out headlands and capes where migrants might make landfall or to frequent the few remaining mud flats in the hope of finding the rarest of the migrant waders, Spoon-billed Sandpiper, Asian Dowitcher, and Nordmann's Greenshank. For the visiting birder, however, mid-winter and late-spring to early summer are the best seasons.

Certain winter specialties arrive late (in November or December) and leave early (in February or March). These include both Hooded and White-naped Crane in Kyushu, and Baikal Teal in Honshu. Steller's Sea Eagle also arrive late, but a few stay in Hokkaido into April, and occasionally an immature bird may summer there. Clearly these are some of the more sought-after winter species and a winter trip should be planned around them. Visitors to Kyushu in March have been lucky enough to find cranes, but a visit starting then is really too late since several species could be missed, yet it is far too early for the majority of the summer visitors, especially the more interesting flycatchers and *Locustella* warblers.

An earlier start, in January or February, is preferable. January is the month to guarantee the presence of Baikal Teal (although these are now becoming rare). February is the peak time for eagles in Hokkaido, and the beginning of March sees the return migration of the southern cranes (the Japanese Crane can be seen in any month in Hokkaido). A visit of three to four weeks starting in late January or early February is ideal. Those with plenty of time might contemplate leaving Japan for Taiwan or elsewhere in Southeast Asia before returning for the summer birds in late May or June. Visitors to Japan at any season should plan to visit east Hokkaido, central Honshu, the Izu Islands, Kyushu, and the Nansei Shoto at the very least if they hope to find a good cross-section of Japanese birds.

The English bird names used here have been chosen for standardization with the forthcoming "Avifauna of Japan" and new edition of the field guide, and are based on a number of sources, particularly my own *Checklist* (second edition), *Birds of the World: A Checklist* (Clements), and *List of Recent Holarctic Bird Species* (Voous). Alternative English names are also given in the Checklist and Index. Lack of space has prevented the inclusion of complete bird lists for each locality; however, the species for which each site is notable are listed by season, and most of these should be found relatively easily; those listed as rarities include species rare for the site in question and for Japan. Do not expect any of these, but with luck you may see one or two, especially if you visit the site several times. The Index to Bird Species and Sites will enable the reader to locate sites where a particular species can be found. Wide-ranging common species, such as Black Kite, Rock Dove, Rufous Turtle Dove, Common Skylark, Barn Swallow (summer), Black-backed Wagtail, Brown-eared Bulbul, Japanese Bush Warbler, Great Tit, Japanese White-eye, Carrion and Jungle Crow, Gray Starling, Black-faced Bunting, Eurasian Tree Sparrow, and Oriental Greenfinch are omitted from the lists since these can be found at virtually all sites. It should also be remembered that birds may linger from one season to the next, but may not necessarily appear in both lists.

I recommend that, in addition to this guide, visitors should be equipped with the *Field Guide to the Birds of Japan*, a good travel guide, a train and subway map of Tokyo, a Mapple road map, a compass, a basic Japanese phrase book, and a spirit of adventure.

No matter how single-minded your pursuit of birds or other wildlife, it is impossible to escape some degree of cultural exposure, especially when visiting areas off the beaten track. For advice in such situations and for background reading to prepare for the country's unique customs and etiquette, please refer to the travel guides included in the Bibliography.

Situation and Topography

The long archipelago of Japan, lying off the east coast of the Asian continent, stretches from latitude 20°N to 45°30'N and is adjacent to the Soviet Union in the north, and Taiwan (Republic of China), the People's Republic of China, and South Korea (Republic of Korea) in the south. The four main islands are, from north to south, Hokkaido (a little smaller than Ireland), Honshu about the size of the United Kingdom, Shikoku (a little smaller than Sardinia), and Kyushu (a little larger than Taiwan). Other related island groups are the Nansei Shoto, lying in an arc between Kyushu and Taiwan; the broken string of islands including the Izu, Ogasawara, and Iwo islands, extending 1,000 km south of Tokyo into the Pacific Ocean; and the southern Kurile Islands (currently occupied by the Soviet Union), extending northeast from eastern Hokkaido.

The land area of Japan is approximately 370,000 km², of which nearly seventy-five percent is mountainous. The spine of the main island, Honshu, has several peaks over 3,000 m high, with Fuji-san (3,776 m) being the highest. As a result of the topography, most rivers are short and fast-flowing, hillsides and valleys are steep, and the major plains, such as those of Kanto and Tokachi, consist of silt deposited from the erosion of the mountains.

Climate and Seasons

As the Japanese archipelago extends through many degrees of latitude, while the north has a prevailing subarctic climate, the south is subtropical. Cold northwesterly winds in winter and warm southeasterly winds in summer make the climate both colder and hotter seasonally than other countries in similar latitudes. Japan's great length also results in there being almost two months' difference between the start of the seasons in Okinawa and in Hokkaido. Rainfall is very heavy, averaging 1,600 mm throughout the country and reaching 4,000 mm in some regions, most of it falling in the rainy and typhoon seasons.

Winter: Winter weather is characterized by a northwesterly airstream from Siberia. Extremely cold winds blow across the Japan Sea, acquiring a great deal of moisture on the way, and from December until March they bring heavy snowfalls (as much as 4 m) to the Japan Sea coast, to the western slopes of the central mountain range of Honshu, and to the north. The Pacific coastal climatic zone in the lee of the mountains, on the other hand, is characterized by an invigorating cold but dry winter climate (and rainy, humid summers). In Hokkaido snow can fall from October onward, and there is continuous snow cover from December to March or April. Sea ice reaches the north and east coasts of Hokkaido from about the end of December and stays until early March. It is especially spectacular along the Okhotsk coast, on Shiretoko Hanto, and at Nosappu Misaki. Further south winter comes later and is milder. Kyushu has little snow and the Nansei Shoto and Ogasawara none at all, but the winters in the south are cool or cold, sometimes with rain. Temperatures throughout Japan are lowest in January and February, but sub-zero temperatures occur in the hills and mountains from October/November onward. Average temperatures in winter are −10°C to 0°C in Hokkaido, 3°C to 8°C in Honshu, and 5°C to 9°C in Kyushu. Great regional variation occurs in winter, from extremely cold in the north (as low as −30°C) to hot in the south (+25°C).

Spring: Though the weather is cool at first, the first warm spring wind, or *Haru Ichiban*, usually occurs in March near Tokyo, and from then on temperatures climb steadily. Pleasant springlike weather begins in March in southern Japan, while winter weather continues in the north. Average temperatures of 10°C reach southern Kyushu in early March, central Honshu in late March to early April (after the first week of April temperatures rise and cherry blossoms bloom in central Honshu), and Hokkaido in early May, with cherry blossoms blooming there from mid-May in the west to late May or even early June in the north and east.

The Rainy Season: In early summer the Okhotsk marine air mass moves south. This cool, humid air mass causes the rainy season so characteristic of the warmer parts of Honshu and southern Japan. The movements of the rain front vary from year to year, but the rainy season, called *Tsuyu* or *Baiu*, lasts for just over a month from early June, starting in the south in the first week of June and moving steadily north, reaching northern Honshu by late June. In this season rain can be torrential and prolonged, sometimes hampering birding. It does not reach Hokkaido, however, where warm summer weather interspersed with showers is typical from June onward.

Summer: Summer is dominated by air currents from the southwestern Pacific, particularly the Bonin (subtropical) marine air mass moving north, leading to an oppressive combination of high temperatures and humidity. Summer temperatures are uniformly high throughout the country, often exceeding 30°C, though they are somewhat lower in Hokkaido (especially in the east). The weather remains fine throughout July and August, although off northern Honshu and especially the south coast of Hokkaido, where the humid southern air meets the cool oceanic surface, dense fog is frequent, especially in the mornings. Average temperatures during this season range from 20°C in Hokkaido to 27°C in Kyushu. In August thunderstorms in the late afternoon and evening are typical of mountainous regions. At first high temperatures are combined with high humidity, but then the humidity drops, and, from mid-August on, so does the temperature, coinciding with the arrival of the typhoons.

The Typhoon Season: Typhoons start in June but are more prevalent in late summer and autumn, especially in September and October, and affect the region from Okinawa to Tokyo. These tropical low pressure storms move north from the southwest Pacific near the Philippines, the Marianas, and the Ogasawara Shoto, usually tracking northeast just off the Japanese archipelago. Many of them strike the Pacific coast of Japan from Okinawa to central Honshu, bringing strong destructive winds, heavy rain, sudden flooding, and high seas. They also bring vagrants to Japan and carry many pelagic seabirds closer to land than at other times of the year.

Autumn: From September onward the air temperature and humidity decline steadily, and from mid-October on cool weather is to be expected, with typhoons and autumn rains prevailing. October is characterized by fine cool weather moving in from Siberia, accompanied by the first waves of winter bird migration, including the ducks, thrushes, and buntings that cross the Japan Sea. The autumn colors from late September in the north to early November in the south are glorious.

Natural Phenomena

Japan is prone to extremes not only of weather but also of destructive phenomena. In addition to the rainy and typhoon seasons, Japan experiences innumerable earthquakes, mostly on a small scale, and quite frequent volcanic eruptions. While the casual visitor and even the long-term resident is unlikely to be lucky enough to observe volcanic activity first-hand, it is more than likely that one or more tremors will be felt by anyone staying in central Honshu. The tell-tale sign of a minor quake is the gently swinging light cord. Larger quakes are self-evident, but if in doubt, head for the nearest strengthened part of the building, for example near a support pillar, or under a sturdy table. If you are in town, don't rush outside.

Ocean Currents

The two main currents affecting Japan are the Black.Current and the Kurile Current. The former, a warm current, sweeps northeast along the southern part of the archipelago, part of it flowing into the Japan Sea as the Tsushima Current, while the main body of water flows along the Pacific coast heading out into the North Pacific between 35° and 40°N. The Kurile Current is cold and flows south down the Pacific coast of Japan. The region where these two currents meet is rich in plankton and one of the best fishing grounds in the world, and as a consequence it has abundant seabirds and, at certain seasons, marine mammals. The Tokyo–Hokkaido ferries pass through this region.

Vegetation

The climate and topography of Japan are ideal for the development of forests, which cover nearly sixty-eight percent of the country. While sixty-two percent of forests are *reported* to be still in a natural state, the majority have in fact been modified to varying degrees. Areas of Japan still in a virgin state account for less than twenty-three percent of the land area, and most of this is in northern Honshu and Hokkaido.

The north–south extent of Japan and the various climatic zones have resulted in four main forest types: subarctic coniferous, cool-temperate broad-leaved deciduous, warm temperate evergreen, and subtropical. In addition to its latitudinal extension, Japan has an altitudinal range from sea level to 3,776 m. With decreasing temperatures at higher altitudes there is a marked transition of vegetation. Thus subarctic coniferous forests, which in Hokkaido occur in the lowlands of the east and north, occur commonly only on high mountain ranges as far south as central Honshu, and in isolated areas even further south.

Avifauna

The avifauna of the Japanese archipelago shares much with that of the adjacent islands and peninsulas, particularly Taiwan, Korea, the Kurile Islands, and Sakhalin, and it should be seen in this context. However, Japan also has many unique birds. Studies of the birds of Japan, beginning with those of Blakiston, Pryer, and Seebohm in the 1880s, have discussed the faunal and avifaunal differences between various parts of the region. Most notable of all is the separation of Hokkaido from Honshu by the Tsugaru Strait, a crucial divide through which passes the zoogeographical line now known as the Blakiston Line.

The second important division is that between the northern, or Palearctic, region and the southern, or Oriental, region. There is disagreement over the precise position of this: some favor the Watase Line between Yakushima and Amami Oshima, others the Hachiouka Line between Miyakojima and the Yaeyama Shoto. Although generally impoverished in biological terms relative to the main islands, the Nansei Shoto shows many more southern characteristics than do other areas of Japan.

Other important divisions are the Tsushima Line, separating Kyushu from Korea, the Hatta Line, separating Hokkaido from Sakhalin, and the Yamashina Lines, dividing the Kurile Islands into three regions and separating Hokkaido from Kamchatka.

The complex of Sino-Manchurian, Siberian, and Oriental elements, with the addition of several endemic species, makes the Japanese avifauna a particularly fascinating Asian cross-section. By 1974, 200 species were known to have bred in Japan, 154 in Hokkaido, 159 in Honshu, 91 in Shikoku, and 94 in Kyushu. Depending on which taxonomy one consults there are approximately 20 endemic and essentially endemic birds and at least 40 species that, given the political systems of Japan's neighbors and the restrictions on travel, can be seen more easily in Japan than anywhere else.

Sakhalin, just to the north of Hokkaido, is very similar to Siberia in its avifauna, and while Hokkaido lacks quite a number of Siberian species, it is characterized by species of northern origin and forms the southern limit of a number of northern residents, notably, White-tailed Eagle, Hazel Grouse, Japanese Crane, Blakiston's Fish Owl, Gray-headed Woodpecker, Lesser Spotted Woodpecker, Marsh Tit, and Pine Grosbeak. In addition, several summer visitors, such as Northern Hobby, Eurasian Wryneck, Sand Martin, Siberian Rubythroat, Gray's Grasshopper Warbler, and Yellow-breasted Bunting, breed only here in Japan. From the south, many more species extend as far north as Hokkaido, but do not reach Sakhalin. Thus Hokkaido also forms the northern limit of many southern species. The southern islands of the Kurile chain, including Kunashiri, Eterofu, and Uruppa (i.e., north to the first Yamashina Line), form an extension of the Hokkaido avifauna.

From Honshu south, birds fall into several different categories. First, there are several relict species, some, such as Rock Ptarmigan, as a result of climatic changes, and others, such as Japanese Crested Ibis (now extinct in the wild in Japan), as a result of human disturbance. Other species are of southern origin and have not fully adapted to cooler regions. These occur no further north than central and northern Honshu and include such species as Intermediate Egret, Greater Painted Snipe, and Japanese Woodpigeon. Many more species, including some endemic species, such as Green Pheasant, Copper Pheasant, and

Japanese Green Woodpecker, are restricted to Honshu, Shikoku, and Kyushu and do not occur in Hokkaido.

Some species of Sibero-Manchurian origin, such as Eurasian Nutcracker, have Honshu as their southern limit, while birds of Sino-Manchurian origin have a general distribution that includes Shikoku and Kyushu but not necessarily Okinawa. Some, such as Gray Starling and Eurasian Skylark, have penetrated north as far as Sakhalin. Birds in this group—occurring south as far as Kyushu but no further—are, for example, Ural Owl, Brown Dipper, and Northern Wren. In addition, certain species have ranges that include the Nansei Shoto as well as the rest of Japan but do not breed any further south, such as Japanese Pygmy Woodpecker and Narcissus Flycatcher.

The avifauna and fauna of the Nansei Shoto are of great interest and importance. Here the northern limit of the Oriental region and the southern limit of the Palearctic region meet, with elements from both regions mixing and with some unique insular endemics having evolved. Notable here are Ryukyu Robin, which ranges throughout the island chain from the Danjo Gunto islands, west of Kyushu, to the Yaeyama group; Ryukyu Scops Owl and Ryukyu Minivet, which range from Amami Oshima to Iriomotejima; Amami Woodcock, which occurs from Amami Oshima to Okinawa; Lidth's Jay and the newly described Amami Thrush, which are restricted just to Amami Oshima; and Pryer's Woodpecker and Okinawa Rail, which are restricted to the northern third of Okinawa. A number of southern species—Cinnamon Bittern, Purple Heron, Crested Serpent Eagle, Barred Buttonquail, Slaty-legged Crake, White-breasted Waterhen, Roseate and Black-naped Tern, Red-capped Green Pigeon, Pacific Swallow, and Chinese Bulbul—just reach Japan in this region.

Several other Japanese islands also have unique species. The Izu Islands boast Izu Island's Thrush and Ijima's Warbler; the Ogasawara and Iwo island groups have Bonin Petrel, Matsudaira's Petrel, and Bonin Islands Honeyeater (several other species and subspecies endemic to the Ogasawara Shoto are already extinct), and Short-tailed Albatross is known to breed only on Torishima (although breeding is now suspected on the Senkaku Islands). Japanese Murrelet and Japanese Woodpigeon are limited to islands primarily around southern Japan.

In addition to the effects of latitude and the separation of islands or island groups on distribution, the mountains of central Honshu enable some northern species, such as the Eurasian Nutcracker, to breed further south, and the warm current along the Pacific coast allows other species, such as the Eastern Reef Egret, to breed further north than might otherwise be expected. Several species are currently extending their range naturally into or within Japan (Little Swift, Red-rumped Swallow, and Forest Wagtail). Several others (Chinese Bamboo Partridge, Common Pheasant, Collared Dove, and Black-billed Magpie) have been introduced and have thrived, while many more have escaped from captivity, some of which may survive to spread, such as the Red Avadavat. Although there have been recent gains, there have also been some losses, both of species and of subspecies: the endemic Bonin Woodpigeon, Ryukyu Woodpigeon, Miyako Kingfisher, Kittlitz's Thrush, and Bonin Islands Grosbeak have all disappeared for ever.

Migration

The formation of the Japanese archipelago involved first the elevation of mountain ranges along the Asian continental coast from the middle of the Pliocene onward, the occurrence of depressions in the Japan Sea and Okhotsk Sea areas in the Tertiary period, and the formation of the Tsugaru Strait, isolating Hokkaido, and the Tsushima Strait, separating Kyushu from Korea, from the third glacial period on. Bird migration routes developed in relation to these changes along the Asian continental coastline and the elevation of mountain ranges. Initially a major route is presumed to have extended along the then Asian continental coast, eventually becoming the Kurile Islands, Hokkaido, Honshu, Kyushu, Nansei Shoto to Taiwan route. Routes along the coasts of the then newly formed Okhotsk Sea depression led to an extra route down what is now Sakhalin, while further south migration routes along the then coasts of the Japan Sea depression led to current routes from Asia to Japan via the Noto Hanto and down the eastern side of peninsular Korea into southwestern Japan and Kyushu. The formation of the East China Sea depression led to a further route extending along what is now the continental coast of the East China Sea, some birds crossing directly from Kyushu to Taiwan and missing out the Nansei Shoto.

Because of Japan's geographical position, mountainous terrain, and various climatic zones, the classification of birds into various categories is not an easy one. Although some are clearly residents, winter visitors, summer visitors, migrants, or accidentals, some make altitudinal migrations and others are resident within the country but make local migrations. In some cases, such as that of the Oriental Greenfinch, certain subspecies breed here but move south and are replaced in winter by different subspecies from further north.

"Japanese" birds come from as far north as the arctic coasts and tundra of Siberia and even Alaska, and range as far west as Burma, southwest to the Malay Peninsula, and south to the Philippines, New

Guinea, and even as far as Tasmania. The study of migration through Japan, while reasonably advanced (the bird ringing scheme in Japan is organized by the Yamashina Institute for Ornithology), still has many gaps that radar studies or even field observation would help fill. In recent years migration routes of raptors, including Common Buzzard and Northern Sparrowhawk, have been observed to occur across the straits from southwest Hokkaido to northwest Honshu, and a major migration route has been discovered for Chinese Sparrowhawk through the Nansei Shoto. No doubt many more discoveries await the field worker in the next decade.

Fauna

The mammalian fauna of Japan has been influenced in much the same way as the avifauna by the complexities of climate, topography, and vegetation, but since most species are terrestrial they are more greatly affected by the separation of the Japanese islands from the Asian continent and the temporal extent of the land bridges. Thus, while some wide-ranging Asian species are represented in Japan, others are absent or are represented by closely related forms that have evolved in isolation into separate species, such as Japanese Macaque and Japanese Serow. Approximately 130 species of mammals, including several introduced species, are reported from Japan, nearly thirty percent of which are endemic.

The fauna of Japan although primarily Palearctic in origin, as is the avifauna, is a complex of southeast Asian, Korean–Chinese and Siberian–subarctic animals. Zoogeographically, Hokkaido belongs to the continental region along with China and Siberia, and its mammalian fauna is characterized by the presence of Brown Bear, Sable, and Asiatic Pika. As with the avifauna, Blakiston's Line marks the southern limits of the distribution of these species.

Honshu, Shikoku, and Kyushu all belong to the Central Japanese Region, with affinities to southern and eastern Asia, and are characterized by the presence of such mammals as Japanese Macaque, Asiatic Black Bear, Badger, Japanese Serow, Giant Flying Squirrel, and Japanese Dormouse, and by the presence of Japanese Giant Salamander (now rare), the world's largest amphibian. Several more species have distinct subspecies on either side of Blakiston's Line, such as Racoon Dog and Sika Deer.

At the other end of Japan, the Nansei Shoto, which became separated rather early on from Asia and Japan, has a unique fauna and is as exciting for its mammals, reptiles, and amphibians as for its birds: Black Rabbit and Spinous Mouse are endemic to the forests of Amami

Oshima; a small endemic subspecies of Wild Boar occurs throughout the Nansei Shoto, Crocodile Salamander occurs only in Okinawa; fruit bats occur from Okinawa south; and on Iriomotejima there is the endemic Iriomote Wild Cat. Another wild cat, the Small-eared Cat, occurs in Japan only on the island of Tsushima in the straits between South Korea and Kyushu.

The sea north of central Honshu belongs to the north Pacific region, and in winter and spring Northern Fur Seals are commonly seen. The Okhotsk Sea north of Hokkaido is in the arctic region and is visited by northern species such as Steller's Sea Lion, while the seas south of central Honshu belong to the Indo–western Pacific region and are frequented by flying fish, hammerhead sharks, bright coral fish, sea snakes (in the Nansei Shoto), and turtles. Many species of whale, porpoise, and dolphin migrate by Japan, passing the Pacific Coast.

As is the fate of islands around the world, Japan has suffered its extinctions. The last wolf disappeared in the nineteenth century, and Brown Bear is likely to vanish in the early part of the twenty-first century, both as a result of persecution. The Otter is probably extinct as a result of habitat destruction, but may just be surviving in parts of Shikoku. While some species have been lost, other, non-native species have been introduced, including Mink, Masked Palm Civet, Formosan Tree-squirrel, Muskrat, and Nutria.

PRACTICAL INFORMATION

Since this is a guidebook to birding sites in Japan, I have left the task of providing general historical, cultural, and travel information to the specialist guidebooks, several of which are listed in the Bibliography. Of these, my own preference is for *Japan: A Travel Survival Kit*.

I have tried to give briefly all the essential information for reaching the sites described here either in the "How to Get There" sections or on the maps. To save space, I have sometimes given directions using just one railway or bus line, even though there are alternatives. At railway and bus stations, if you say the name of the place or the line you want slowly and clearly, you should have no problems. Despite the language barrier, travel is made easier by the helpful attitude of the Japanese toward foreigners.

Certain Japanese words appear repeatedly in the text, particularly in place-names, such as *hanto* (peninsula), *ike* (pond), *kaigan* (coast), *kawa* or *-gawa* (river), *ko* (lake), *misaki* (cape), *numa* (marsh), *-san* or *yama* (mountain), and others in travel directions, such as *sen* (railway line). It will be more useful when asking for directions or further information if you use these rather than the English translations, which are unfamiliar to most Japanese.

The description of each site is accompanied by a map, in which I have used ···· to indicate recommended routes, and ∗ to denote the best birding spots.

Transport

Public transport is very efficient, and transferring between different forms of transport is usually simple since in most towns and cities the train and bus stations and taxi ranks are very close together, if not adjacent. On the whole, long-distance buses are either not available, or not worthwhile because of the time they take. Most sites can be reached by a combination of train and bus, or by car. Where no other form of transport exists, there are almost invariably taxis. For long-distance journeys, take either trains or ferries, or, if you can afford to, planes. Most people travel on national holidays, and particularly at New Year, during "Golden Week" at the end of April and the beginning of May, and in mid-August, so if you cannot avoid traveling at these times, make sure you book transport and accommodation well in advance.

Trains vary greatly in speed and, accordingly, in price. The basic ticket charge is for the distance to be traveled, and additional supplements are paid for faster trains, for reserved seats, and for sleepers. In order of speed and expense, from the slowest (cheapest), the trains are the local *kakueki* that stop at each station; the express, or *kyuko*; the limited express, or *tokkyu*; and finally the superexpress (bullet train, or *Shinkansen*). Sleeping cars, or *shindaisha*, are available on many long routes, for example from Tokyo to Kyushu or Hokkaido, or across Hokkaido.

If you are traveling a long way by train, stock up with fruit and liquids before you board. The over-heated or over-air-conditioned atmosphere quickly becomes very dry and drinks on board are expensive. A large percentage of Japanese people smoke and non-smoking cars are few, although they have increased in recent years. On trains and buses the stops are brief (usually less than a minute) but are usually announced in advance, so listen carefully, and be ready to alight.

Visitors planning extensive rail travel should obtain a condensed railway timetable in English from the Japan National Tourist Organization (JNTO) and should invest in a Japan Rail Pass before arriving (they cannot be purchased once inside Japan). These provide unlimited travel over a given period on the Japan Railway (JR) lines, although not on some private lines that run mainly in or near the major cities.

For those staying in Tokyo, *The Tokyo Transit Book* by Garry Bassin clearly describes and illustrates the city's transportation systems, including connections to the airports.

For those with plenty of time and a desire to economize, **boats** offer a good alternative since they connect all the main islands on a daily basis and provide good opportunities for seawatching; they are also the cheapest form of long-distance travel. They are clean and comfortable, and the service is generally very good, although it declines in the south, from Kagoshima down the island chain to Taiwan. Economy class consists of a large communal tatami-matted area with blankets and pillows available, and the boats also have cabins of various sizes. There is usually a shop and a restaurant on board, and the longer routes have

Japanese-style baths, an experience definitely not to be missed on board a swaying ship.

The southern boat trips are mostly birdless in winter, but the voyage from Tokyo to Hokkaido is an absolute must for anyone with the slightest interest in seabirds, and is good at all seasons. Boats traveling up the Japan Sea coast are also frequent, but there are fewer birds. Any birder with interest in seabirds but with little time might consider a side trip from Tokyo to Miyakejima and Hachijojima in the Izu Islands.

Air travel is a reasonable but birdless solution for those with little time and sufficient finances. An efficient network of flights on three carriers (ANA, JAL, and TDA) connects most areas of Japan and, of course, all the major cities.

Cars are useful particularly in Hokkaido, Kyushu, or Okinawa, or in other rural areas where the distances to be covered are large. Driving is on the left. It takes a while to get used to the fact that road numbers marked on the maps are rarely shown on signs on the roads, while those indicated on signs on the roads rarely appear on the maps! Patience, a compass, and an eye for the detail of the characters that appear on the road signs are necessary. An international driving license is essential if you plan to rent a car.

On the whole give the roads in central Honshu a miss. Apart from the expense, which is considerable, speed limits are very low (usually 30–50 kmph), and the roads are poorly signed and usually crowded. Particularly within Tokyo, but also in all other cities and towns, it is extremely difficult to park, and to travel away from Tokyo at any speed means taking the expressways, which are often crowded at the weekend and levy heavy tolls. The best approach is to travel to your destination by public transport, then hire a car locally. Car rental offices can invariably be found at airports and major stations.

If you are a visitor with visions of buying a car and then selling it at the end of a trip, feasible in some countries, forget it. Among all the bureaucratic requirements involved in buying a car is proof that you have a place to park it.

The best **maps** are the large-format, soft-cover Mapple series published by Shobunsha and updated every year. One volume covers the whole of Japan, and slimmer volumes are devoted to the different regions. They are available at most large bookshops, and I have found them to be both the clearest and the most accurate. They are in Japanese, but so too are most road signs. English-language maps are of little use since you cannot compare the road signs with the name of your destination.

Timetables and prices of course change. Rail, boat, and plane timetables are published monthly in book form in Japan. It is important, therefore, to check in advance wherever possible with either the Japan Travel Bureau (JTB) or the Japan National Tourist Organization (JNTO), both of which have English-speaking staff in many of their offices in Japan. They also have offices in many other countries.

If you are willing to do away with timetables altogether and trust your luck, you could always try **hitchhiking**. Japan must rank as one of the safest, if not *the* safest, country in the world, making hitching extremely easy. The novelty of carrying a *gaijin* (foreigner) or the opportunity for a free English conversation lesson is irresistible to many drivers, and often they will be embarrassingly generous, sometimes to the extent of taking you all the way to your destination even when they are not going anywhere near it. Hitching has all the disadvantages of car travel of course, but once on the expressway (try at night and accept mainly trucks) it can be quite fast. I have enjoyed many birding trips this way, meeting people along the way. It is of course infinitely cheaper and can often be hilariously funny. In Kyushu, in a single winter trip, I had people stop their cars because they thought I wanted to cross the road, stop because they thought I wanted directions, and stop just to stare, but nothing that happened to me could match the experience of one German couple I met. After standing in the rain for a while they thought that they were finally in luck when a car stopped. A little girl got out, bowed, handed them an umbrella, got back into the car, and her parents drove off!

It is helpful to carry a pocket dictionary or phrase book. Some people go to great lengths to copy out the characters (*kanji*) for the place they want to go to and hold them up as a sign. Remember, however, that the Japanese are unused to hitchhikers, don't really understand the idea too well, and are very literally minded. I have asked drivers if they are going to a certain town only to be told no, but have got in any way to find that they were going virtually all the way there, though not *actually* there. That I would be able to hitch again after they turned off just hadn't occurred to them.

Accommodation

Unless you are flying with China Airlines, you will arrive in Japan at Narita Airport, inconveniently located 60 km from the center of Tokyo in Chiba Prefecture. It is two hours from Tokyo by either a combination of bus and train or by the "Limousine bus" that goes to the major hotels in Tokyo. The airport is closed at night and all the accommodation in the immediate vicinity is expensive. In the nearby town of Narita, however, try the Kirinoya Ryokan, 58 Tama-cho, Narita, Chiba-ken ☎(0476)22-

0724. Situated close to Narita-san, a famous shrine, it is only 15 min on foot from Narita Station, which is a 20-min bus ride from the airport. It is useful for individuals or small groups, but ask someone to book ahead in Japanese, perhaps at the information desk at the airport.

Anyone arriving by China Airlines will land at Haneda Airport, only 25 min from central Tokyo by Monorail. Haneda is also the starting point for internal flights in Japan.

An abundance of accommodation is available, ranging from huts in the mountains (*yamagoya*) to the finest Western-style hotels and Japanese-style inns (*ryokan*) in the cities. On the whole, anywhere you stay will be very comfortable and extremely clean; tap water is potable throughout the country. Many of the accommodations I have listed have some special attraction for birders, such as their proximity to sites or their having an owner/manager who is interested in birding himself. I have tried only to recommend places that I have used personally or that have been strongly recommended to me. Usually a wide range of good accommodation will be available nearby. For further information travelers should consult one of the travel guides or travel organizations listed in this book. However, remember that unless otherwise instructed, the Japan Travel Bureau (JTB) will almost invariably try to book you into either expensive Western-style hotels or expensive ryokan. They do have information on the cheaper *minshuku* (see below) as well, but you must ask for it.

Arriving in Tokyo for the first time is an extremely bewildering experience, with a confusing variety of accommodation and eating places. I suggest that budget travelers arriving in Tokyo contact Okubo House, Hyakunin-cho 132, Shinjuku-ku ☎(03)361-2348, since this is a well-known traveler's hostel with beds for as little as ¥1,400. It is a 2-min walk from Shin-Okubo Station on the Yamanote Line (which circles inner Tokyo), one stop north of Shinjuku.

Budget travelers will find **youth hostels**—and thus an International Youth Hostel Card—invaluable, since at less than ¥3,000 per night hostels often offer the only cheap accommodation available. Furthermore, carrying a sheet sleeping bag will save you ¥100–¥500 per night. The quality of the food varies from decidedly dull to excellent. You can often cook your own food in the kitchen, but ingredients usually work out almost as expensive as the meals provided. Although there is no age limit, the meetings, curfew, and noise bear witness to the fact that hostels are used almost exclusively by youngsters.

For those wishing for a little more privacy and a more typical Japanese experience, **minshuku** are highly recommended. For ¥4,000–¥4,500 per person per night including two meals, they provide no-frills family accommodation. Similar to minshuku are the lodgings called *kokuminshukusha* that are government-run and are located at scenic places. Ryokan in the country are often as cheap as minshuku, while others offer better service but are sometimes very expensive, so check first. Membership of the Wild Bird Society of Japan (Nihon Yacho no Kai) will often entitle you to discounts at the accommodation I have listed.

When you stay in Japanese-style accommodation, whether minshuku or ryokan, I can offer the following few pointers in etiquette. In brief, the basic rule is to watch your hosts—the Japanese are a quiet reserved people unlikely to criticize your blunders. Instead, try to prevent them. Bathing is for relaxation, washing being done outside the tub so that soap is not introduced into the water, which will be used by others. In Japanese accommodation, Japanese meals may be served in your room or in a communal dining room. Do not expect courses, or for that matter choice, as menus are invariably fixed in reasonably priced accommodation. Eating is almost always done with chopsticks, although as a foreigner you may be presented with cutlery. While most visitors can adjust quite quickly to Japanese food, others find one meal in particular difficult to get used to—Japanese breakfast. This consists of rice, fish, raw egg, seaweed, and miso soup. Lunches and dinners can be found for about ¥1,000 at cheap restaurants; at Western-style hotels and many Japanese and foreign restaurants, of course, the sky is the limit.

Beds are uncommon, except in Western-style hotels. Instead, *futon* quilts are put out at night and taken up each morning. In ryokan and some minshuku this will be done for you during your evening meal and during breakfast, but in others you have to do it yourself. Cotton robes, or *yukata*, are usually provided for sleeping in and can be worn to the bathroom, to the dining room, and, with the addition of wooden-soled sandals (*geta*), for an evening stroll at hot spring (*onsen*) resort towns. Both men and women should remember to wrap the yukata left over right. Towels are rarely provided, so carry your own.

Service in Japan is excellent and a paying customer is welcomed with open arms, whether fashionably dressed or in rugged outdoor clothes. Just remember to note whether shoes are lined up outside and, if so, remove yours. And remember, *never* wear footwear other than socks on tatami mats.

Western-style hotels are generally the most expensive (from ¥7,000 per night without meals), and they are not widely available outside the major cities or sightseeing areas. There are also **business hotels**, which are cheaper Western-style hotels for traveling businessmen (usually

¥5,000–¥7,000 per night without meals). For those looking for reasonably priced comfortable Western-style hotel accommodation in Tokyo, I recommend the Aoyama Shanpia Hotel, 2-14-15 Shibuya, Shibuya-ku, Tokyo 150; ☎(03)407-2111, which is very close to the Wild Bird Society of Japan headquarters, and not far from Shibuya Station.

In Tokyo, buy any film or camera equipment you need from the Yodobashi or Sakuraya shops, just outside the east exit of Shinjuku Station on the Yamanote Line. Just around the corner from them is Kinokuniya bookstore, which has the Mapple maps, English-language maps and guidebooks, and all the hiking maps you will need if you plan a trip to the mountains.

Although shops open late (between 09:30 and 10:00), many stay open all evening and all day Sunday too. In addition to shops, ubiquitous vending machines make virtually everything available from books and batteries to food and drinks. The ready availability of ice-cold drinks and ice cream in summer and hot coffee in cans in winter make the naturalist's life an easy, albeit slightly expensive, one.

If you are in Tokyo for a while and want an opportunity to meet locals over a cup of tea or coffee or just escape the rain to write up notes, try one of the conversation lounges advertised in the monthly *Tokyo Journal*, such as the "Com Inn English Conversation Lounge." It is a good place to while away a few hours of darkness or bad weather. Newspapers and music are provided. A small entrance fee entitles native English speakers to unlimited tea or coffee from 16:00–22:00 in return for talking to anyone who wants to try out his or her English. It is a 3-min walk from Ebisu Station, one stop south of Shibuya Station on the Yamanote Line. There is a map to it on the left inside the station before you go out through the ticket barrier.

Equipment

The bare necessities of course include binoculars, a field guide, and a notebook. For viewing seabirds, waterbirds, and shorebirds, a telescope and tripod are extremely useful. Public transport is crowded so keep your luggage to a minimum. During spring and autumn, include a sweater and a jacket in your luggage; in summer, light cotton clothing is adequate, but carry insect-repellent. From spring to autumn Japanese birders often carry a collapsible umbrella and drape a small towel around their necks. Both are extremely practical—the umbrella as condensation-free protection from sudden downpours on humid days, and the towel for brow mopping, as a sweat band, or to protect the back of the neck from the sun.

The mountain regions have pleasant cooler weather in summer, attracting visitors from the hot, humid lowlands, but winters are severe. Deep snow prevents walking away from the roads In many areas in the west and north in winter unless you are equipped with skis or snowshoes. Mid-winter is cold enough for down jackets, hats, scarves, and gloves even in and around Tokyo, although you will find buildings and trains overheated. Those heading for Hokkaido to view the cranes and eagles in winter should be prepared for temperatures as low as −15°C, with the windchill factor making it feel even colder.

Japan makes no change from winter to summer time, and the days are on the whole shorter than expected by most visitors. In the evenings it is light only until about 19:30 in the summer, and it gets dark two to three hours earlier in the winter. However, it gets light very early, between 03:00 and 04:00 in summer and between 05:30 and 06:30 in winter. There is some variation from north to south, but as a general rule do not rely on any evening birding other than "owling." Instead, get up early and get several hours in before breakfast.

Useful Addresses and Telephone Numbers

Friends of the Earth: 501 Shinwa Building, 9-17 Sakuragaoka-cho, Shibuya-ku, Tokyo 150; ☎(03)770-6308.

Fuji Tours International: (Mr. Totsuka or Mr. Hoshikawa) Ryuwa Bldg., 2-3-5 Yuraku-cho, Chiyoda-ku, Tokyo 100; ☎(03)571-4811.

Japan National Tourist Organization (JNTO): 1-6-6, Yuraku-cho, Chiyoda-ku, Tokyo 100; ☎(03)502-1461.

Japan Travel Bureau (JTB): 1-13-1 Nihonbashi Chiyoda-ku, Tokyo 103; ☎(03)273-1611.

Japan Travel Phone: ☎(03)502-1461 for English-language assistance.

The Ornithological Society of Japan: Dr. H. Morioka, Department of Zoology, National Science Museum, Hyakunin-cho, 3-23-1, Shinjuku-ku, Tokyo 160; ☎(03)364-2111.

TRAFFIC (Japan) & World Wildlife Fund (Japan): 7th Floor, Nihon Seimei Akabanebashi Bldg., 3-1-14, Shiba, Minato-ku, Tokyo 105; ☎(03)769-1716.

Wild Bird Society of Japan (WBSJ): 5th Floor, Aoyama Flower Building, 1-1-4 Shibuya, Shibuya-ku, Tokyo 150; ☎(03)406-7141.

The Yamashina Institute for Ornithology: 115 Tsutsumine-aza, Konoyama, Abiko, Chiba Prefecture 270-11; ☎(0471)82-1101.

The Wild Bird Society of Japan

Birdwatching and bird conservation in Japan are promoted by the Wild Bird Society of Japan (WBSJ), a private organization founded in 1934. Its purpose is to protect birds and their habitats, to conduct and commission research concerning the status and habitat of birds in Japan, and to encourage more people to enjoy birdwatching. Some of the society's achievements include having Bean and White-fronted Goose added to the national protected birds list, thereby saving them from being hunted, encouraging the government to protect the habitat of Pryer's Woodpecker in Okinawa, and setting up several bird sanctuaries.

In association with local governments, the WBSJ maintains the following sanctuaries so that people can enjoy and learn about birds. No admission is charged.

1. Lake Utonai Sanctuary (in Hokkaido; administered solely by the WBST)
2. Fukushima City Kotori-no-Mōri Sanctuary (in Fukushima Prefecture)
3. Oi Bird Park (in Tokyo)
4. Kaga City Kamo-ike Sanctuary (in Ishikawa Prefecture)
5. Keep Kiyosato Sanctuary (in Yamanashi Prefecture)
6. Yokohama Nature Sanctuary (in Kanagawa Prefecture)
7. Himeji Nature Sanctuary (in Hyogo Prefecture)

More sanctuaries are planned and the society is working in cooperation with other organizations to establish sanctuaries in other Asian countries.

Other activities include the "Save the Birds Campaign" to preserve Asian birds and their habitats, and a campaign to prevent the poaching of goshawks. The WBSJ is also involved in various conservation activities, such as protecting wetlands and mud flats, and tries to be aware of any decisions made in Japan that may affect birds or other wild animals. The WBSJ is also involved in cooperative, international research, particularly in East Asia, and organizes conferences and symposia.

The WBSJ has seventy local chapters that are engaged in local conservation issues and research as well as in organizing birdwatching trips. With the support of members, the WBSJ has been able to establish the Wild Bird Protection Fund and the Japanese Crane Protection Fund.

The WBSJ conducts annual nationwide waterfowl and wader counts and international sea eagle counts, studies the habitat and distribution of birds, and investigates cases of poaching. It publishes the monthly magazine *Yacho* for its members, the annual scientific journal *Strix*, and has published various books on Japanese birds, including copublishing the *Field Guide to the Birds of Japan* and this guide with Kodansha International.

The headquarters of the society includes a shop selling books, tapes, and other birdwatching accessories.

You can help the work of the society by becoming a member. For details, write to the Membership Secretary, Wild Bird Society of Japan, 5th Floor, Aoyama Flower Building, 1-1-4, Shibuya, Shibuya-ku, Tokyo 150, Japan, ☎(03)406-7141.

Tokyo and Environs

1. Meiji Jingu, Tokyo　明治神宮
Good birding months: Sept.–May

Meiji Jingu (Meiji Shrine), dedicated to Emperor Meiji (1852–1912) and his consort, is one of the finest Shinto shrines in Japan. Built of plain cedar timbers and set in extensive grounds covering 73 ha, it is a green haven amid Tokyo's characteristic concrete. When the park was established in the 1910s, 100,000 trees were donated from all over Japan, and these have now matured. The park has ponds, open grassy areas, and wide footpaths, and is an excellent mixed woodland site. This is as good a place as any to start birdwatching in Japan, since it has many of the species typical of the Kanto area and central Honshu, and is the best place in the Tokyo area to see Varied Tit and Azure-winged Magpie. In winter the North Pond (Kita-ike) attracts small numbers of waterbirds, including Little Grebe and Common Kingfisher. Up to a hundred Mandarin Duck can be found tucked away in the shadier areas under trees around the pond and may even be flushed from the woods. (If you miss them here, try nearby Shinjuku Gyoen.) Also in winter, watch for thrushes feeding on the ground among the leaf litter in the woods. To see most birds, visit in the early morning or late in the afternoon on weekdays, when visitors are fewest, and keep to the woods, near the pools, and on the narrower paths away from the shrine itself. In spring (April and May) and autumn (September and October), the woods and the inner iris garden attract migrant warblers and fly-catchers. The South Pond (Minami-ike) attracts herons and egrets.

BIRDS AND SEASONS
All year: Little Grebe; Black-crowned Night Heron; Little Egret; Chinese Bamboo Partridge; Japanese Pygmy Woodpecker; Varied Tit; Azure-winged Magpie.

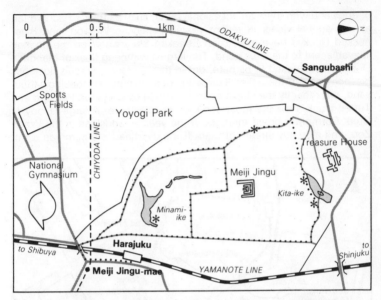

Spring & Autumn: Common Cuckoo; Eye-browed Thrush; Eastern Crowned Warbler; Blue-and-White, Gray-streaked (autumn only), and Narcissus Flycatcher.

Winter: Mandarin Duck; Common Teal; Mallard; Spot-billed Duck; Northern Shoveler; Common Kingfisher; Red-flanked Bluetail; Daurian Redstart; White's, Brown, Pale, and Dusky Thrush; Bull-headed Shrike; Eurasian Jay; Hawfinch.

HOW TO GET THERE

The nearest station is Harajuku on the Yamanote Line (Tokyo's circle line). Leave by the southern exit, which is nearest Shibuya, turn right out of the station, walk uphill about 100 m, then turn right again across a broad bridge over the railway tracks. The entrance is ahead and slightly to the right. Map boards show the main paths, the shrine, and the museum.

2. Shinobazu-no-ike, Tokyo 不忍池

Good birding months: Oct.–April

Ueno Water Zoo (Ueno suijo dobutsuen), part of Ueno Zoo, and the contiguous Shinobazu-no-ike (Shinobazu Pond), the lotus pond, form one corner of central Tokyo's Ueno Park, a famous cherry-blossom-viewing spot in early April. From October to April the ponds attract huge flocks of duck and with them an occasional rarity, such as Baer's Pochard (an almost annual visitor in recent years), American Wigeon, and Ring-necked Duck. I have even seen Streaked Shearwater on the boating lake adjacent to the lotus pond. The largest wintering flock of Mandarin Duck in Tokyo used to be here, but in the last few years this flock has disappeared. Northern Pintail replaced them, in numbers topping a thousand, but recently they have been swamped by Common Pochard and Tufted Duck, now the most common species here. A large colony of Great Cormorant breed throughout the year on an island in the Water Zoo, and a steady stream of them flying overhead is a common sight.

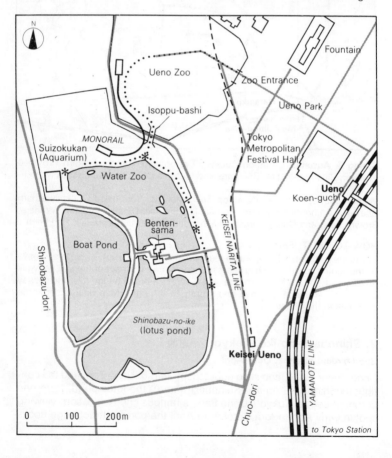

BIRDS AND SEASONS

All year: Great Cormorant; Spot-billed Duck; Common Moorhen; Azure-winged Magpie.
Winter: Little Grebe; Great Egret; Eurasian Wigeon; Common Teal; Mallard; Northern Pintail; Northern Shoveler; Common Pochard; Tufted Duck.
Rarities: American Wigeon; Ring-necked Duck; Baer's Pochard.

HOW TO GET THERE

From Tokyo Station: 25 min by train and on foot.
Ueno Station is on the Yamanote Line, four stops north of Tokyo Station. Leave by the west, or park, exit (Koen-guchi) and cross the park to the entrance of the zoo. Once inside, follow the route of the zoo monorail down to the Water Zoo. The pond is no more than a 10-min walk from Ueno Station. The two halves of the pond (Water Zoo and lotus pond) are separated by a one-way turnstile, making it impossible to walk from one side to the other except when leaving the zoo. The lotus pond alone can be visited without entering the zoo.

3. Oi Yacho Koen and Shioiri-no-ike, Tokyo 大井野鳥公園

Good birding months: Jan.–Dec.
Best birding months: April–May, Aug.–Oct.

This is an excellent small (3.2 ha) site hidden in the grim industrial and commercial area close to Haneda Airport on the western shore of Tokyo Bay. Oi Yacho Koen (Oi Wild Bird Park) was established by the Tokyo Metropolitan Government and is due to be expanded to 26 ha in 1989. It is managed by the WBSJ and is manned from Wednesday to Sunday by two of their staff. This whole area was reclaimed from the bay, and what was until recently a large reedbed is now mostly developed warehouse property. The main pool (Shioiri-no-ike), currently outside the bird park, however, remains very attractive to birds. It is suitable for a half-day trip from central Tokyo, and its popularity makes it a good place to meet local birdwatchers.

Oi has a remarkably long bird list for such a small urban reserve and is a must at any season. It is one of the best places for migrant shorebirds in Tokyo, and many rarities have visited, including Pied Avocet and Lesser Yellowlegs. In late April and May and again in September and October, migrant flycatchers and bulbuls pass through. Barn Swallow flocks appear in autumn with small numbers of Sand Martin (which only breed in Hokkaido). In winter there are many herons, duck, coot, moorhen, snipe, and gulls, and Bull-headed Shrike, Daurian Redstart, and Common Reed Bunting visit.

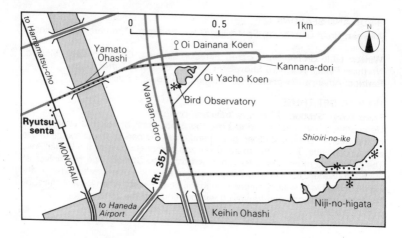

BIRDS AND SEASONS

All year: Black-crowned Night Heron; Little and Great Egret; Spot-billed Duck; Water Rail; Common Moorhen; Common Coot; Kentish Plover; Common Sandpiper; Fan-tailed Warbler.

Spring & Autumn: Black-winged Stilt; Little Ringed and Mongolian Plover; Red-necked Stint; Dunlin; Black-tailed and Bar-tailed Godwit; Marsh Sandpiper; Common Greenshank; Green, Wood, and Terek Sandpiper; Common Black-headed Gull; Common and Little Tern; Sand Martin; Blue-and-White, Gray-streaked, Asian Brown, and Narcissus Flycatcher.

Summer: Yellow Bittern; Gray Heron (late summer to winter); Greater Painted Snipe; Little Tern; Black-browed and Oriental Reed Warbler.

Winter: Gray Heron; Common Teal; Mallard; Northern Pintail; Northern Shoveler; Eastern Marsh Harrier; Eurasian Kestrel; Common Snipe; Common Black-headed, Black-tailed, Common, and Herring Gull; Long-eared and Short-eared Owl; Daurian Redstart; Dusky Thrush; Bull-headed Shrike; Meadow, Rustic, and Common Reed Bunting.

Rarities: Great Bittern; Oriental Pratincole; Common Ringed Plover; Spoon-billed Sandpiper; Japanese Marsh Warbler.

HOW TO GET THERE

From Tokyo Station: 45 min by train and on foot.

Take the Yamanote Line to Hamamatsu-cho Station. Change to the Monorail, which runs to Haneda Airport, and get off at the second stop, two stops before Haneda at Ryutsu-senta Station (a 15-min ride). It is a further 15–20 min on foot from the station.

4. Gyotoku, Chiba Prefecture　行徳

Good birding months: Jan.–Dec.
Best birding months: April–May, Sept.–Oct.

Sanctuary address: 4-22-11, Fukuei, Ichikawa-shi, Chiba 272-01; ☎(0473)57-9046. Open every day except Monday and the day after public holidays.

Gyotoku, an enclosed area of mud flats, pools, and reedbeds on re-claimed land near the north shore of Tokyo Bay, consists of the Imperial Shinhama Duck Refuge (29 ha; closed to visitors) and the Shinhama Bird Reserve/Gyotoku Wildlife Protection Area (54 ha), which can be viewed from an observatory and from a few points along peripheral roads. The observatory opened in 1976 and was expanded in 1979 to cope with the large number of visitors. The observatory has a full-time warden, a library, a museum, displays, and telescopes.

Gyotoku, rewarding at any time of year, is most popular in April, May,

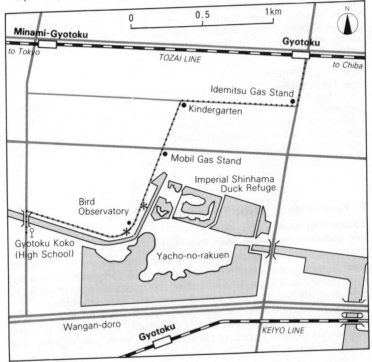

September, and October, when migrant shorebirds drop in. In winter, there are vast numbers of duck, particularly Greater Scaup (between 30,000 and 100,000). Baikal Teal, uncommon winter visitors, stay inside the duck refuge and hence are difficult to see, although they sometimes fly over the reserve area. Watch for Black-crowned Night Heron and Gray Heron in front of the observatory, and Eastern Marsh Harrier hunting the reedbed in winter. Little Tern are common spring visitors, and Yellow Bittern and Oriental Reed Warbler haunt the reedbed in summer.

BIRDS AND SEASONS
All year: Black-crowned Night Heron; Gray Heron; Spot-billed Duck; Green Pheasant; Common Moorhen; Black-winged Stilt; Kentish Plover.
Spring & Autumn: Little Ringed, Mongolian, and Pacific Golden Plover; Great Knot; Red-necked Stint; Dunlin; Sharp-tailed Sandpiper; Whimbrel; Eurasian Curlew; Marsh Sandpiper; Common Greenshank; Wood, Terek, and Common Sandpiper; Gray-tailed Tattler; Ruddy Turnstone; Little Tern.
Summer: Yellow Bittern; Oriental Reed Warbler.
Winter: Eurasian Wigeon; Gadwall; Common Teal; Mallard; Northern Pintail; Northern Shoveler; Greater Scaup; Eastern Marsh and Hen Harrier; Gray Plover; Dunlin; Black-tailed Gull; Short-eared Owl.
Rarities: Baikal Teal

HOW TO GET THERE
From Tokyo Station: 1 hr by train and on foot.
The reserve is easily reached by taking the Tozai subway line to Gyotoku Station, from which it is a 25-min walk to the observatory. Alternatively, get off the train at Minami-Gyotoku (the stop before Gyotoku) and take a bus from Bus Stand 2 outside the station to Gyotoku Koko. Walk back over the small bridge, turn right onto a narrow road, and continue until you see water on your right and the observatory on your left. This walk takes about 10 min.

5. Yatsu-higata, Chiba Prefecture 谷津干潟
Good birding months: Jan.–Dec.
Best birding months: April–May, Aug.–Oct.

This small (40 ha) inland mud flat, reputedly the best place in the Kanto area for spring and autumn migrant waders, is completely surrounded by roads and buildings. A tidal flooding basin for the adjacent canalized river, this site has its high tide two hours later than Tokyo Bay.

Spring (April and May), autumn (early August on), and winter provide the best birdwatching, with a host of herons, egrets, gulls (the rare Saunders's Gull has appeared here), and shorebirds congregating. This

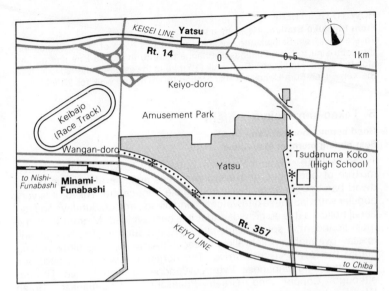

is the most reliable place during autumn in Japan to look for the uncommon Great Knot. It is also well worth visiting to look for rarities, such as Spoon-billed Sandpiper, Asian Dowitcher, and Nordmann's Greenshank, while Eastern Curlew can be seen year-round. From October onward duck arrive. Altogether, 171 species have been recorded here. Like Oi Yacho Koen (3), this is a good place to meet Japanese birdwatchers on the weekend.

BIRDS AND SEASONS
Spring & Autumn: Little Ringed, Kentish, Mongolian, Pacific Golden, and Gray Plover; Great Knot; Red-necked and Long-toed Stint; Sharp-tailed Sandpiper; Dunlin; Broad-billed Sandpiper; Black-tailed and Bar-tailed Godwit; Whimbrel; Eurasian and Eastern Curlew; Marsh Sandpiper; Common Greenshank; Wood, Terek, and Common Sandpiper; Gray-tailed Tattler; Black-tailed Gull.
Summer: Little and Great Egret; Spot-billed Duck; Kentish Plover; Eastern Curlew; Black-tailed Gull; Little Tern.
Winter: Gray Heron; Eurasian Wigeon; Common Teal; Mallard; Spot-billed Duck; Northern Pintail; Northern Shoveler; Eastern Marsh Harrier; Common Buzzard; Eurasian Kestrel; Peregrine; Kentish and Gray Plover; Eastern Curlew; Common Black-headed and Black-tailed Gull.
Rarities: Red Knot; Spoon-billed Sandpiper; Asian Dowitcher; Nordmann's Greenshank; Saunders's Gull.

HOW TO GET THERE
From Shinjuku Station: 1½ hr by train.
Take a train from Shinjuku or Akihabara (two stops north of Tokyo Station) on the Sobu Line to Nishi-Funabashi. Change there to the Keiyo Line and go one stop to Minami-Funabashi. Then walk (15 min) to the estuary. Alternatively, take the Keisei Line from Ueno to Yatsu Station (50 min) and walk for 20 min.

6. Takao-san, Tokyo   高尾山
Good birding months: Jan.–Dec.
Best birding months: May–June

Takao-san (600 m), on the western outskirts of Tokyo, is covered with a mixture of deciduous and evergreen trees and the ubiquitous dense dwarf bamboo, or *sasa*. Easily accessible from central Tokyo, it is very popular with Japanese birdwatchers and hikers, and on Sundays and national holidays it is so crowded that it is best avoided. Migrant birds are most abundant in spring, early summer, and autumn. The best plan is to stay overnight, which allows peaceful early morning birdwatching before the day's visitors arrive. The commoner woodland birds are here, including Japanese Pygmy Woodpecker and Varied Tit, but although Copper and Green Pheasant and Japanese Green Woodpecker are still present, they are uncommon. Staying overnight is essential to see the Giant Flying Squirrel that live in the tall trees around the temple at the top of the mountain and begin to glide through the forest at dusk.

BIRDS AND SEASONS
All year: Northern Goshawk; Chinese Bamboo Partridge; Copper and Green Pheasant; Ural Owl; Japanese Green, Great Spotted, and Japanese Pygmy

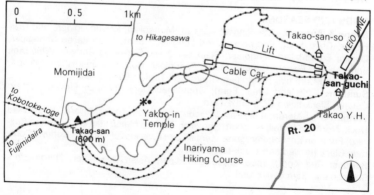

Woodpecker; Gray Wagtail; Northern Wren; Willow, Varied, and Coal Tit; Azure-winged Magpie; Japanese Grosbeak.

Summer: Crested Honey Buzzard; Japanese Sparrowhawk; Gray-faced Buzzard; Little Cuckoo; Brown Hawk Owl; Dollarbird; Ashy Minivet; Gray Thrush; Stub-tailed Bush Warbler; Eastern Crowned Warbler; Blue-and-White and Narcissus Flycatcher.

Winter: Red-flanked Bluetail; Daurian Redstart; White's, Brown, and Pale Thrush; Goldcrest; Common Bullfinch; Hawfinch; Gray, Meadow, and Rustic Bunting.

HOW TO GET THERE

From Shinjuku: 1 hr by train.
Take the Keio Line from Shinjuku Station to Takao-san-guchi. Either walk up the hillside paths or take the cable car to the top and then walk down.

Accommodation: Stay overnight at the top of the mountain at Yakuo-in temple ☎(0426)61-1115, which serves good vegetarian food; at the base of the mountain at Takao Youth Hostel ☎(0426)61-0437, next to the museum near the station; or at Takao-san-so ☎(0426)61-0306, a kokuminshukusha near the cable car station.

7. Tamagawa, Tokyo　多摩川

Good birding months: Jan.–Dec.
Best birding months: Aug.–May

Tamagawa (Tama River) drains the western part of the Kanto plain and flows into the west side of Tokyo Bay north of Kawasaki and immediately south of Haneda Airport. This wide shingle river is banked with concrete in many places, and although not particularly clean, some sections of the upper reaches, 20 or more km inland, still attract large flocks of duck in winter, providing excellent birdwatching from October to April. The small mud flats near the mouth of the river are host to a wide variety of shorebirds during the migration seasons and, to a lesser extent, also in winter.

In winter, scan the large flocks of the commoner dabbling ducks that teem on the upper river for small numbers of Falcated Teal and Gadwall and an occasional American Wigeon. Smew are here in small flocks from November onward. Oriental Ibis occasionally seen here are free-flying birds from the nearby Tama Zoo. Check the vegetation near the river edge for finches, buntings, and Fan-tailed Warbler, and along the river edge for Water Pipit, Japanese Wagtail, and, where it is shingly, Long-billed Plover. This is the best site for the latter within easy reach of Tokyo, and they can be found easily at any season. Such a large concentration of birds as this often attracts predators, such as Peregrine. You

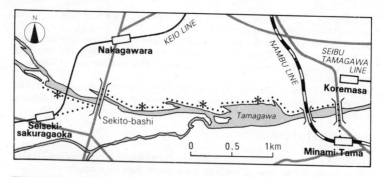

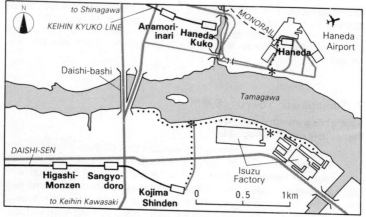

can walk along either bank of the upper reaches, but the east bank has more open access for a greater length.

On the first Sunday of every month the WBSJ holds bird walks. Meet at the west exit of Seisekisakuragaoka Station on the Keio Line at 08:15 from July to September and at 10:00 from October to June.

The Tamagawa river mouth is also well worth a half-day visit from Tokyo, particularly from August to May. The best area is on the south bank overlooking a reedbed, a small island, and mud flats, as the tide is rising. The second week of August is notable as it is the peak of the autumn wader passage. If you have an hour to spare before or after a flight from Haneda Airport, visit the north bank, which is only a 5-min walk from the terminal building.

BIRDS AND SEASONS

All year: Little Grebe; Great Cormorant; Black-crowned Night Heron; Little and Great Egret; Spot-billed Duck; Greater Scaup; Common Moorhen; Long-billed and Kentish Plover; Common Sandpiper; Common Kingfisher; Japanese Wagtail; Blue Rock Thrush; Fan-tailed Warbler; Red Avadavat.

Spring & Autumn: Yellow Bittern; Striated Heron; Little Ringed, Mongolian, Pacific Golden, and Gray Plover; Great and Red Knot; Red-necked Stint; Curlew Sandpiper; Dunlin; Broad-billed Sandpiper; Black-tailed and Bar-tailed Godwit; Whimbrel; Spotted Redshank; Common Greenshank; Terek Sandpiper; Gray-tailed Tattler; Ruddy Turnstone; Little Tern.

Summer: Yellow Bittern; Black-tailed Gull; Little Tern; Common House Martin; Oriental Reed Warbler; Gray-headed Bunting.

Winter: Gray Heron; Eurasian Wigeon; Falcated Teal; Gadwall; Common Teal; Mallard; Northern Pintail; Northern Shoveler; Common Goldeneye; Smew; Eastern Marsh Harrier; Eurasian Kestrel; Peregrine; Red-necked Stint; Dunlin; Common Snipe; Common Black-headed, Black-tailed, Common, and Herring Gull; Water Pipit; Gray Wagtail; Daurian Redstart; Brown and Dusky Thrush; Bull-headed Shrike; Hawfinch; Meadow, Rustic, and Common Reed Bunting.

Rarities: Ruddy Shelduck; American Wigeon; Green-winged Teal (*A. crecca carolinensis*) (at the river mouth in winter); Spoon-billed Sandpiper; Nordmann's Greenshank (river mouth in autumn). In 1983–84 and 1984–85 a Long-billed Dowitcher wintered here, and at the end of 1985 the first Bonaparte's Gull for Asia was recorded.

HOW TO GET THERE

To the upper reaches: 30 min by express train.
Take the Keio Line from Shinjuku Station (on the Yamanote Line) to Seisekisakuragaoka Station, which is a 5-min walk from the river. Alternatively, take the Odakyu Line from Shinjuku Station to Noborito. At Noborito change to the Nambu Line and go five stops to Minami-Tama Station. From Minami-Tama it is a 20-min walk to the river's east side. For anyone staying south of Tokyo, the Nambu Line runs from Kawasaki, easily reached by train from Tokyo, Shinagawa, or Yokohama.

To the river mouth: 1 hr by train.
Take the Yamanote Line to Shinagawa, transfer to the Keihin Kyuko Line and take a train south to Keihin Kawasaki Station. Change to the Keihin Kyuko branch line (Daishi-sen) and travel east to the end of the line at Kojima Shinden. Leave the station, walk for 40–50 m in the direction the train was heading, then turn left and keep straight on north until you reach the south riverbank (10–15 min). Explore the riverbank eastward to the end of the path (about 1.5–2 km) and westward to the bridges. Check the small island out in the river. Alternatively, take the Monorail from Hamamatsu-cho (on the Yamanote Line) to Haneda Airport (20 min), then a taxi (10 min) to the south end of Daishi-bashi (Daishi Bridge), under which Common House Martin breed. Walk eastward from there.

Accommodation: These sites are best visited on day trips from central Tokyo.

8. Futagoyama, Kanagawa Prefecture 二子山

Good birding months: Jan.–Dec.
Best birding months: May–June

Futagoyama is an area of low hills near Tokyo between the two residential districts of Zushi and Hayama. A broad track runs along the bottom of a wooded valley beside a stream. Smaller tracks branch off, but quickly disappear. After 3–4 km the track ends and becomes a narrow path climbing hills covered with mixed forest, scrub, and some planted cryptomeria. All except the cryptomeria have a good ground flora, with *sasa* predominating. In winter, in addition to the resident common woodland species, various thrushes can be found along the valley bottom, and from late autumn Gray Bunting can be found among the Black-faced Bunting flocks that skulk in the *sasa*.

In spring and early autumn raptors pass through, and in summer it is excellent for Japanese Paradise Flycatcher, up to three pairs of which nest in shady areas close to the stream. The male's song is a loud, quite unmistakable—"tski-hi-hoshi, hoi-hoi-hoi." Common Kingfisher and Blue-and-White Flycatcher also inhabit the forest along the stream, and Japanese Night Heron are reported to occur here.

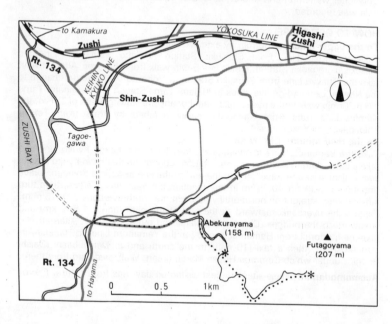

BIRDS AND SEASONS

All year: Chinese Bamboo Partridge; Japanese Green and Japanese Pygmy Woodpecker; Long-tailed and Varied Tit.

Spring & Autumn: Crested Honey Buzzard; Japanese Sparrowhawk; Gray-faced Buzzard.

Summer: Brown Hawk Owl; Common Kingfisher; Eastern Crowned Warbler; Blue-and-White and Japanese Paradise Flycatcher.

Winter: White's, Pale, Eye-browed, and Dusky Thrush; Gray Bunting.

Rarities: Japanese Night Heron.

HOW TO GET THERE

From Tokyo: 1 hr 40 min by train and on foot.

Take a JR train from Tokyo Station to Zushi (55 min). Alternatively, take the Keihin Kyuko Line from Shinagawa Station to Shin-Zushi, changing at Kanazawa Hakkei. It takes about 30 min on foot from Shin-Zushi Station to the entrance of the valley, and 35 min from Zushi Station. By taxi it takes about 10 min.

Accommodation: This site is easily visited on a day trip from central Tokyo, although a variety of accommodation is available in the Zushi area.

9. Miyakejima, Tokyo　三宅島

Good birding months: Jan.–Dec.
Best birding months: April–June

Miyakejima, one of the chain of the Izu Islands that extends out into the Pacific Ocean, is about 160 km south of Tokyo. Oshima, the northernmost island of the group, famous for its volcano (which erupted in 1986) and its camellias, and Hachijojima, to the south of Miyakejima, are the most popular with tourists. From a naturalist's point of view, however, Miyake offers the greatest wealth of flowers, and birds that are both common and tame. Good at any season, the best time for a visit is between April and June.

The island is nearly circular, 8 km from north to south and 7.5 km from east to west, with an area of 55.1 km^2. Its scenery is dominated by the 815-m-high volcano Oyama, whose slopes are cloaked with subtropical evergreen forest. Oyama erupted in 1962 and 1983, and the resultant lava fields are clearly visible at the northeast and southwest ends of the island.

The population of about 4,500 depends on agriculture, fishing, and tourism for its livelihood. There are villages all around the island and small fields protected by hedges near the road.

In winter the climate is dry and relatively mild, while in summer it is hot and humid. Temperatures range from 7°C in February to 28°C in

August. More than 3,000 mm of rain fall annually, mostly during the early summer rainy season and the typhoon season.

More than five hundred species of wild plants have been recorded, and the avifauna includes several species and subspecies endemic to the Izu Islands. Of particular note are the Izu Islands Thrush, Ijima's Warbler, and the large, chestnut-cheeked island race of Varied Tit (*P. v. owstoni*). Other interesting species, although not endemic to the Izu Islands, are Japanese Murrelet, Japanese Woodpigeon, Collared Scops Owl, Japanese Robin, and Middendorff's Warbler.

The best birdwatching area is around Tairo-ike, a 2,000-year-old, 1.2 km^2 lake at the south end of the island. A footpath encircles the lake through forest where Ijima's Warbler is abundant. This active and very vocal warbler that breeds only in the Izu Islands arrives in late March or early April and stays until September. The attractive but secretive Japanese Robin, arriving in May and staying until September (although some are said to be resident), is also fairly common here. They prefer dense vegetation, occur on or near the ground, and are best located by their song, which ends in a dry rattle.

In the evenings Eurasian Woodcock display over Tairo-ike, giving their double display calls—a low grunting "ung-ung" and a sibilant "twissick." Also watch for them over the road at night. Look out also for Brown Hawk Owl on wires and posts beside the road, listening for their repeated, rhythmical, "hoo-oo, hoo-oo" double call-note. Other night birds likely to be encountered are Black-crowned Night Heron, which visit Tairo-ike at dawn and dusk, and the resident Collared Scops Owl. The latter is uncommon, however, and only calls in early winter and early spring. Its varied calls include a repeated, catlike "mew, mew," a strong "kwee-kwee," and a whistling "pew-u, pew-u." The secretive and nocturnal Japanese Night Heron is a very uncommon summer visitor that breeds in the forest. The best chance of seeing it is to visit the shore of Tairo-ike at dawn and dusk, but remember that the common species is also here. Between seven and eight at night you may also hear the strange "gya-gya" calls and the fluttering of Streaked Shearwater as they come to their nesting burrows on the slopes of Oyama. There is a huge colony of Streaked Shearwater on Mikurajima, south of Miyakejima, and large numbers feed offshore from Miyakejima.

In summer the call of Little Cuckoo, sounding just like its Japanese name, "Ho-to-to-gi-su," is often heard, although this is a difficult bird to see. Bamboo Partridge is common and similarly more likely to be heard than seen. Males and females sing in duet, repeating again and again their loud "weep and sweep" calls, starting very fast and gradually slowing down.

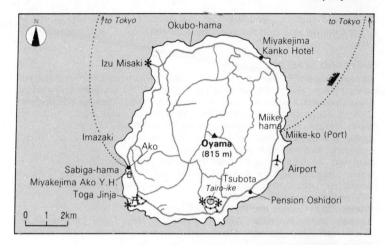

The endemic Izu Islands Thrush, also found on Hachijojima and on Oshima in winter, is particularly common on Miyakejima, and seeing fifty or more a day is not unusual. They feed on the ground, especially in gardens, tea plantations, and other cultivated areas, wherever there is damp soil and leaf litter, and their song, "gyororo-ji," is heard in the early morning and evening.

Dense grassland and rough scrub around the edges of woodlands on Izu Misaki (Cape Izu) in the northwest, the cape in the southwest near Toga Jinja (Toga Shrine), and the upper slopes of Oyama are the habitat of Middendorff's Warbler. This is a late summer visitor, arriving in mid-May. The race here (*L. o. pleskei*) is sometimes treated as a separate species from that breeding in Hokkaido (*L. o. ochotenis*). In the same habitat, keep an eye out for the Fan-tailed Warbler, although it is not common.

Look for Eastern Reef Egret and shorebirds around the coast, and for Fork-tailed Swift around low cliffs. The capes, particularly Izu Misaki, are interesting during the spring migration season since migrants, such as Latham's Snipe, Wandering Tattler, Hoopoe, and other rarities visit.

The first three hours out from Miyake on the ferry journey back to Tokyo are best for seawatching, especially for Japanese Murrelet, which breed on Sanbon-dake, a group of islets to the southwest of Miyakejima, and Tristram's Petrel, which sometimes occur in quite large numbers. In spring, look out for skuas; Pomarine are the commonest, but you may also see other species. There are phalaropes in spring and summer, and keep an eye open for albatrosses. In winter Great Crested and Red-necked Grebe, various gulls, and murrelets are present at sea.

BIRDS AND SEASONS

All year: Streaked Shearwater; Tristram's Petrel; Temminck's Cormorant; Black-crowned Night Heron; Eastern Reef Egret; Osprey; Chinese Bamboo Partridge; Green Pheasant; Black-tailed Gull; Japanese Murrelet; Japanese Woodpigeon; Collared Scops Owl; Japanese Pygmy Woodpecker; Blue Rock Thrush; Izu Islands Thrush; Fan-tailed Warbler; Varied Tit; Bull-headed Shrike.

Spring & Autumn: Cattle Egret; Latham's Snipe; Common Sandpiper; Ruddy Turnstone; Red-necked Phalarope; Pomarine Skua.

Summer: Black-footed and Laysan Albatross; Sooty and Short-tailed Shearwater; Japanese Night Heron (very uncommon); Gray-faced Buzzard; Eurasian Woodcock; Little Cuckoo; Brown Hawk Owl; Fork-tailed Swift; Japanese Robin; Middendorff's Warbler; Ijima's Warbler.

Winter: Great Crested and Red-necked Grebe.

Rarities: Oriental Pratincole; Wandering Tattler (in May); Arctic, Long-tailed, and South Polar Skua; Hoopoe (March/April); Greater Short-toed Lark; Japanese Yellow Bunting.

HOW TO GET THERE

From Tokyo: 1 hr by plane, 7 hr by boat.

There are two flights a day each way between Tokyo's Haneda Airport and Miyakejima Airport, operated by Air Nippon ☎(03)552-6311. Winter flights may be cancelled because of bad weather.

The ferry to Miyakejima, operated by Tokai Kisen Co. ☎(03)432-4551, runs several days a week. Boats leave Tokyo Hinode Sanbashi pier, a 10-min walk east of Hamamatsucho Station (on the Yamanote Line), at 22:10 and arrive at Miyakejima at 04:50. The cheapest fare in July and August is about ¥6,000, while at other seasons it is about ¥4,000. Boats go every day in July and August, but not on Tuesdays in other months. Since the ferry leaves late at night and arrives at Miyakejima early in the morning, there is little chance of seeing anything other than Streaked Shearwater, so it is better to fly there and return by boat. Boats leave Miyakejima at 13:20 and arrive at Tokyo at 19:20.

Buses run around the island seven or eight times a day and timetables are posted at bus stops. Taxis are available at the airport, and both cars and bicycles may be rented.

Accommodation: There are various minshuku and ryokan, and Miyakejima Ako Youth Hostel ☎(04994)5-0100, as well as camp sites at Miike-hama, Sabiga-hama, and Okubo-hama.

The best place for birders to stay is at Pension Oshidori (Mandarin Duck) ☎(04994)6-0346. (The owners do not speak English.) It is about 5 min southwest of the airport by car, and the nearest bus stop is Miyake-mura Kominkan. Book in advance, especially for weekends and on national holidays, which are usually very busy. Alternatively, stay at Miyakejima Kanko Hotel ☎(04994)2-0230 on the northeast coast.

10. Ogasawara Shoto, Tokyo   小笠原諸島

Good birding months: Jan.–Dec.
Best birding months: May–Aug.

This small group of subtropical islands, 1,000 km south of Tokyo, is also known as the Bonin Islands and forms part of a long island chain stretching through the Izu Islands down to the Iwo (Volcano) Islands. As oceanic islands they lack the faunal diversity found on offshore islands, but the several endemic races and species found here are fascinating if you have an interest in island biogeography. Admittedly, most of the endemic birds have unfortunately disappeared, including the Bonin Islands Grosbeak and Kittlitz's Thrush, neither of which has been seen since the naturalist J. H. von Kittlitz landed at Port Lloyd, Peel Island (Chichijima), in June 1828 and collected specimens. The Bonin Islands Honeyeater, however, is still common on Hahajima, where it occurs widely in forests, gardens, and among fruit (papaya) trees.

Other island endemics include races of Common Buzzard, Japanese Woodpigeon (now seemingly extinct too), Brown-eared Bulbul, and Japanese Bush Warbler. The endemic island race of the White-eye has now unfortunately been diluted by birds of the nominate race introduced from the mainland.

Being so far south and so far out in the Pacific, tropical seabirds are common. In fact the surrounding seas have an abundance of seabirds found nowhere else in Japan, except around some of the uninhabited islands in the southern Nansei Shoto.

The best chance of seeing Short-tailed Albatross in Japan is from the boat to Ogasawara Shoto in winter. By the morning after departure from Tokyo the *Ogasawaru Maru* is already well south of Torishima, where the species' only proven breeding grounds are, so for a chance of seeing one, get up at dawn to start seawatching. Both Laysan and Black-footed Albatross breed on Mukojima in winter, and many can be seen from the ferry during this season.

Wedge-tailed Shearwater and Bulwer's Petrel are common around the islands, Matsudaira's Petrel follow the boat north of Chichijima, and between the islands both Audubon's Shearwater and Bonin Petrel are relatively easy to see. The best seawatching is just north of Chichijima and just north of Hahajima. Brown Booby are common around Hahajima. There is a breeding colony just off the south cape, and you should also find Brown Noddy and, if you are lucky, perhaps Red-tailed Tropicbird or Lesser Frigatebird.

On Hahajima the best birdwatching area is around Motochi village, where the mouth of the Otanigawa and the school grounds encourage various shorebirds to stop over on migration and to winter. Keep an eye

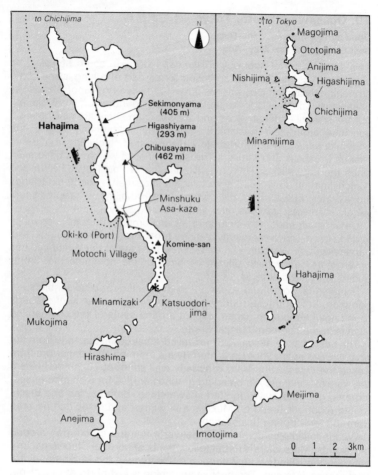

open for other unusual migrants too—Hoopoe have been seen here in March. Walk along the roads north or south from the village to watch the honeyeaters—they are common and tame—look for birds among the papaya, banana, and tobacco plantations, as well as in the surrounding woodland, and walk to Minamizaki to watch the boobies.

It is worth visiting Ogasawara at any time of the year, but for seabirds from spring to autumn is best. The snorkeling and fishing are excellent throughout the year, and the whole atmosphere of the islands, particularly Hahajima, is very relaxing.

Goats have been introduced on Chichijima, and cats occur on both islands. The only mammal of note is the endemic fruit bat, although this now seems to be rare. A large toad is very common on Hahajima, African Mai-Mai (snails) are everywhere, and land and hermit crabs are common.

BIRDS AND SEASONS

All year: Bulwer's Petrel; Brown Booby; Common Buzzard; Blue Rock Thrush; White's Thrush; Bonin Islands Honeyeater.

Summer: Bonin Petrel; Streaked, Wedge-tailed, Sooty, Short-tailed, and Audubon's Shearwater; Matsudaira's and Tristram's Petrel (near the Izu Islands); Greater Crested Tern; Brown Noddy.

Winter: Laysan and Black-footed Albatross.

Rarities: Short-tailed Albatross; Red-tailed Tropicbird; Red-footed and Masked Booby; Lesser Frigatebird; Sooty Tern; Black Noddy.

HOW TO GET THERE

From Tokyo: 28 hr by boat to Chichijima.

Take the *Ogasawara Maru* from Hinode Sanbashi pier, a 10-min walk east of Hamamatsu-cho Station (on the Yamanote Line). The cheapest single fare in summer costs ¥24,000; cabins are available at higher prices. The boat departs at 10:00 and takes 28 hr to reach Chichijima, the main island of the group, most popular with tourists and least interesting for birdwatchers. From Chichijima, catch the connecting boat, the *Hahajima Maru*, which takes 2 hr 20 min to get to Hahajima (¥3,000 single fare). The *Hahajima Maru* leaves Hahajima at 09:00 to connect with the *Ogasawara Maru*, leaving for Tokyo at noon and reaching there the following day at 17:30. The ferry from Tokyo operates only five times a month. The round trip of six days allows for a stay of three nights on Hahajima. For schedules and bookings, telephone the shipping company, Ogasawara Kaiun ☎(03)451-5171.

If you have plenty of time and enjoy sea-watching there is a slower, cheaper (¥17,500, including meals) cargo boat, the *Kyosho Maru*, which takes 50 hr to reach Chichijima and 4 hr to Hahajima. This boat passes Torishima in daylight and thus provides the very best opportunity for looking for Short-tailed Albatross. In winter the seas are rougher and the sailing schedules more erratic. Allow at least ten days for the round trip at that season. From Tokyo Station (Marunouchi South Exit), take a bus (No. 16) to Toyomi-suisan-futo and get off at Toyomi-keisatsu-sho-mae. For schedules and prices contact Kyosho Maru ☎(03)533-2671.

There are no flights to Ogasawara, and Hahajima has no land transportation.

Accommodation: Since camping is prohibited, stay at Minshuku Asa-kaze ☎(04998)3-2131 (the owners speak English), or Minshuku Kinsho ☎(04998)3-2141.

Central Honshu

11. Kotoku-numa, Ibaraki Prefecture　古徳沼

Good birding months: Jan.–Dec.
Best birding months: Jan.–Feb.

Despite recent industrial development and its proximity to Tokyo, much of Ibaraki Prefecture retains a market-garden atmosphere thanks to a mild climate and an abundance of level land and good soil. With mountains in the north, plains in the south, several lakes, and the Pacific coast, it is a varied prefecture with several good spots for birding that can be comfortably visited in a weekend, such as Hi-numa (12) and here at Kotoku-numa. Although small (about 150 m by 300 m), this reservoir, surrounded by deciduous woods and conifer plantations, along with nearby Kenmin no Mori (Kenmin Forest), attracts a wide variety of species, including some interesting specialties such as Copper Pheasant and Gray Bunting. Like many other good Japanese winter birding spots, it attracts a good variety of waterfowl. Quite a large flock of Whooper Swan can be seen here at close range and thus it is popular with Sunday visitors.

There is a regular wintering flock of Falcated Teal at Kotoku-numa, and sometimes they are joined by Baikal Teal. Both of these extremely attractive Asian duck can be very difficult to find in Japan since they are so local in distribution. Baikal Teal winter from central Honshu southward and can only be found from November until March. Sites close to Tokyo where both species can be found are few.

The reservoir attracts not only waterfowl but also Common Snipe and wagtails. In the adjacent woods both species of pheasant occur along with a wide variety of resident and wintering woodland birds, such as Japanese Pygmy Woodpecker, Daurian Redstart, Dusky and Pale Thrush, and several species of buntings. Olive-backed Pipit feed on the

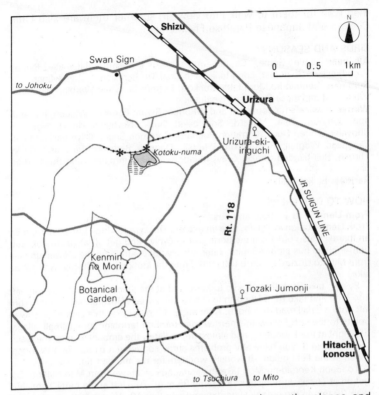

ground among the trees, and in the low scrub on the slopes and beneath the conifers there are usually small flocks of Yellow-throated Bunting and with them a few Gray Bunting. The former, with its yellow head, black face mask, black throat, and dark crest, is the most attractive of all the buntings wintering in Japan. It is commoner in the west of Japan and even breeds on Tsushima (48), but from central Honshu northward it is uncommon. Gray Bunting, on the other hand, are inconspicuous and skulk among the *sasa*. Around the farms and rice fields nearby are Bull-headed Shrike and Hawfinch.

Kenmin no Mori, a 65-ha area of woodland with 10 km of nature trails, was planted to commemorate the hundredth anniversary of the beginning of the Meiji period. Both Copper and Green Pheasant can be seen here too. Listen for them rustling among the leaf litter as they feed, then wait for them to walk into view. In summer there are also Little Cuckoo and Japanese Paradise Flycatcher.

BIRDS AND SEASONS

All year: Little Grebe; Copper and Green Pheasant; Japanese Pygmy Woodpecker; Goldcrest; Long-tailed and Coal Tit; Eurasian Jay; Hawfinch.

Summer: (Kenmin no Mori) Little Cuckoo; Eastern Crowned Warbler; Blue-and-White and Japanese Paradise Flycatcher.

Winter: Bewick's (uncommon) and Whooper Swan; Eurasian Wigeon; Falcated and Common Teal; Mallard; Spot-billed Duck; Northern Pintail; Northern Shoveler; Tufted Duck; Common Pochard; Common Snipe; Olive-backed Pipit; Japanese Wagtail; Red-flanked Bluetail; Daurian Redstart; Pale and Dusky Thrush; Bull-headed Shrike; Gray, Meadow, Yellow-throated, and Rustic Bunting.

Rarities: Baikal Teal.

HOW TO GET THERE

From Ueno: 2 hr by train and bus.

From Ueno Station in Tokyo, take an express (*tokkyu*) to Mito (1 hr 20 min), then an Ibaraki Kotsu bus from the north exit to Omiya and get off at Urizura-eki(station)-iriguchi bus stop (40 min). Alternatively, take a train on the JR Suigun Line from Mito to Urizura or Shizu (30 min). From the station it is a 40-min walk to the lake.

By car, take Rt. 6 from Tokyo to Mito, and at the junction with Rt. 51 turn left into Mito and take Rt. 118 north to Omiya and bypass Urizura town center. Turn left onto a small road to Johoku. After about 1 km a sign with a picture of a swan points to the left. Follow this narrow road through farmland and a small village, turn right at the T-junction, and almost immediately the embankment of the reservoir is visible. If you have any problems show someone a picture of a Whooper Swan in the field guide—it worked wonders for me the first time I went!

To reach Kenmin no Mori take the same bus as above from Mito Station, but get off at Tozaki Jumonji bus stop (after 35 min). Turn left at the traffic lights and walk 20 min to the botanical garden and a further 10–15 min to the entrance of Kenmin no Mori.

Accommodation: A wide variety of accommodation is available in Mito, or visit on a day trip from Tokyo.

12. Hi-numa, Ibaraki Prefecture 涸沼

Good birding months: Jan.–Dec.

Hi-numa is a large lake (about 800 ha) lying 12 km southeast of Mito. From March to May it attracts egrets, ducks, and waders; from May to August Gray-headed Bunting breed here; and in September Crested Honey Buzzard, Gray-faced Buzzard, Common Buzzard, and various

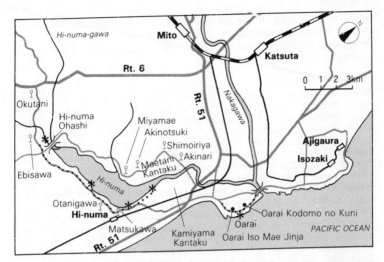

shorebirds pass through on migration. In winter a wide range of common waterfowl occur, with among them a small flock of Great Crested Grebe, including a few Black-necked Grebe, usually a few Falcated Teal (at the west end of the lake), and sometimes Bean Goose and Whooper Swan. White-tailed Eagle sometimes reach this far south and Osprey occasionally visit, while the lake's list of rarities have included a wintering flock of Canvasback (in 1982–83 and 1983–84).

Around the lake in winter there are plenty of Dusky Thrush and Rustic Bunting and occasionally Snow Bunting. In spring on the surrounding fields there are Pacific Golden Plover and Northern Lapwing, and in rough vegetation and reeds there are buntings. Just before the rice is planted in the spring, look for egrets, ducks, and shorebirds at Maetani Kantaku and Kamiyama Kantaku.

In summer Oriental Reed Warbler and Gray-headed Bunting sing from the reedbed at Akinari, and from May till August near Hi-numa Ohashi, look for Yellow Bittern, Spot-billed Duck, Ruddy Crake, Greater Painted Snipe, and Black-browed Reed Warbler. In autumn various birds of prey pass through on migration, and some, such as Common Buzzard and Eurasian Kestrel, remain to winter here.

From late April and early May nearby Oarai Kaigan is attractive to Whimbrel, Ruddy Turnstone, and sometimes to Wandering Tattler. Shearwater pass offshore on their northerly migration in May and June and can be seen both here and off the mouth of the Nakagawa. In winter at both areas there are divers, Ancient Murrelet, shorebirds including Sanderling, cormorants, scoter, Harlequin Duck, and gulls. In spring and autumn, check the pines near the beach for *Phylloscopus* warblers and flycatchers.

BIRDS AND SEASONS

Spring & Autumn: Streaked, Sooty, and Short-tailed Shearwater; Crested Honey Buzzard; Gray-faced and Common Buzzard; Eurasian Kestrel; Pacific Golden Plover; Sharp-tailed Sandpiper; Common Snipe; Whimbrel; Spotted Redshank; Common Greenshank; Wood Sandpiper; Ruddy Turnstone; Eastern Crowned Warbler; Blue-and-White Flycatcher.

Summer: Yellow Bittern; Spot-billed Duck; Ruddy Crake; Common Coot; Greater Painted Snipe; Little Ringed Plover; Common Sandpiper; Fan-tailed Warbler; Black-browed and Oriental Reed Warbler; Gray-headed Bunting.

Winter: Red-throated and Black-throated Diver; Great Crested and Black-necked Grebe; Temminck's and Pelagic Cormorant; Whooper Swan; Bean Goose; Eurasian Wigeon; Falcated Teal; Gadwall; Mallard; Spot-billed Duck; Northern Shoveler; Common Pochard; Tufted Duck; Greater Scaup; Harlequin Duck; Common and Velvet Scoter; Common Goldeneye; Smew; Goosander; Common Buzzard; Osprey; Eurasian Kestrel; Peregrine; Kentish Plover; Northern Lapwing; Sanderling; Dunlin; Common Sandpiper; Black-tailed, Common, Herring, and Slaty-backed Gull; Ancient Murrelet; Dusky Thrush; Meadow, Gray-headed, Rustic, and Common Reed Bunting.

Rarities: American Wigeon; Canvasback; White-tailed Eagle; Wandering Tattler; Snow Bunting.

HOW TO GET THERE

From Ueno: 2½–3 hr by train and bus.

From Ueno Station in Tokyo take an express (*tokkyu*) to Mito, then from Mito either a JR bus or a Kanto Tetsudo bus (about 30 min), or an Ibaraki Kotsu bus to Oarai. For Maetani and Kamiyama Kantaku (the east end of the lake), take a JR bus bound for Ebisawa and get off at Shimoiriya, Akinari, Matsukawa, or Otanigawa. Or take an Ibaraki Kotsu bus, get off at Shimoiriya or Akinotsuki, and walk between the houses and through the rice fields to the reedbed. For Oarai Kaigan, take the Ibaraki Kotsu bus to Oarai Kodomo no Kuni and get off at Oarai Iso Mae Jinja.

A car is useful for exploring the area around Hi-numa and for visiting other sites in Ibaraki Prefecture, such as Kotoku-numa (11). Cars can be rented from Eki Renta Car ☎(0292)25-9577 at Mito Station.

Accommodation: There are many minshuku and ryokan nearby and in Mito, or visit on a day trip from Tokyo.

13. Ukishima, Ibaraki Prefecture   浮島

Good birding months: May–Sept.

Ukishima marsh, although small (60 ha), is an excellent place for Japanese reedbed birds. It is situated at the southeast corner of Kasumigaura, Japan's second largest lake (after Biwa-ko near Kyoto), in the Suigo-Tsukuba Quasi-National Park. The combination of lake shore and river, reedbed and rice fields makes for an excellent variety of species at Ukishima, including in particular Schrenk's Bittern and Japanese Reed Bunting.

In early spring Water Pipit, Dusky Thrush, and buntings pass through on their way northward, and from May onward Common Black-headed Gull and Little Tern visit the lake. In spring and autumn shorebirds can be found along the muddy shores or on the wet and drying rice fields, while in autumn the lotus ponds sometimes attract Greater Painted Snipe.

During summer the reedbeds become the haunt of both Yellow and Schrenck's Bittern. The former is common and flies across the reedbeds frequently. The latter is more skulking and a little harder to see; its dark chocolate or chestnut-brown back, crown, and tail distinguish it, however, from its sandier-colored cousin. Keep watching across the reedbed and sooner or later both species will fly up and beat leisurely across the marsh.

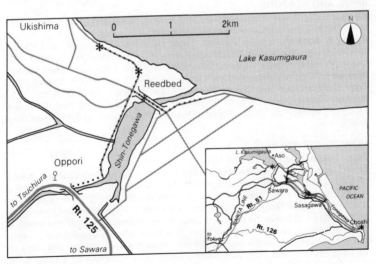

While watching for bitterns you will see and hear Japanese Reed Bunting singing their characteristic "chui-tsui-chirin" song, or giving their rather chatlike "bireet" calls from the reed tops. The male's hood is sooty black and lacks the white mustachial streak of the Common Reed Bunting (which is more likely to be seen here in winter). They remain at Ukishima until September. Then in winter they can be found at nearby Tonegawa (14).

The reeds harbor other songsters too. From May onward the small Black-browed Reed Warbler and the much larger and louder Oriental Reed Warbler sing from the reed tops, while the diminutive, streaky, Fan-tailed Warbler bobs over the reedbed in its display flight with a regular "tseep-tseep-tseep," which changes abruptly to a hard "zit-zit-zit" as it lands.

From November onward birds of prey visit, and harriers can be found quartering the lakeside fields as well as the reedbeds. There are records of the rare Pied Harrier here in early summer, but confusion can arise with males of the Eastern Marsh Harrier, which can be easily mistaken for it.

The best season for a visit is from late spring until early autumn (mid-May until September). Japanese Reed Bunting arrive from April onward and the bitterns from mid-May. An earlier visit may find more shorebirds but no Schrenck's Bittern.

BIRDS AND SEASONS

All year: Little Grebe; Black-crowned Night Heron; Little and Great Egret; Spot-billed Duck; Common Coot; Fan-tailed Warbler.
Spring & Autumn: Greater Painted Snipe; Little Ringed, Kentish, and Pacific Golden Plover; Sharp-tailed Sandpiper; Common Snipe; Whimbrel; Spotted Redshank; Wood Sandpiper; Common Black-headed Gull; Little Tern; Sand Martin.
Summer: Cattle and Intermediate Egret; Yellow and Schrenck's Bittern; Little Tern; Black-browed and Oriental Reed Warbler; Japanese Reed Bunting.
Winter: Tufted Duck; Eastern Marsh and Hen Harrier; Water Rail; Common Moorhen; Water Pipit; Dusky Thrush; Meadow, Rustic, and Common Reed Bunting.

HOW TO GET THERE

From Tokyo: 2 hr by train and bus.

From Tokyo Station, take the Narita Line to Sawara (1½ hr). From Sawara, take a JR bus to Edosaki via Nichiro and get off at Oppori bus stop (25 min), where the road crosses the river. Walk north along the west side of the Shin-Tonegawa (so it is on your right), first past houses, then past fields and paddies, until you come to the reeds and finally the lake. The large bridge crossing the river and marsh is the best place to view the reedbed from. The lake is an easy day trip from Tokyo, but those with a car might explore the area around Kitaura as well and carry on up Rt. 51 to Hi-numa (12), then Kotoku-numa (11). Another way is to go south along the Tonegawa (14) toward Choshi, looking for Japanese Marsh Warbler in any likely looking reedbeds, since they breed and winter along the river.

Accommodation: Either visit from Tokyo or stay in Aso at the minshuku Shiraho-so ☎(0299)72-0831,

14. Tonegawa, Chiba Prefecture 利根川

Good birding months: Jan.–Dec.
Best birding months: May–July

The Tonegawa (Tone River) flows through the center of the Kanto Plain collecting water from north Chiba and Kasumigaura before flowing into the Pacific Ocean at Choshi (15) in Chiba Prefecture. It once flowed out into Tokyo Bay, but its course was diverted to prevent flooding in Saitama Prefecture. Between Kasumigaura and Choshi the river is bordered by rice fields and reedbeds.

The Japanese Marsh Warbler both breeds and winters here. This species has a very localized distribution in Japan, occurring also in Akita and Aomori prefectures in summer, but this site is by far the easiest to

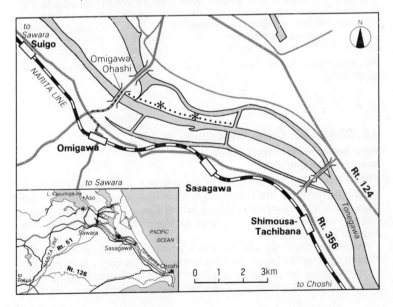

visit from Tokyo. It is a little larger and darker than a Fan-tailed Warbler, with a rounded tail that is brown all the way to the tip, and a distinctive habit of singing during brief circling display flights over the reeds. It displays from late May onward, and thus this is the best time to go looking for it. Japanese Reed Bunting also breed here, and in winter both it and Common Reed Bunting can be found among the reeds and in areas of dry grass.

BIRDS AND SEASONS
All year: Little Egret; Spot-billed Duck; Common Moorhen; Japanese Marsh Warbler; Bull-headed Shrike; Japanese Reed Bunting.
Spring & Autumn: Ruff; Common Snipe; Spotted Redshank; Common Greenshank.
Summer: Yellow Bittern; Eastern Marsh Harrier; Greater Painted Snipe (in rice fields); Little Tern; Fan-tailed Warbler; Black-browed and Oriental Reed Warbler.
Winter: Common Teal; Peregrine; Dusky Thrush; Common Reed Bunting.
Rarities: Great Bittern.

HOW TO GET THERE
From Tokyo: 3 hr by train.
Follow the same route as for Ukishima (13), via Narita and Sawara, but get off at Omigawa, two stops east of Sawara. Walk from the station (or take a taxi) to Omigawa Ohashi (Omigawa Bridge). Cross the bridge, turn right at the far end of the bridge and walk alongside the reedbed for 1 or 2 km. The reeds here harbor both marsh warbler and reed bunting, but if the reeds have been cut or burned you may need to try in the opposite direction, upriver from the bridge.

Accommodation: Either visit from Tokyo or stay in Aso at the minshuku Shiraho-so ☎(0299)72-0831.

15. Choshi-ko, Chiba Prefecture　銚子港
Good birding months: Nov.–March
Best birding month: Feb.

This is the best place in central Honshu to get to know the east Asian gulls. The mouth of the Tonegawa is 1 km wide here, and on the south bank there is the 2 km-long fishing port of Choshi. It is a winter birding site worth visiting from November to March but at its best in mid-February.

Weekday mornings are the most interesting because the sardine fishing boats return laden and followed by gulls. Large flocks of the commoner species are joined by smaller numbers of Glaucous-winged and Glaucous Gull, Black-legged Kittiwake, and occasionally by a Northern

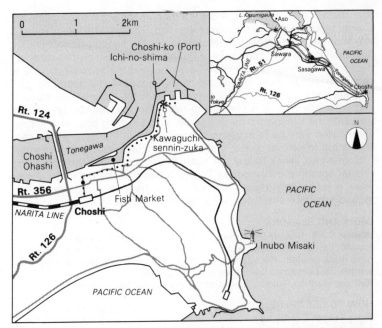

Fulmar or two. When you have had your fill of gulls, look out for the sea duck—there will probably be a few Harlequin Duck on and around the rocks at the river mouth and scoter and merganser further offshore. Temminck's Cormorant are very common, perching on the breakwater within 100 m of the road, and you may also see a few Pelagic Cormorant.

Most notable is the wintering flock of Rock Sandpiper. This bird is a North American species, but each autumn a small group makes its way down the Kurile Island chain instead of down the west coast of America. They visit only two sites in Japan regularly, Kiritappu (34) in east Hokkaido, and here at Choshi. Their movements are erratic and they are difficult to find, but if you search the breakwaters and the rocks beyond at high tide with a telescope you might be lucky. The bird is about the size of a Dunlin but behaves quite differently, and being well camouflaged can easily be overlooked. They are most reluctant to fly, creeping around wet rocks and running to escape the waves.

The outcrop of rocks on the south side of the river mouth near the lighthouse is mostly out of view behind a long sea wall. At the corner near the bus stop, however, there is a monument and a small shrine on a slight rise to the landward side of the road. The extra couple of meters elevation this gives makes it possible to see the sandpipers roosting at high tide and to get good views of Harlequin Duck, which also roost on the rocks. The best rock is immediately beyond the sea wall, behind a section painted yellow with large, black, Japanese characters on it. If they are not in view at first they may well be on the other side of the rock and walk into view. It is possible to reach the sea wall for close-range views of the sandpipers by joining up with a fishing boat at a fishing shop called Tanaka Tsurigu-ten. Also walk down the coast a little past the harbor to look for divers, grebes, Eastern Reef Egret, and Peregrine.

Sometimes skuas follow the gulls, Brent Goose occasionally come this far south, and Wandering Tattler, a bird that prefers rocky shorelines, is reasonably regular in winter. There have been records of Red-legged Kittiwake and Ivory Gull joining the gull flocks here.

BIRDS AND SEASONS
Winter: Black-throated Diver; Red-necked Grebe; Temminck's and Pelagic Cormorant; Eastern Reef Egret; Harlequin Duck; Peregrine; Rock Sandpiper; Common Black-headed, Black-tailed, Common, Herring, Slaty-backed, Glaucous-winged, and Glaucous Gull; Black-legged Kittiwake.
Rarities: Northern Fulmar; Brent Goose; Wandering Tattler; Pomarine Skua.

HOW TO GET THERE
From Tokyo: 2 hr by train.
From Tokyo Station, take an express on the Narita Line and Sobu Honsen, which goes via Chiba to Choshi. From the station, either walk or take a Chiba Kotsu bus to Kawaguchi and Kurohai Jutaku, get off at the Kawaguchi-sennin-zuka bus stop at the corner of the harbor (about a 15-min ride), and walk back along the south side of the river, looking out to the north across the river mouth, breakwaters, and harbor. Also watch the sea and rocks offshore from the river mouth, and the river from Choshi Ohashi (Choshi Bridge).

Accommodation: A variety of accommodation is available in Choshi; however, this site is easily visited on a day trip from Tokyo.

16. Oku-Nikko, Tochigi Prefecture　奥日光
Good birding months: Jan.–Dec.
Best birding months: Oct.–March, May–June

Nikko is one of Japan's most renowned and attractive sightseeing areas, with its famous Toshogu Shrine, its famous carvings of a sleeping cat and the "see-no, hear-no, speak-no-evil" monkeys, and many buildings of the Tokugawa period (1603–1867). The nearby hills, forests, and lakes are equally well known for hiking and birdwatching.

For those looking for a more relaxing atmosphere than Nikko itself, it is better to stay at Yumoto Onsen, or in Oku-Nikko (1,400 m). From October to mid-November the trees around Chuzenji-ko, Nantai-san, Kirikomi-ko, and Karikomi-ko are a superb blaze of color. At Senjogahara, a 1,000-ha area of marsh, river, ponds, and forest, the tints are more muted—soft-brown marsh grass and sedge, and silver-barked birch with yellowing leaves.

Trails cross Senjogahara, branching in several places (see map), but I recommend following the trail along the river to Yuno-ko to see Gray Wagtail and Brown Dipper and the beautiful Yutaki waterfall. The trees beside the river attract the commoner woodland birds. Mallard are resident along the river, Common Teal frequent the marshier places, and Latham's Snipe and Water Rail summer and breed in the marshes.

The route to Nantai-san passes through forests of dark green pines and paler larches. Here woodpeckers, Goldcrest, and Coal Tit are common. Both Red-flanked Bluetail and Eye-browed Thrush may be seen in winter, although they are more likely to be heard, since they prefer the shadier parts of the forest to the edges. Bluetail have a low "tuc-tuc" call and usually perch within one or two meters of the ground. The thrushes have a thin whistling call, feed on the ground, and are most likely to be seen as they fly up when disturbed.

Another pleasant walk passes Kotoku Bokujo (Kotoku Ranch), where the trail climbs over low hills, passing through mixed and coniferous forest and *sasa*—an excellent area for mushrooms in the autumn. The trail passes two small lakes, Kirikomi-ko and Karikomi-ko, then rejoins the road above Yuno-ko. In winter there are Spot-billed Duck, Tufted Duck, Common Pochard, and Smew at Yuno-ko.

Summer, from May onward, is the best time to walk this route, with Hodgson's Hawk Cuckoo, various warblers and flycatchers, Japanese Robin, and Siberian Blue Robin in the woods, Japanese Yellow Bunting in the Kotoku area, and Common House Martin overhead.

In autumn Gray-streaked and Asian Brown Flycatcher pass through, and even in late autumn Narcissus Flycatcher are still here. White-backed Woodpecker are resident and Japanese Accentor move here from their breeding grounds in the higher mountains. The latter are very secretive, feeding on the ground under the trees or among the *sasa*. Look for them especially on the paths. Rocky areas, even alongside the main roads, sometimes attract wintering Alpine Accentor. In winter, search the shore of the small pond (Kotoku-numa) and the stream just below the ranch for Solitary Snipe and Japanese Wagtail. Toward the end of October several species of buntings, finches, and thrushes arrive, and in some winters a Great Gray Shrike visits.

In winter Chuzenji-ko (Lake Chuzenji) attracts a few species of waterbird, including Slavonian Grebe, but for the rest of the year it is not interesting. In Nikko itself the river harbors Japanese Wagtail and Brown Dipper, and in the giant cedars around Toshogu Shrine there are Azure-winged Magpie.

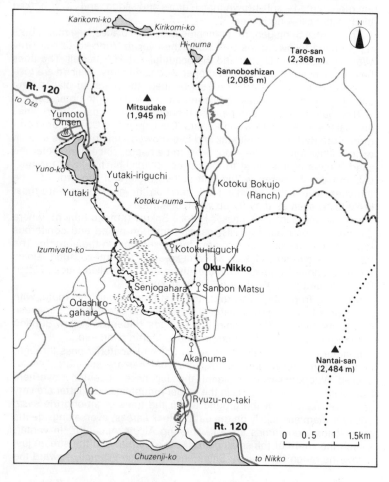

The combination of autumn colors, lakes, and waterfalls, and the presence of some very attractive autumn and winter birds make Oku-Nikko a pleasant holiday destination. In summer the area has a host of birds and flowers. In winter birds are scarcer, but snow on the surrounding mountains makes the scenery even more beautiful for hiking in.

Early in the morning or late in the afternoon, listen for the call of the Sika, the largest forest deer in Japan. Most deer have a rough, almost barking, call, but the Sika has a strange, plaintive whistle that carries far. Japanese Macaque too are often to be seen in the Nikko area, especially alongside the main road below Irohazaka (the winding mountain road up to Chuzenji-ko).

If you visit the Toshogu Shrine in Nikko itself, on the broad approach path there is still sometimes a man using a Varied Tit to tell fortunes, a relic of old customs. And the shrine itself has more bird and animal carvings than any other shrine I know.

BIRDS AND SEASONS
All year: Mallard; Ural Owl; Great Spotted, White-backed, and Japanese Pygmy Woodpecker; Japanese Wagtail; Brown Dipper; Northern Wren; Goldcrest; Long-tailed, Willow, Varied, and Coal Tit; Eurasian Nuthatch; Common Treecreeper; Azure-winged Magpie.
Summer: Common Teal; Water Rail; Latham's Snipe; Japanese Green Pigeon; Hodgson's Hawk Cuckoo; Common and Little Cuckoo; Common House Martin; Japanese Robin; Siberian Blue Robin; Siberian, Gray, and Brown Thrush; Stub-tailed Bush Warbler; Eastern Crowned, Pale-legged, and Arctic Warbler; Blue-and-White and Narcissus Flycatcher; Russet Sparrow; Japanese Yellow and Gray-headed Bunting.
Autumn: Gray-streaked, Asian Brown, and Narcissus Flycatcher.
Winter: Slavonian Grebe; Eurasian Wigeon; Spot-billed Duck; Common Pochard; Tufted Duck; Common Goldeneye; Smew; Goosander; Common Buzzard; Japanese and Alpine Accentor; Red-flanked Bluetail; Stonechat; Eyebrowed and Dusky Thrush; Brambling; Eurasian Siskin; Long-tailed Rosefinch; Common Bullfinch; Hawfinch; Meadow and Rustic Bunting.
Rarities: Solitary Snipe; Great Gray Shrike; Pallas's Rosefinch.

HOW TO GET THERE
From Asakusa Station, Tokyo: 3 hr by train and bus.
In Tokyo, take the Ginza subway line to Asakusa, walk a short distance to Matsuya department store, where the Tobu Nikko Line Station is situated. A special express takes 1 hr 45 min and a limited express 2 hr 10 min to Tobu Nikko Station. In Nikko, take a Tobu bus for Yumoto Onsen from the stop in front of the railway station to Aka-numa bus stop (1 hr) (closest to the approach to Senjogahara), or Sanbon Matsu bus stop. The former is more convenient for a day-trip to Senjogahara, the latter for a walk up Nantai-san.

Accommodation: Nikko has many first-class hotels and two youth hostels, but most birdwatchers will want to go straight to Oku-Nikko. From Sanbon Matsu bus stop (on Rt. 120), cross the road to a gift-shop, turn right past it up a track and take the next left. On the right there is a pleasant minshuku called Sanso Photo ☎(0288)55-0169, which caters to hikers and birders.

Alternatively, stay at an onsen hotel. In this case, stay on the bus until it passes Yuno-ko and get off at Yumoto Onsen. A variety of accommodation is available, all with the advantage of a hot spring bath at the end of a day out in the field. In summer there is a camp site at Yumoto.

17. Karuizawa, Nagano Prefecture 軽井沢

Good birding months: Jan.–Dec.
Best birding months: Dec.–March, May–June

Karuizawa is situated amongst forested hills, 145 km northwest of Tokyo, at the foot of the active Asamayama volcano (2,542 m), which is covered with Japanese larch and white birch forests. This area is a cool summer retreat for Tokyoites, particularly in July and August, and is one of the most famous birdwatching regions in Japan.

The combination of altitude (about 1,000 m), mixed deciduous and coniferous forests, and the Yukawa make this an attractive place to visit for walking and birdwatching. Many birds found here are not found in the Tokyo area. The two best birdwatching seasons are from mid-May to late June (bird song is most enjoyable from about May 20 to June 10) and from December to March. The woodlands alongside the river from Hoshino Onsen and the trees and gardens around the holiday houses are excellent for birdwatching. Below are some recommended walks.

1. From Naka-Karuizawa along the Yukawa via Hoshino Onsen, Yacho no Mori, and Kose Onsen.

From Naka-Karuizawa walk northward along the Yukawa to Hoshino Onsen, then turn right past the New Hoshino Hotel and walk along Kose-rindo forest road (best in winter). This track passes the entrance to Yacho no Mori on your right (best in summer) and continues all the way to Kose Onsen through very attractive mixed deciduous forest. This is by far the best birding walk and should not be missed. Most species can be found along the river, up in the Yacho no Mori, or around clearings in the forest (e.g., Jungle Nightjar). Copper Pheasant should be looked for near streams in winter (it is very secretive in summer), and Green Pheasant and Japanese Green Woodpecker around gardens.

You can return by bus from Kose Onsen to Karuizawa or continue on foot via Kyu-Karuizawa. A good forest road branches off to the left past the camp site, just after you leave Kose going south.

2. Along the Yagasakigawa.

Walk east from Karuizawa Station until the road crosses the river—at this point it seems more like a ditch in its concrete channel. Turn left and follow the river up to its source in the hills. There are many small roads, summer houses, gardens, and mature trees in this area, and consequently plenty of birds. The roads do not always follow the river closely and you will need to wend your way a little to remain close to it.

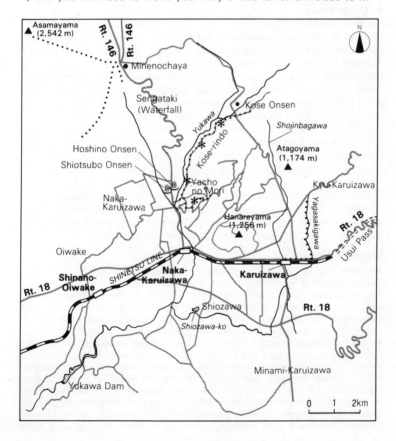

3. Asamayama.

Drive or take a taxi up to the head of the road that passes Hoshino Onsen (about 20 min). On the left, trails lead uphill to Asamayama and downhill through excellent forest. Arrive early in the forest here, because the cicada noise can be deafening later. At about 1,800 m, this is a pleasant walk through natural forest, with a chance of some high-altitude birds. In May, June, and July, look for Eurasian Nutcracker, Red-flanked Bluetail, Stonechat, Arctic Warbler, Sooty Flycatcher, and Common Bullfinch.

4. Other areas.

For meadow birds in summer, such as Stonechat and Gray-headed Bunting, try Minami-Karuizawa Golf Course or the area north of Oiwake. Between Karuizawa and Naka-Karuizawa, lying to the north of the railway line and the main road, is Hanareyama. Around its northern flanks the forest is worth looking in during summer for Siberian Blue Robin and the secretive Siberian Thrush if you have missed it along the Yukawa. The song of the latter is a fluty "kiron-tsee," not to be confused with the similar song of the Brown Thrush, which is "kiron-kiron-tsee." Northeast of Karuizawa Station, near the ice-skating rink, from May onward look for Ruddy Kingfisher, Brown Thrush, and Blue-and-White and Narcissus Flycatcher. Also explore south of Karuizawa by car. Latham's Snipe and Gray-headed Bunting breed in abandoned rice fields here.

Mammals to look for at night or early in the morning include the Racoon Dog, Red Fox, Japanese Serow (which occur on Asamayama but are uncommon), Japanese Squirrel, Japanese Hare, and the Giant Flying Squirrel (in large nest boxes along the Yukawa trail).

BIRDS AND SEASONS

All year: Copper and Green Pheasant; Japanese Green Pigeon; Ural Owl; Crested Kingfisher (uncommon); Japanese Green, Great Spotted, and Japanese Pygmy Woodpecker; Japanese Wagtail; Brown Dipper; Northern Wren; Goldcrest; Long-tailed, Willow, and Coal Tit; Eurasian Nuthatch; Common Treecreeper; Eurasian Jay; Azure-winged Magpie; Eurasian Nutcracker; Common Bullfinch; Japanese Grosbeak; Hawfinch; Meadow Bunting.

Spring & Summer: Mandarin Duck; Northern Goshawk; Japanese and Northern Sparrowhawk; Gray-faced and Common Buzzard; Latham's Snipe; Hodgson's Hawk Cuckoo (from the first week of May), Common (from the second week of May), Oriental (from the last two or three days of April), and Little Cuckoo (around May 15–20); Brown Hawk Owl; Jungle Nightjar; Fork-tailed Swift; Ruddy Kingfisher; Common House Martin; Olive-backed Pipit; Ashy Minivet; Siberian Blue Robin; Red-flanked Bluetail; Stonechat; White's, Siberian, Gray, and Brown Thrush; Stub-tailed Bush Warbler; Fan-tailed Warbler; Black-browed Reed

Warbler; Eastern Crowned, Pale-legged, and Arctic Warbler; Blue-and-White, Sooty, Asian Brown, and Narcissus Flycatcher; Red-cheeked Starling; Japanese Yellow (uncommon) and Gray-headed Bunting.

Autumn & Winter: Japanese and Bohemian Waxwing; Japanese Accentor; Daurian Redstart; Dusky Thrush; Brambling; Common Redpoll; Red Crossbill; Long-tailed Rosefinch; Yellow-throated Bunting.

Rarities: Solitary Snipe, a little known wintering bird in Japan, is occasionally found alongside both the Yukawa and Yagasakigawa. Look for it where the banks are muddy or overhanging with vegetation. Pallas's Rosefinch is sometimes encountered in winter feeding on seed heads protruding through the snow alongside forest tracks. Japanese Waxwing is also a species to look for; although not present every winter this bird quite regularly visits the Yukawa area. Hoopoe, normally a rare spring visitor to small islands in the south and west of Japan, bred for the first time in the Karuizawa area in 1983 and have returned each summer since. Listen for their regular "hoop-oop-oop-oop" calls. Japanese Paradise Flycatcher and Tiger Shrike sometimes occur in summer but are very uncommon.

HOW TO GET THERE

From Ueno: 2 hr by express (*tokkyu*).
From Nagano: 1 hr by train.
From Ueno Station in Tokyo, take the Shinetsu Line (platform 15) to Naka-Karuizawa (look for Azure-winged Magpie on wires on the way). For Hoshino Onsen, walk (25 min), or take a rental car, bus, or taxi from the station (5 min). For Kose Onsen and Kose-rindo, get off at Karuizawa Station and take a JR bus to Kose Onsen (20 min), then walk from Kose to Hoshino Onsen along the Yukawa. In summer, take the night train leaving Ueno about midnight and arriving at Karuizawa before dawn.

Accommodation: Hotels, ryokan, minshuku, youth hostels, and camp sites are plentiful in the Karuizawa area, but Shiotsubo Onsen Hotel ☎(0267)45-5441 and Hoshino Onsen Hotel ☎(0267)45-5121 are famous among birders for their woodland setting and the wide variety of birds at the feeders. Both are, however, somewhat expensive, so for cheaper accommodation, try Ariake Lodge ☎(0267)45-3096, a minshuku between Naka-Karuizawa Station and Hoshino Onsen. Avoid the crowded high summer season and the New Year period.

18. Ura-Myogi, Gunma Prefecture　裏妙義

Good birding months: Jan.–Dec.

Ura-Myogi is an area of outstandingly beautiful mountain and forest scenery between Tokyo and Karuizawa. To the south of Yokokawa, the nearest town, the Nakagigawa winds through a steep-sided, forested valley with high crags on both sides. The mountains here are reminiscent of those in old Japanese or Chinese landscape paintings, and be-

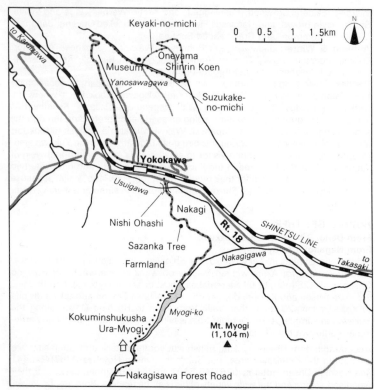

tween them lies Myogi-ko, a small reservoir. To the north of Yokokawa lies Oneyama Shinrin Koen, a forest park opened in 1904 as an experimental forest, with many native and foreign species of tree. In 1973, it was opened to the public. The path to the park is a pleasant walk through orchards of plums and apples and mixed woodland and follows the Yanosawagawa part of the way.

Resident birds include Long-tailed Tit and Varied Tit, both of which are common in the Nakagigawa valley. Look out for Crested Kingfisher and Brown Dipper along the river and Northern Wren in damp wooded gullies. The winding country lane that runs south down the valley passes a large Sazanka tree, a kind of evergreen Camellia, with small rose-pink flowers that open from January onward. This tree has been declared a national monument, since although not of great stature as trees go, it is remarkably large for its species. Its winter flowers sometimes attract birds fond of nectar, such as Japanese White-eye, while Russet Sparrow and Japanese Grosbeak have also been seen here. Around the nearby Nakagi village there are Chinese Bamboo Partridge, Japanese and Gray Wagtail, Bull-headed Shrike, Azure-winged Magpie, and in winter Dusky Thrush and Rustic Bunting. In early spring Common Bullfinch visit the fruit trees around the village to eat the buds.

There is quite a large flock of Mallard on the Myogi-ko reservoir in winter, and this sometimes attracts other species, such as Common Teal, Smew, and occasionally even Baikal Teal. Once this was one of the best winter sites for Mandarin Duck (from mid-October until March), with more than 500 birds, but the numbers are declining due to disturbance by boats and fishermen. Look for small flocks under the trees along the far bank of the reservoir.

The many rocky crags beyond the reservoir attract various birds of prey. Golden Eagle breed nearby and remain in the valley throughout the winter, and resident Northern Goshawk, Northern Sparrowhawk, and Common Buzzard may also be encountered. In summer, look carefully for Crested Honey Buzzard and Gray-faced Buzzard, and in winter for Eurasian Kestrel and Peregrine.

In summer, further along the Nakagisawa forest road it is possible to see Ruddy Kingfisher, Gray Thrush, and Blue-and-White Flycatcher. In winter there are Japanese and Alpine Accentor, Red-flanked Bluetail, Rosy Finch, and Long-tailed Rosefinch. The accentors move to lower altitudes when snow covers higher ground. They are often very tame and feed on open slopes, sometimes beside the road.

In summer in Oneyama Shinrin Koen, all four species of cuckoo can be heard, as well as Brown Hawk Owl and Jungle Nightjar. Around dawn (between 04:00 and 06:00) is best, when White's and Gray Thrush, Blue-and-White, Narcissus, and Japanese Paradise Flycatcher, and Stub-tailed Bush Warbler can all be heard. Winter is the best time to look for Copper Pheasant, and among the flocks of commoner buntings there may well be a few Yellow-throated and Gray Bunting, and Long-tailed Rosefinch. There are of course common woodland birds such as woodpeckers, Red-flanked Bluetail, and Daurian Redstart. Both species of waxwing appear during the winter, but, as elsewhere in Japan, their numbers and movements are unpredictable.

In winter you will probably hear the chittering of Japanese Squirrel, even if you don't see them. Japanese Macaque descend from the mountains and are occasionally to be seen foraging in the Nakagigawa valley. Look for them along the edge of the forest and crossing the road. They give a gruff alarm bark when disturbed.

BIRDS AND SEASONS

All year: Northern Goshawk; Northern Sparrowhawk; Common Buzzard; Golden Eagle; Chinese Bamboo Partridge; Copper Pheasant; Crested Kingfisher; Great Spotted and Japanese Pygmy Woodpecker; Gray and Japanese Wagtail; Brown Dipper; Northern Wren; Goldcrest; Long-tailed and Varied Tit; Azure-winged Magpie; Common Bullfinch; Japanese Grosbeak.

Summer: Crested Honey Buzzard; Gray-faced Buzzard; Japanese Green Pigeon; Hodgson's Hawk Cuckoo; Common, Oriental, and Little Cuckoo; Brown Hawk Owl; Jungle Nightjar; Ruddy Kingfisher; White's and Gray Thrush; Stub-tailed Bush Warbler; Narcissus, Blue-and-White, and Japanese Paradise Flycatcher.

Winter: Mandarin Duck; Common Teal; Mallard; Smew; Eurasian Kestrel; Peregrine; Japanese and Bohemian Waxwing; Japanese and Alpine Accentor; Red-flanked Bluetail; Daurian Redstart; Dusky Thrush; Bull-headed Shrike; Russet Sparrow; Brambling; Eurasian Siskin; Rosy Finch; Long-tailed Rosefinch; Hawfinch; Gray, Meadow, Yellow-throated, and Rustic Bunting.

Rarities: Baikal Teal.

HOW TO GET THERE

From Ueno Station: 3 hr by train and on foot.

From Ueno Station in Tokyo, take the Shinetsu Line and get off at Yokokawa Station (2 hr). It is a 40-min walk south to Myogi-ko reservoir along the Nakagisawa forest road.

Accommodation: If you continue along the forest road, which follows the Nakagigawa, you will reach Matsuida Choei Kokuminshukusha Ura-Myogi ☎(0273)95-2631, 5 km from the station. If you are staying there overnight but don't fancy the walk, they will pick you up from the station. Since this is situated in the best area for birds, staying there allows for pre-breakfast birding. Alternatively, visit from Tokyo or Karuizawa (17).

If you want to eat or drink in Yokokawa while waiting for a train back to Ueno or on to Karuizawa, the more-than-100-year-old Oginoya restaurant just opposite the station entrance serves good food and coffee. Incidentally, this area is famous for *kama-meshi*, a rice dish served with meat and vegetables in an attractive earthenware pot that you get to keep if you buy it as a take-away.

19. Tanzawa, Kanagawa Prefecture　丹沢

Good birding months: Jan.–Dec.
Best birding months: May–June

East Tanzawa, with its natural conifer forests and cypress and cedar plantations, is a pleasant area for hiking at any season, with good chances of encountering interesting birds and mammals. The azaleas and other wild flowers are attractive during summer and the autumn colors are splendid. Interesting at all seasons, Tanzawa is, however, best

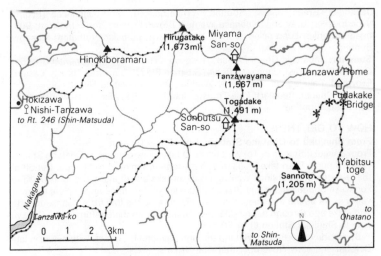

for birds in May and June. The area is famous among Japanese bird-watchers for being home to the nearest pair of Hodgson's Hawk Eagle to Tokyo. Other birds of note here are Copper Pheasant, Hodgson's Hawk Cuckoo, Gray Thrush, and Japanese Robin. Brown Dipper are common along fast-flowing rivers and streams, and look out for Crested Kingfisher along the rivers and at the trout farm. It is, in addition, a very good area for other wildlife.

In winter there are many of the common buntings and finches in the forest, and among them it is always worth checking for Gray Bunting. Hike up to the top of Togadake (1,491 m) for flocks of Rosy Finch, but since the area sometimes has heavy snow, it is advisable to have suitable hiking gear.

Sika Deer are the commonest mammals, and can be seen here at any season, but their mournful whistling calls are best heard in the autumn. The somewhat secretive Japanese Serow occurs on higher slopes, while lower down in the woods there are the more easily seen Racoon Dog, Red Fox, Giant Flying Squirrel, Japanese Squirrel, and Japanese Hare. Two of Japan's larger mammals, the Wild Boar and the Asiatic Black Bear, also occur in this region, but as a result of hunting and disturbance, both are very shy and it requires a great deal of patience to see them.

BIRDS AND SEASONS
All year: Northern Sparrowhawk; Hodgson's Hawk Eagle; Copper Pheasant;

Japanese Green, Great Spotted, White-backed, and Japanese Pygmy Woodpecker; Gray and Japanese Wagtail; Brown Dipper; Northern Wren; Bull-headed Shrike; Long-tailed, Varied, and Coal Tit; Eurasian Nuthatch; Meadow Bunting.
Summer: Japanese Green Pigeon; Hodgson's Hawk Cuckoo; Oriental Cuckoo; Oriental Scops Owl; Japanese Robin; Siberian Blue Robin; Gray Thrush; Eastern Crowned, Pale-legged, and Arctic Warbler; Blue-and-White Flycatcher.
Winter: Daurian Redstart; Pale Thrush; Brambling; Rosy Finch; Hawfinch; Gray and Rustic Bunting.

HOW TO GET THERE
From Shinjuku to Ohatano Station: 1 hr 10 min by train.
From Shinjuku Station in Tokyo, take an Odakyu Line express to Ohatano Station (1 hr 10 min). Then take a bus to Yabitsu-toge (45 min) or to Minoge. Get off at the last stop and continue walking north (or take a taxi) along the forest road to Fudakake Bridge (about 2 hr 30 min). Turn left at the bridge and explore the river valley as far as the trail goes. Alternatively, hike up the trail from Yabitsu-toge to Togadake and through to Shin-Matsuda Station. From there return by the Odakyu Line to Shinjuku Station (1 hr 20 min).

By car, drive north from Hatano through beautiful hill forest, with colors in late October and early November that rival Nikko's.

Accommodation: At Fudakake, stay at Tanzawa Home ☎(0463)75-3272, a kokuminshukusha; or on Togadake, in the mountain hut Sonbutsu San-so ☎(0468)88-1113.

20. Yamanaka-ko, Yamanashi Prefecture　山中湖
Good birding months: Jan.–Dec.

The Fuji Five Lakes (Fuji Go-ko) lie in an arc around the northern flank of Fuji-san (21). Yamanaka-ko, the largest and highest of the five (646 ha, and 981 m above sea level), northeast of Fuji-san, is easily accessible from Tokyo. The lake is surrounded by mature forests, with parklike woodland in areas developed for vacation homes. Early morning bird-watching here is very good. The best areas are around Asahigaoka, where there is a maze of small roads through excellent mixed woodland with beautiful larch trees, at Chaya-no-dan, and around the Kenei camping area.

Three species of woodpecker occur here and include the Japanese Green Woodpecker, which has a whiplike "kwip-kwip-kwip" call. Brown Thrush are especially common in gardens, often feeding on the lawns, while Gray Thrush are more often seen up in the woodland canopy. The "kiron-kiron-tsee" of the former and the chuckling, fluty notes of the latter fill the early morning air. In summer, in addition to the thrushes, look out for Japanese Paradise Flycatcher, and, if you are lucky, you may find Ashy Minivet and Siberian Thrush. You may also find displaying Latham's Snipe and should see Eurasian Woodcock in early summer. Gray and Japanese Wagtail can be seen along streams or feeding on the lawns of the houses, while Common House Martin breed under the eaves of buildings along the lake shore.

The lake itself is rather poor for birds, although a pair of Mute Swan breed (and produce a mixture of normal and "Polish" cygnets) and Common Moorhen can be seen near the shore, but it is well worth visiting the reedbed along the northeast shore, just west of Hirano. Oriental Reed Warbler are common summer visitors here, with their distinctive song, "kara-kara-grik-grik-grik, gurk-gurk," issuing from reed or bush tops. Another reedbed inhabitant is the Yellow Bittern. This small member of the heron family usually stalks along the edge of the reeds where, with its tawny plumage, it is well camouflaged, but it occasionally takes wing and flies across the reed tops.

In winter there are many of the commoner duck on the lake, with a few Falcated Teal and Common Goldeneye, and every year in early January there are a few Whooper Swan. From March onward the ducks can be seen displaying. In most years a few Pallas's Rosefinch are seen near the lake, and Japanese Waxwing sometimes appear. Wandering young Golden Eagle occur at nearby Kawaguchi-ko and sometimes remain throughout the winter.

BIRDS AND SEASONS
All year: Mute Swan; Northern Goshawk; Northern Sparrowhawk; Common Moorhen; Japanese Green, Great Spotted, and Japanese Pygmy Woodpecker; Gray and Japanese Wagtail; Northern Wren; Long-tailed, Willow, Varied, and Coal Tit; Eurasian Nuthatch.
Summer: Yellow Bittern; Ruddy Crake; Latham's Snipe; Eurasian Woodcock; Common, Oriental, and Little Cuckoo; Common House Martin; Olive-backed Pipit; Ashy Minivet; Siberian Blue Robin; White's, Siberian, Gray, and Brown Thrush; Stub-tailed Bush Warbler; Black-browed and Oriental Reed Warbler; Eastern Crowned Warbler; Blue-and-White, Narcissus, and Japanese Paradise Flycatcher; Brown Shrike.
Winter: Whooper Swan; Eurasian Wigeon; Falcated Teal; Mallard; Tufted Duck; Common Goldeneye; Smew; Goosander; Japanese Waxwing; Eurasian Siskin; Long-tailed Rosefinch; Meadow, Yellow-throated, and Rustic Bunting.
Rarities: Golden Eagle; Pallas's Rosefinch.

HOW TO GET THERE
From Shinjuku: 2 hr 10 min by bus or train.
From Shinjuku Station in Tokyo, go by Chuo Kosoku bus to Yamanaka-ko, or by

train from Shinjuku to Gotemba or Kawaguchi-ko stations. Buses connect both towns and pass the lake. Yamanaka-ko is 35 min from either station. Get off at

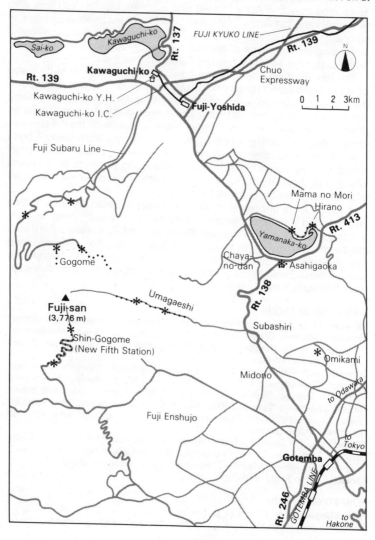

the road junction at Asahigaoka on the south shore of the lake and explore the woodlands. Later in the day, take a bus to Hirano (15 min), walk north and then west around the lake to visit the reedbeds and Mama no Mori (Mother's Forest), with its lookout point for views across the lake. During the summer buses also run from Hamamatsu-cho in Tokyo to the Fifth Station of Fuji-san on Sundays and national holidays except from mid-July until the end of August, when buses are daily.

Accommodation: In the Yamanaka-ko area, near Fuji Enshujo, is Fuji Takamura Ryokan ☎(0555)62-0690, while close to Kawaguchi-ko is Kawaguchi-ko Youth Hostel ☎(0555)72-0630. There are also hotels at both lakes. Avoid the area during the Golden Week holidays in late April and early May, during the school holidays from about July 20 to the end of August, and in the last week of October and the first week of November (autumn color viewing), when it is crowded.

21. Fuji-san, Yamanashi and Shizuoka Prefectures 富士山
Good birding months: Jan.–Dec.
Best birding months: May–July

The symmetrical cone of Fuji-san (3,776 m), extremely beautiful from a distance or from the air, is known throughout the world. Its slopes are cloaked in forest, and the road up the mountain passes through a wide variety of zones in just a few kilometers: mature deciduous forests, then stands of conifers, giving way to increasingly stunted birches and pines, until finally it is too high for even them to survive in the loose volcanic tephra. Here at the tree line is the Fifth Station (Gogome; app. 2,500 m) and the end of the road.

The flora of Fuji-san is a rich one—more than 2,000 species have been recorded—ranging from lowland forest to high alpine species, and birds too are much in evidence. The best season to visit the Fuji-san area is from mid-May to early July when both flowers and birds are at their best. In July and August many people climb the trail from the Fifth Station to the summit during the night in order to greet the dawn.

From the Fifth Station the mountain loses some of its attraction. The trail climbs up over loose gravel, for the most part gray but interspersed with dark rust red, and after summer Sundays there is also a horrendous amount of litter, but if you are lucky enough to have a clear day, the view from the top is excellent and well worth the hike.

The weather here is unpredictable, and while it is wise to take precautions against sunburn you may also encounter chilling low cloud. Even in June there can be fresh snow on the peak, and low temperatures and lack of vegetation result in sparse bird life. Above the Fifth Station it is almost birdless, but Fork-tailed Swift hawk around the mountainside after high-flying insects, while around many of the rest stops there are Alpine Accentor. In 1960 Rock Ptarmigan were introduced here from the Japan Alps, but they have not thrived. A few are said to remain wherever there is low, heathlike vegetation above the tree line, but I have never seen one.

Walking is easy at the tree line, as there are several trails up to the peak and around the contour. At this altitude, look for Olive-backed Pipit and Red-flanked Bluetail among the smaller trees, and for Japanese Accentor feeding on the ground beneath patches of stunted conifers and singing from their tops.

To see a wide range of species, make two or three stops on the way up or down, one at the tree line and one or two around the second and third stations, anywhere between 1,000 m and 2,000 m. As most people bypass the middle-level forests by going up to the Fifth Station in cars and buses, there are few trails left, but these are the most rewarding forests, with the widest variety of species. Here you will find Japanese Sparrowhawk, Japanese Green Pigeon, two or more species of cuckoos, thrushes, flycatchers, warblers, and perhaps a Japanese Paradise Flycatcher or a Siberian Thrush. If you can stay late in the evening at or just below the tree line, you may be lucky enough to hear the steady "hoo-hoo, hoo-hoo" of Brown Hawk Owl, and during early spring, the deep, hoarse notes of Ural Owl. On summer evenings, listen for Jungle Nightjar, which sing from perches, usually at the very top of a tree. Their song is a regular "chockchock-chockchock," continuing for minutes at a time.

There are two main routes to the Fifth Station. The old Fifth Station (Gogome) on the north flank can be reached by bus from Kawaguchiko, while the new Fifth Station (Shin-Gogome) on the south flank can be reached by bus from Gotemba Station. There is also a road up the east side from Subashiri to Umagaeshi, which in my opinion is the best of the three for birdwatching. Beyond Umagaeshi the metaled surface ends and the woodlands are well worth exploring in search of Siberian Blue Robin, Narcissus Flycatcher, and thrushes, including Siberian Thrush. Try to birdwatch on at least one of these roads at dawn.

The woodlands around Midono, between Gotemba Station and Subashiri, have Japanese Paradise Flycatcher, and Gray and Brown Thrush, while at Omikami, east of Subashiri, there are Japanese Yellow Bunting in the summer and Yellow-throated Bunting in winter.

The area is easily reached from Tokyo in a day, but deserves several. May is the best month, when all the summer birds are arriving, but each season brings different colors and different birds. The autumn is especially beautiful from late September to late October.

Fuji-san's forests are home to several mammals. Red Fox occur at all levels—I have found their tracks in snow on the summit—and on the upper forested slopes you may encounter a strange goatlike antelope, the Japanese Serow. It browses on low vegetation and is extremely hardy, surviving the winter even in areas with deep snow. In the lower forests, watch for Sika, and in autumn, listen for their long, whistled call. There are also Yellow Marten and Japanese Squirrel.

BIRDS AND SEASONS

All year: Northern Goshawk; Northern Sparrowhawk; Common Buzzard; Copper and Green Pheasant; Ural Owl; Great Spotted and Japanese Pygmy Woodpecker; Northern Wren; Japanese and Alpine Accentor; Red-flanked Bluetail; Goldcrest; Long-tailed, Willow, Varied, and Coal Tit; Eurasian Nuthatch; Eurasian Nutcracker; Common Bullfinch; Meadow Bunting.

Summer: Crested Honey Buzzard; Japanese Sparrowhawk; Gray-faced Buzzard; Japanese Green Pigeon; Hodgson's Hawk Cuckoo; Common, Oriental, and Little Cuckoo; Brown Hawk Owl; Jungle Nightjar; Fork-tailed Swift; Common House Martin; Olive-backed Pipit; Ashy Minivet; Japanese Robin; Siberian Blue Robin; White's, Siberian, Gray, and Brown Thrush; Stub-tailed Bush Warbler; Pale-legged and Arctic Warbler; Blue-and-White, Sooty, Asian Brown, Narcissus, and Japanese Paradise Flycatcher; Japanese Yellow Bunting.

Winter: Brambling; Eurasian Siskin; Red Crossbill; Long-tailed Rosefinch; Rustic Bunting.

HOW TO GET THERE

From Shinjuku: 2½ hr by train and bus.

From Shinjuku Station in Tokyo, Odakyu Line express trains run four times a day directly to Gotemba Station, getting there in less than two hours. For more frequent but less direct services, check with your travel agent. Direct buses run from Hamamatsu-cho and Shinjuku stations to Kawaguchi-ko, Yamanaka-ko, and Motosu-ko. Buses from Shinjuku also go to Gotemba, and from there many buses climb to the southern Fifth Station. A few buses a day run between Kawaguchi-ko and the northern Fifth Station. Roads ascend to 2,400 m and from there a hike to the peak takes 4–5 hr up and 2–3 hr down.

By car, take the Chuo Expressway to Kawaguchi-ko, then the toll road called Fuji Subaru Line to the Fifth Station.

Accommodation: Fuji-san can be visited from Hakone (22), Yamanaka-ko (20), and from Tokyo, or stay in Gotemba where there is plentiful hotel accommodation.

22. Hakone, Kanagawa Prefecture 箱根

Good birding months: Jan.–Dec.
Best birding months: May–June

Situated between the Izu Peninsula and Fuji-san, Hakone is part of the Fuji-Hakone-Izu National Park. It is an extremely popular year-round holiday area, and a weekend retreat for businessmen. Second homes, company vacation houses, tennis clubs, golf courses, first-class hotels, and a skyline highway all testify to the sightseeing attractions of the area. But holiday crowds and jammed roads should not deter anyone out for a country walk. This is a large, well-forested, mountainous region, the highest peak being Hakoneyama (1,438 m). The area is highly volcanic, with many hot springs, and beautiful rivers, gorges, and Ashi-no-ko all combine to make this region attractive.

If you want to combine your birdwatching with other attractions and are willing to brave the crowds, time your visit to coincide with the cherry blossoms in April, the azaleas in May, or the maple leaves in October and November.

Ashi-no-ko, a beautiful crater lake, is famous for its fish and for its reflection of Fuji-san. A broad paved path snakes along its northeastern shore through woodland alive with bird song on summer mornings—most of the summer visitors occur here.

The path passes the Hakone Jumoku-en (Hakone Arboretum), between Kojiri and Hakone Prince Hotel. It is well worth entering. White's Thrush frequent the park even in winter, and in the summer its mournful, two-note (one low and one high) whistle can be heard at night. Here the loud "ho-to-to-gi-su" of the Little Cuckoo, and the mournful "oh-ah-oh" of the Japanese Green Pigeon are the background against which Japanese Grosbeak whistle. Great Spotted and Japanese Pygmy Woodpecker are usually tapping or drumming somewhere here, and look out especially for Japanese Green Woodpecker.

Hakone is the most convenient and best-known site close to Tokyo to look for another Japanese specialty, Japanese Yellow Bunting. The distribution of this bird is not well-known in Japan, where it is probably now quite rare. At Ashi-no-ko, however, you may encounter one in summer along the east shore of the lake. I have found them feeding on or close to the ground in low vegetation around the edge of woods in Jumoku-en and singing from treetop perches on forested slopes above the footpath. The song is a pleasant "chip-in, chin-chin, chee-chee-chee-che-rui." It has similar alarm and flight notes to Black-faced Bunting.

Watch for Azure-winged Magpie near the hotel and along the lake shore, and check overhanging branches for Mandarin Duck. Mandarin

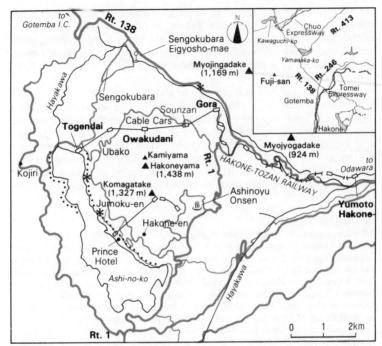

breed here but are very secretive, and if you miss them at the lake, look for them along the Hayakawa. Various duck winter on Ashi-no-ko, including a flock of Mandarin. In the woods at this season Dusky Thrush, Hawfinch, and Meadow Bunting are all common.

North of the lake is a marshy area near Sengokubara where a few Latham's Snipe display from April to June and where Green Pheasant, Brown Shrike, and Gray-headed Bunting all breed. There are also Common Kingfisher, reed warblers, and three species of wagtails. A rich profusion of marsh flowers is best seen here from May to July.

By afternoon Sengokubara and the eastern shore of the lake may be too busy for your liking; then it is time to take a walk along the west shore trail to look for more Japanese Yellow Bunting or to hike in the mountains.

If you enjoy hiking, take a bus from Odawara to Owakudani and walk to Kamiyama (about 1 hr 30 min), then on another hour to Komagatake (1,327 m). A cable car descends from Komagatake to the lakeshore close to Hakone Prince Hotel. On the hike to Komagatake, watch for

Olive-backed Pipit and Japanese Accentor in low trees and bushes near the summit, and also Japanese Yellow and Gray-headed Bunting. In winter along the same course you should still find accentors, along with Long-tailed Rosefinch and Common Bullfinch. From this peak in a double volcanic range there is a marvelous view across Ashi-no-ko to Fuji-san.

Along the Hayakawa, a good area to watch is above Gora, about half a kilometer north of a snow tunnel on Rt. 138 at Momiji-en. But anywhere a track or road goes down to or crosses the river is just as good. Look for Mandarin Duck along shadier stretches, Brown Dipper and Japanese Wagtail in rocky, faster-running sections, and listen for the harsh "chek-chek" of the Crested Kingfisher. In summer, in the woods near the river, listen for the rapid descending whistle of the Ruddy Kingfisher. In the Odawara area, look out for Little Swift and Red-rumped Swallow.

BIRDS AND SEASONS
All year: Mandarin Duck; Green Pheasant; Common and Crested Kingfisher; Japanese Green, Great Spotted, and Japanese Pygmy Woodpecker; Gray and Japanese Wagtail; Brown Dipper; Northern Wren; Japanese Accentor; White's Thrush; Long-tailed, Willow, Varied, and Coal Tit; Eurasian Nuthatch; Eurasian Jay; Azure-winged Magpie; Japanese Grosbeak; Meadow Bunting.
Summer: Latham's Snipe; Japanese Green Pigeon; Hodgson's Hawk Cuckoo; Common, Oriental, and Little Cuckoo; Little Swift; Ruddy Kingfisher; Red-rumped Swallow; Olive-backed Pipit; Japanese Robin; Siberian Blue Robin; Gray and Brown Thrush; Stub-tailed Bush Warbler; Black-browed and Oriental Reed Warbler; Eastern Crowned Warbler; Blue-and-White, Asian Brown, and Narcissus Flycatcher; Brown Shrike; Japanese Yellow and Gray-headed Bunting.
Winter: Common Teal; Northern Pintail; Common Pochard; Tufted Duck; Smew; Pale and Dusky Thrush; Long-tailed Rosefinch; Common Bullfinch; Hawfinch.

HOW TO GET THERE
From Tokyo: 4 hr by train and bus.
From Shinjuku Station in Tokyo, take an Odakyu Line express to Odawara (1 hr 35 min), or from Tokyo Station a "Kodama" Shinkansen (42 min) or ordinary JR train (1 hr 30 min). From the south exit of Odawara Station, take a bus to Kojiri on the northeast shore of Ashi-no-ko, via Owakudani or Sengokubara, or to Hakone-en on the east shore. For Sengokubara, get off at Sengokubara Eigyosho-mae bus stop (after about 1 hr from Odawara). Both are suitable starting places for a birding walk. An attractive way to reach the lake, if you have the time to spare, is by the narrow-gauge Hakone-Tozan railway from Odawara Station up the valley to Gora (800 m).

Gora is the start of a long series of cable cars running first to Sounzan, then Owakudani—a volcanically active area with steam and mud springs—then continuing across the highlands before descending by way of Ubako (900 m) to Togendai near the lake shore. There are several trails from Owakudani, including one to Komagatake.

The Hakone area is most easily explored by car, and with an early start it is possible to visit the lakeside woods, afterwards heading for the eastern slopes of Fuji-san and Yamanaka-ko, exploring all three areas in one day. Cars can be rented at Odawara Station.

Accommodation: Hakone Prince Hotel ☎(0460)3-7111 is the best hotel in the area, and there are many more hotels and ryokan of all grades in Hakone itself, but try the Kinokuniya Lodge ☎(0460)3-7045 at Ashinoyu Onsen. Budget travelers will prefer Hakone Sounzan Youth Hostel ☎(0460)2-3827, which is open from mid-March until mid-November and which is a 2-min walk from Sounzan Station. It is also possible to take a bus from Odawara Station, get off at Sounzan, and walk from there to the hostel.

23. Hegurajima, Ishikawa Prefecture　舳倉島

Best birding months: April–May, Sept.–Oct.

The tiny island of Hegurajima lies 50 km north of Wajima on Noto Hanto. It is less than 2 km by 1 km in area, and has a coastline of just 6 km and a maximum elevation of only 30 m. Numerous vagrants have been found here, and many species uncommon elsewhere in Japan occur regularly here on spring and autumn migration. The best seasons for a visit are from late April to late May and from late September until the end of October.

Birdwatching begins as the boat leaves Wajima harbor, or even before, if the spring migration of Red-necked Phalarope is in full swing. On the way to the island there are Streaked Shearwater, Temminck's Cormorant, and possibly Japanese Murrelet. Once on the island, most of the regular Japanese migrants can be found. The island is particularly attractive to flycatchers, warblers, and buntings, but raptors also pass over, and considering the island has a rocky coastline, a surprising number of shorebirds visit the bays. Visit the area around the lighthouse in the morning to look for tired migrants and walk on the open grassland areas near the northern and southern capes, and along the line of pines that runs north–south the length of the island.

On some mornings, the northern part of the island is reminiscent of eastern Hokkaido coastal meadows and marshes. Siberian Rubythroat, Stonechat, and Yellow-breasted Bunting stop over, set up temporary territories, and sing; the only thing that breaks the image is the presence of Oriental Reed Warbler singing at the same time.

It is possible to visit the island for a long weekend from Tokyo, but a

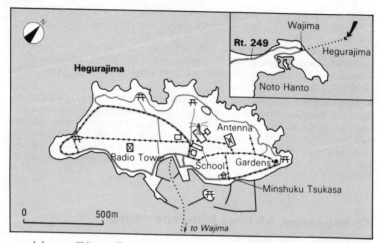

week here will be well rewarded. The list of birds to expect in a three- or four-day stay reads like a list of all Japan's summer visitors, with a touch of eastern China and eastern Siberia thrown in. On most days in spring it is easy to see over 60 species, a difficult feat anywhere else in Japan. The all-time record day total for Japan stands now at 106 (May 1985 and September 1986, both by my Hokkaido Birdathon team), but on this tiny island I have seen 98 species in one day, making it without doubt the best single birding spot of its size in Japan, and personally I rank it as my second most favorite site after Furen-ko (33).

Most of the same migrants appear both in autumn and in spring, although generally fewer species occur in autumn. What is lost in numbers, however, is often made up for by the appearance of rare species.

The island list already stands at over 275, and almost every year it produces surprises, anomalies, and new species. Where, for example, are the supposedly sedentary Japanese Woodpigeon and Eurasian Nutcracker going to and from, and why are Japanese Yellow Bunting relatively common here but so rare on the mainland?

BIRDS AND SEASONS

Spring & Autumn: Black-throated Diver; Streaked Shearwater; Temminck's and Pelagic Cormorant; Black-crowned Night Heron; Japanese and Chinese Sparrowhawk (spring); Northern Hobby; Peregrine; Ruddy Crake; Mongolian Plover; Whimbrel; Terek Sandpiper; Gray-tailed Tattler; Ruddy Turnstone; Red-necked Phalarope; Black-tailed Gull; Japanese Murrelet; Japanese Green Pigeon;

Hodgson's Hawk Cuckoo; Common and Oriental Cuckoo; Oriental Scops Owl; Jungle Nightjar; Dollarbird; Hoopoe; Greater Short-toed Lark; Richard's and Olive-backed Pipit; Yellow Wagtail; Ashy Minivet; Japanese Waxwing; Japanese Robin; Siberian Rubythroat; Siberian Blue Robin; Red-flanked Bluetail; Daurian Redstart; Siberian, Gray, Brown, Pale, Eye-browed, and Dusky Thrush; Black-browed and Oriental Reed Warbler; Eastern Crowned, Pale-legged, and Arctic Warbler; Blue-and-White, Sooty, Gray-streaked, Asian Brown, Mugimaki, Tricolored, and Narcissus Flycatcher; Black-naped Oriole; Tiger, Bull-headed, and Brown Shrike; Red-cheeked Starling; Brambling; Japanese Grosbeak; Gray, Meadow, Japanese Yellow, Gray-headed, Yellow-throated, Tristram's, Rustic, Little, and Yellow-breasted Bunting.

Autumn: Shore Lark; Eurasian Nutcracker; Pallas's Rosefinch; Pine Grosbeak; Lapland Bunting.

Rarities: Japanese Night Heron; Swinhoe's Egret; Little Curlew; Japanese Wood-pigeon; Rufous-tailed Robin; Gray-backed Thrush; Yellow-browed Warbler; Daurian Starling; Pine, Yellow-browed, and Chestnut Bunting.

HOW TO GET THERE

From Kanazawa: 5 hr by train and boat.

From Ueno Station in Tokyo, take an express (*kyuko*) train to Kanazawa, or the Shinkansen from Tokyo Station to Maebara (2½ hr) and there change to the Hokuriku Honsen Line bound for Kanazawa. It is also possible to fly to Komatsu Airport, then take an airport bus to Kanazawa Station. From Kanazawa Station, take a JR train on the Nanao Line to Wajima (3 hr 10 min), then walk 15 min to Wajima harbor. Long-distance buses from Kanazawa bus terminal to Wajima are regular and more frequent than trains.

The boat *Hegura* takes 1 hr 50 min to get to the island, setting out once a day at 08:30 and leaving the island at 14:30. The boat schedule is somewhat dependent on the tide and the weather, particularly in autumn, and the boat is sometimes cancelled, so check with the boat company, Hegura Koro ☎(0768) 22-4381.

Accommodation: The night before the ferry, stay at Minshuku Hakuto-en in Wajima ☎(0768)22-2178, and on the island stay at Minshuku Tsukasa ☎(0768) 22-8713.

24. Katano Kamo-ike, Ishikawa Prefecture 片野鴨池

Good birding months: Jan.–Dec.

Sanctuary address: 2-1, Katano-cho, Kaga-shi, Ishikawa 922-05; ☎(07617)2-2200. Open every day, 08:30–17:00.

Katano Kamo-ike (1.5 ha during summer, flooding to about 6 ha in winter) at Kaga, close to the Japan Sea Coast, is a popular wintering

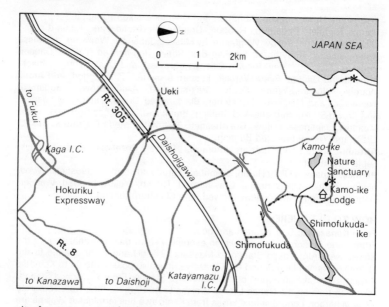

site for many waterfowl (up to 10,000 duck and 1,000 geese), but is best known for its Baikal Teal, which spend part of the winter there. As elsewhere in Japan, and apparently the rest of Asia too, numbers have declined and large flocks are now irregular. However, it is still annual here. In 1984 the lake became a WBSJ sanctuary and now has a full-time warden and a nature center.

The whole area is worth exploring since the rice fields around the lake have many birds, as do nearby woods and the Japan Sea coast, making for a good variety of species in one small area. In autumn and winter, look for geese, gulls, plovers, snipe, and pipits in the fields, and Azure-winged Magpie, thrushes, and Gray Starling wherever there are trees. At the lake itself are Greater White-fronted and Bean Goose, Bewick's Swan, various duck including Baikal Teal, and a flock of up to 80 Great Cormorant. This concentration of waterfowl attracts several species of raptor.

In the woods between Katano Kamo-ike and the sea are Green Pheasant, woodpeckers, tits, buntings, and occasionally, in winter, wax-wings, Chinese Grosbeak, Common Redpoll, and Red Crossbill. Offshore there are grebes, Ancient Murrelet, gulls, and sea ducks, and along the rocky coast there are cormorants and Eastern Reef Egret.

BIRDS AND SEASONS

All year: Temminck's Cormorant; Eastern Reef, Little, and Great Egret; Gray Heron; Mallard; Spot-billed Duck; Green Pheasant; Great Spotted and Japanese Pygmy Woodpecker; Blue Rock Thrush; Long-tailed and Coal Tit; Azure-winged Magpie.

Summer: Little Grebe; Common Teal; Japanese Green Pigeon; Red-flanked Bluetail; Bull-headed Shrike; Japanese Grosbeak; Yellow-throated Bunting.

Winter: Red-throated and Black-throated Diver; Little, Red-necked, and Black-necked Grebe; Great and Pelagic Cormorant; Bewick's Swan; Bean and Greater White-fronted Goose; Mandarin Duck; Eurasian Wigeon; Falcated Teal; Gadwall; Baikal and Common Teal; Northern Pintail; Northern Shoveler; Common Pochard; Tufted Duck; Common and Velvet Scoter; Smew; Red-breasted Merganser; White-tailed Eagle; Eastern Marsh and Hen Harrier; Northern Goshawk; Northern Sparrowhawk; Common Buzzard; Peregrine; Common Coot; Greater Painted Snipe; Northern Lapwing; Common Snipe; Common Black-headed, Black-tailed, Common, and Herring Gull; Black-legged Kittiwake; Ancient Murrelet; Water Pipit; Japanese Waxwing; Pale and Dusky Thrush; Common Redpoll; Red Crossbill; Chinese Grosbeak.

Rarities: Swan, Lesser White-fronted, and Snow Goose; Ruddy Shelduck; Steller's Sea Eagle.

HOW TO GET THERE

From Kanazawa: 1–2 hr by train, then on foot or by taxi.

Go by local train (expresses don't stop) on the Hokuriku Honsen Line from Kanazawa to Daishoji (1 hr), then walk for 50 min or take a taxi (10 min). From Komatsu Airport it is a 20-min taxi ride. Walk along the Daishojigawa, along Rt. 305 to the north, and through the rice fields south of the lake via Ueki, Iminosawa, and Shimofukuda. Just to the east of Katano Kamo-ike, another pond called Shimofukuda-ike also attracts many birds.

Accommodation: Try Hashimoto Ryokan ☎(07617)2-0606, in front of Daishoji Station, Tokugetsu-so ☎(07617)2-1138, or Katano-so Kokuminshukusha ☎(07617)3-2500.

25. Kamikochi and the Japan Alps 上高地/日本アルプス

Good birding months: May–Aug.
Best birding months: May–June

Kamikochi, in the middle of the Japan Alps National Park and one of the most scenic places in Japan, is situated on the Azusagawa in a narrow basin surrounded by peaks. At 1,500 m it is the starting point for a number of hiking trails and is *the* mountaineering center for the National Park. Mountaineering was first introduced into Japan by the Reverend

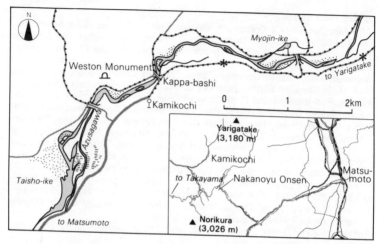

Walter Weston, who dubbed these mountains, once shunned as the home of the gods and goblins, the Alps, and inadvertently led to their ever-increasing popularity among city-weary Japanese. The peaks here are spectacular, with spear-shaped Yarigatake (3,180 m), known as the Matterhorn of Japan, dominating the landscape although Hotakadake is slightly higher. The view from the top of these mountains is unforgettable. The whole chain of the Alps stretches off to the north, while way off to the south, on the skyline, is a tiny cone—Fuji-san!

In summer the Azusagawa valley is lush and green, with mixed woodlands and trails running alongside the shingly river. Hiking is pleasant both for the scenery and for birdwatching. Kamikochi is an ideal base from which to explore the lower wooded areas, and as a starting point for hikes at higher altitudes to see Rock Ptarmigan, or Thunderbird. A good trail runs along the south side of the Azusagawa all the way up the valley. After a fairly long level stretch, the trail climbs steadily, then more steeply, up to the ridge below Yarigatake. Mountain huts halfway along the valley and on the ridge make it an easy hike that, with an early start, can be done in one day, but it is best spread over two days to allow time for birding. The climb up to the top of Yarigatake is only for the very fit, but otherwise the trail is not too difficult. I recommend a whole day up on the ridge exploring southwest from Yarigatake in search of Rock Ptarmigan, which like rock-strewn areas, particularly around creeping pine. Alpine Accentor are common around high mountain huts, and you may be lucky enough to see a Golden Eagle. The best time to visit is from the end of May until mid-June. For the higher parts of the mountains, July and August are best.

BIRDS AND SEASONS
Summer: Mandarin Duck; Mallard; Northern Goshawk; Golden Eagle; Eurasian Kestrel; Rock Ptarmigan; Common Sandpiper; Hodgson's Hawk Cuckoo; Little Cuckoo; Crested Kingfisher; Japanese Pygmy Woodpecker; Japanese Wagtail; Ashy Minivet; Brown Dipper; Northern Wren; Japanese and Alpine Accentor; Japanese Robin; Siberian Blue Robin; Siberian, Gray, and Brown Thrush; Arctic Warbler; Goldcrest; Blue-and-White, Asian Brown, and Narcissus Flycatcher; Long-tailed, Willow, Varied, and Coal Tit; Eurasian Nuthatch; Common Treecreeper; Common Bullfinch; Japanese Grosbeak.
Rarities: Hodgson's Hawk Eagle.

HOW TO GET THERE
From Matsumoto: 2 hr by train and bus.
From Shinjuku Station in Tokyo, take an express train to Matsumoto (3 hr 30 min). Change there to a local train (Matsumoto Densetsu), get off at Shin-shima-shima (30 min), and from there take a bus to Kamikochi (1 hr 20 min).

By car, take Rt. 158 west from Matsumoto to Nakanoyu Onsen, then turn north to Kamikochi (6 km). If you don't have time to hike for the higher-altitiude birds, drive south from Kamikochi to Nakanoyu Onsen, turn west there onto Rt. 158, then take the Skyline road south and up to Mt. Norikura for ptarmigan and both accentors near the parking area at the top, and nutcrackers lower down.

Accommodation: Tokuzawa-en ryokan ☎(0263)95-2508 is recommended by the WBSJ.

26. Ogasayama, Shizuoka Prefecture 小笠山
Good birding months: Jan.–Dec.
Best birding months: May–July

This low, forested mountain with steep cliffs a mere 260 m high has more than 1,300 species of plants and is also home to some interesting birds, most notably Japanese Night Heron.

The best season is in early summer when along the trail to the top of Ogasayama it is possible to see Crested Honey Buzzard, Gray-faced Buzzard, Little Cuckoo, and several species of flycatcher. Continue over the top of the mountain and explore the forested river valleys, particularly along damp streamsides, in search of Japanese Night Heron. If you can, stay in the evening to listen for their deep booming call.

In winter, along the same route, there are hawks, buntings, and finches, in addition to the commoner woodland species.

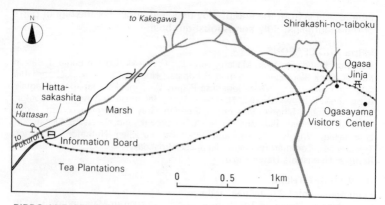

BIRDS AND SEASONS

All year: Japanese Green, Great Spotted, and Japanese Pygmy Woodpecker; Northern Wren; Long-tailed, Willow, and Coal Tit; Meadow Bunting.
Summer: Japanese Night Heron; Crested Honey Buzzard; Gray-faced Buzzard; Little Cuckoo; Blue-and-White, Narcissus, and Japanese Paradise Flycatcher.
Winter: Northern Goshawk; Northern Sparrowhawk; Eurasian Siskin; Common Bullfinch; Yellow-throated and Rustic Bunting.

HOW TO GET THERE

From Tokyo: 3 hr by train and on foot.
From Tokyo Station, take the Shinkansen to Shizuoka (1 hr 30 min), change to a local train on the Tokaido Line, get off at Fukuroi (1 hr). From Fukuroi it is a 20-min ride on a Totetsu bus to Hattasan via Bodai. Get off at Hattasakashita. From Hattasakashita it is a 10-min walk to the start of the forest trail.

Accommodation: It is best to stay in Shizuoka, where there is a variety of accommodation.

27. Kisogawa, Mie Prefecture 木曽川

Good birding months: Jan.–Dec.
Best birding months: Jan.–Feb.

The Kisogawa, Nagaragawa, and Ibigawa all join to flow into Ise Bay south of Nagoya, and in winter they attract many egrets, gulls, and large flocks of duck, with smaller numbers of grebes, Great Cormorant, and sometimes Bewick's Swan. The major attraction for most visiting birders, however, will be the flock of Baikal Teal that comes every winter, although in dwindling numbers. They come late and depart early, staying from late November until late February. While searching for them, you will probably find small numbers of Falcated Teal and possibly even American Wigeon.

The winter waterbirds also include Gray Heron, Common Black-headed Gull, Northern Lapwing, and Dunlin. Along the riverbanks, look out for flocks of finches and buntings, and overhead watch for raptors. Northern Goshawk occur in the area, Peregrine roost in the line of ancient pine trees known as "Senbon Matsubara," and Eastern Marsh Harrier regularly hunt over the reedbeds.

The area east of the Kisogawa in spring attracts ducks and waders. Sandpipers, Spotted Redshank, and Greater Painted Snipe like the lotus fields, and Gray-headed Lapwing nest in the area. The reedbeds along the river have breeding Yellow Bittern, Oriental Reed Warbler, and Fan-tailed Warbler, and Common Cuckoo lay their eggs in the reed warbler and Bull-headed Shrike nests. In late August and early September, migrants are on the move, and these include other species of cuckoo and Red-cheeked Starling.

BIRDS AND SEASONS
Spring & Autumn: Greater Painted Snipe; Spotted Redshank; Wood Sandpiper; Oriental and Little Cuckoo; Red-cheeked Starling.
Summer: Yellow Bittern; Cattle Egret; Common Cuckoo; Fan-tailed Warbler; Oriental Reed Warbler; Bull-headed Shrike.
Winter: Little and Great Crested Grebe; Great Cormorant; Gray Heron; Bewick's Swan; Falcated, Baikal, and Common Teal; Mallard; Spot-billed Duck; Northern

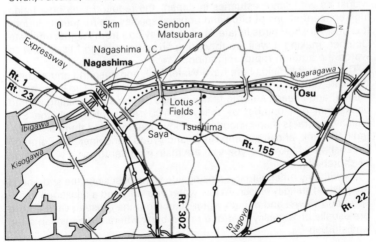

Pintail; Tufted Duck; Goosander; Eastern Marsh and Hen Harrier; Northern Goshawk; Common Buzzard; Peregrine; Northern Lapwing; Dunlin; Common Black-headed Gull; Rustic and Common Reed Bunting.

Rarities: American Wigeon; White-tailed and Steller's Sea Eagle; Merlin.

HOW TO GET THERE

From Nagoya: 30 min by train.

From Shin-Gifu Station, take the Nagoya Tetsudo Takehana Line to Osu (40 min). From Osu, walk south to Sewarizutsumi. South along the river from Osu to Nagashima is about 15 km. From Nagoya Station, take the Kokutetsu Kansai Honsen Line to Nagashima (15 min) or the Kinki Nihon Tetsudo Yamada Line from Kintetsu Nagoya Station to Kintetsu Nagashima (15 min). Walk north to Sewarizutsumi. Alternatively, take the Nagoya Tetsudo Bisai Line from Shin-Gifu Station to Tsushima or Saya, which takes 40 min, and walk west 6 km or 3 km to the river.

Accommodation: A wide variety of accommodation is available in Nagoya.

28. Shiokawa, Aichi Prefecture 汐川

Best birding months: April–May, Aug.–Oct.

The Shiokawa estuary once covered nearly 2,000 ha, but now has almost completely disappeared through reclamation and construction; a mere 280 ha remain, but in this area 221 species have been recorded, many of them shorebirds.

Just as with other estuaries in Japan, the reduced area now holds high concentrations of birds and unusual species are frequently found. It is best for shorebirds in late April and May and from August until late October, making it well worth visiting en route to Irago Misaki (29) to watch the autumn raptor migration.

The vegetable fields here have Water Rail, and in spring and autumn there are Cattle Egret, plovers, and Oriental Pratincole. The latter breed nearby, and in early autumn family parties can be seen building up into flocks that can number as many as 100. Although small, the Shijimigawa attracts many shorebirds at low tide. In spring there are Spotted Redshank, and in autumn Green and Wood Sandpiper and Common Greenshank. Make sure you visit the main mud flat to see a wide range of shorebirds.

As with any other estuary, a rising tide is the best since the shorebirds are pushed steadily closer. At low water you will need a telescope to obtain good views, and at high water search out the roosting sites. These are usually on a grassy field or a raised bank where the birds can sleep undisturbed.

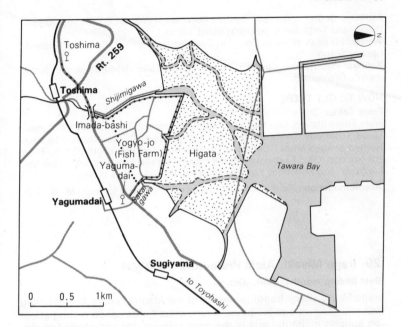

The Shiokawa has a well-justified reputation for attracting rarities. Pied Avocet have, in recent years, become almost regular January visitors, and Greater Yellowlegs, Western Sandpiper, and Buff-breasted Sandpiper have all appeared here.

In winter there are large flocks of both dabbling and diving duck, including most of the commoner species but with Greater Scaup making up the majority of the 100,000-strong flocks.

As you travel south to this or other sites, watch for Gray-headed Lapwing from the train or from the expressway. This rather locally distributed bird frequents rice fields in the central and southern parts of Honshu. Its distinctive black, white, and brown wing pattern makes it immediately recognizable, even from the window of a speeding Shinkansen.

BIRDS AND SEASONS
All year: Water Rail; Gray-headed Lapwing.
Spring & Autumn: Cattle Egret; Oriental Pratincole; Little Ringed, Kentish, Mongolian, Pacific Golden, and Gray Plover; Red-necked Stint; Sharp-tailed Sandpiper; Curlew Sandpiper; Dunlin; Broad-billed Sandpiper; Black-tailed and

Bar-tailed Godwit; Whimbrel; Spotted Redshank; Common Greenshank; Green, Wood, and Terek Sandpiper; Gray-tailed Tattler.
Winter: Eurasian Wigeon; Common Teal; Northern Pintail; Common Pochard; Greater Scaup.
Rarities: Pied Avocet; Common Ringed Plover; Spoon-billed Sandpiper; Nordmann's Greenshank.

HOW TO GET THERE
From Tokyo: 3 hr by train and bus.
From Tokyo Station, take the "Kodama" Shinkansen to Toyohashi (2 hr 10 min). Leave Toyohashi Station by the east exit and take a Toyotetsu bus to Irago Honsen or Irago Misaki. Get off at Toshima bus stop after about 30 min. From the bus stop it is a 15-min walk to the river mouth along the east side of the Shijimigawa. The walk from the Shijimigawa to the Sakaigawa is best.

Accommodation: See the accommodation recommended for Irago Misaki (29).

29. Irago Misaki, Aichi Prefecture 伊良湖岬
Best birding months: Sept.–Oct.

Irago Misaki (Cape Irago), at the tip of the Atsumi Peninsula and jutting out into Mikawa and Ise bays, is renowned for its concentrating effect on autumn migrants, and is the most famous place in Japan for watching migrating raptors. There are also migrants in the spring, which include Gray-faced Buzzard, but, on the whole, birdwatching is better elsewhere in Japan at that season.

If you want to see large numbers of birds of prey in Japan you must visit either the Nansei Shoto between the beginning of September and the end of October, though the diversity of species is not large at any one time, or Irago from the end of the second week of September until the end of the first week of October. A wide variety of birds of prey move southwest together over Irago at this season. After mid-October the raptors decline in number, and small birds are commoner. Thousands of Barn Swallow and Gray Wagtail pass over in September, and there are also large numbers of Japanese White-eye and Eurasian Jay.

Gray-faced Buzzard are the commonest raptor from late September to mid-October, peaking in early October, and with them are lesser numbers of buzzards, hawks, and falcons. From mid-October onward, many hawks and common small birds pass through. The most conspicuous are noisy, undulating flocks of Brown-eared Bulbul.

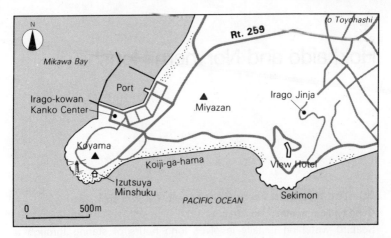

In October, Streaked Shearwater can be seen offshore especially after typhoons, and on the sea in winter are cormorants, gulls, flocks of sea duck, and some alcids and divers.

BIRDS AND SEASONS
All year: Chinese Bamboo Partridge; Blue Rock Thrush.
Spring & Autumn: Streaked Shearwater; Crested Honey Buzzard; Northern Goshawk; Japanese and Northern Sparrowhawk; Gray-faced and Common Buzzard; Northern Hobby; Peregrine; Red-rumped Swallow; Gray Wagtail; Eurasian Jay.
Winter: Black-throated Diver; Temminck's and Pelagic Cormorant; Harlequin Duck; Common Scoter; Red-breasted Merganser; Black-tailed and Herring Gull; Ancient Murrelet.
Rarities: Chinese Sparrowhawk; Merlin.

HOW TO GET THERE
From Tokyo: 4 hr by train and bus.
Follow the directions for Shiokawa. From the east exit of Toyohashi Station, a JR or Toyotetsu bus to Irago Misaki takes about 1½ hr.

Accommodation: Izutsuya Minshuku ☎(05313)5-6178 is recommended if you have a limited budget; otherwise try Irago View Hotel ☎(05313)5-6111.

Hokkaido and Northern Honshu

30. The Northern Ferry Routes　北フェリー航路
Good birding months: Jan.–Dec.

Seabird watching usually involves long hours of staring through a telescope in the teeth of a gale in the hope of birds passing close enough to be identified, special excursions to breeding sites, or special pelagic trips. In Japan, none of this is necessary because the many ferries connecting the islands pass through excellent seabird areas.

Wherever you travel in Japan it is worth considering the ferries as a cheap, comfortable, and interesting alternative to airplanes and trains, and as a way of combining a long, leisurely journey with some exciting seabirds.

The Pacific coast routes have many more birds of more species than those of the Japan Sea coast, although the latter provide a cheap way of traveling and birdwatching between western Honshu and Hokkaido (from Niigata or Maizuru to Otaru, for example).

Of all the ferry routes I have traveled on between Hokkaido and Taiwan, off the Pacific and Japan Sea coasts, the routes from Tokyo to Tomakomai or Kushiro in Hokkaido consistently provide the very best seawatching. Boats leave late in the evening from Tokyo and two nights are spent on board with the whole of the intervening day and the following early morning for seawatching in good waters.

Seabirds sometimes follow the boats but are more often to be seen passing alongside or in flocks around fishing boats waiting for offal to be thrown out. Just as in a forest, birds at sea occur in patches, so don't expect to have birds in view all the time. The best areas are off the coast of Chiba Prefecture and the Rikuchu coast of Iwate Prefecture, which the boat passes in the early morning and in the late afternoon, respectively, on the northbound route. Sanganjima and Hidejima off the

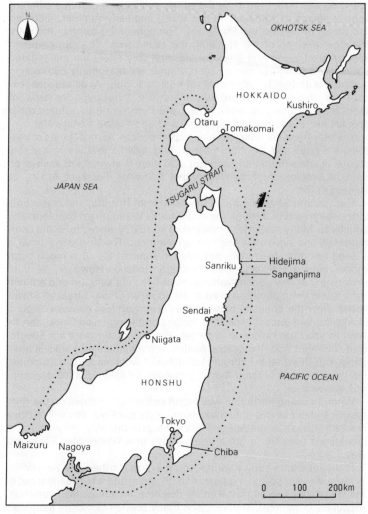

Iwate coast are the breeding ground of Band-rumped Petrel, so look for these especially toward evening.

I have traveled on the northern ferry routes many times but have found no two boat trips to be the same, and in each month a different species seems to dominate. In late spring and early summer, there are thousands of Red-necked Phalarope. Throughout the summer there are the most exciting of the seabirds, the albatrosses. The two common species are Laysan and Black-footed, and very rarely the endangered Short-tailed Albatross can be seen. Petrels are reasonably common in summer, with Leach's abundant off Kushiro in July. At all seasons, except for mid-winter (February), there are thousands, or tens of thousands, of Streaked Shearwater, and from spring to autumn other species join them, particularly Sooty and Short-tailed Shearwater.

In winter there are auks, auklets, and murrelets. At most times of year there are gulls and Northern Fulmar, Fork-tailed Petrel are reasonably regular in late summer and autumn, and there is always a chance of an unusual species, such as Red-legged Kittiwake, Parakeet Auklet, or Horned Puffin.

The Tsugaru Strait separates Hokkaido from Honshu, and Blakiston's Line, which passes through the strait, forms the southern limit for many land birds. Many seabirds, although not so strictly limited by it, are commoner on one side of the line than on the other. The Northern Fulmar is a good example. In winter, and often in summer too, it is much commoner around Hokkaido than northern Honshu. However, as if to underline that few generalizations about birds are safe, on one autumn trip I found them common even as far south as Chiba. Streaked Shearwater show the opposite pattern: they are much less common around Hokkaido. Sea ducks, especially scoters and Long-tailed Duck, can be seen as you near Hokkaido in winter, and in summer there are Spectacled Guillemot and Rhinoceros Auklet. The abundance of auks is most intriguing. One year in February Least Auklet were reasonably common, but there were no Crested Auklet. However, by early April the exact opposite was true.

When traveling north it is well worth getting up at dawn on the third day for an hour or two of birdwatching before docking. You will notice a marked change in the species from the previous day. In winter it is sometimes possible to get a first glimpse of a White-tailed Eagle this way.

From autumn to early summer, you may see Northern Fur Seal lolling at the surface or swimming past. At high speed and when leaping out of the water they can be mistaken for dolphins, which are also common, especially in summer. Theoretically, many species of marine mammals can be seen off the Pacific coast, but in the dozen or so trips I have made, I have only identified Pacific White-sided Dolphin. In summer, there are flying fish, and I have seen rays, the huge moonfish, hammerhead sharks, and Green Turtle.

BIRDS AND SEASONS

All year: Laysan Albatross; Northern Fulmar; Streaked Shearwater; Temminck's and Pelagic Cormorant; Red-necked Phalarope; Pomarine, Arctic, and South Polar Skua; Black-tailed, Herring, and Slaty-backed Gull; Spectacled Guillemot; Japanese Murrelet.

Summer (May to Oct.): Black-footed Albatross; Flesh-footed, Sooty, and Short-tailed Shearwater; Leach's, Swinhoe's, Band-rumped, and Tristram's Petrel; Long-tailed Skua; Common Tern; Rhinoceros Auklet.

Winter (Nov. to April/May): Red-throated and Black-throated Diver; Harlequin and Long-tailed Duck; Common and Velvet Scoter; Gray Phalarope; Common, Glaucous-winged, and Glaucous Gull; Black-legged Kittiwake; Common and Brunnich's Guillemot; Marbled and Ancient Murrelet; Crested and Least Auklet.

Rarities: Short-tailed Albatross; Bonin Petrel; Stejneger's Petrel; Wedge-tailed Shearwater; Fork-tailed Petrel; Red-legged Kittiwake; Pigeon Guillemot; Parakeet Auklet; Horned Puffin.

HOW TO GET THERE

From Tokyo: 31 hr to Tomakomai, west Hokkaido, and 33½ hr to Kushiro, east Hokkaido.

Go to Toyocho Station on the Tozai subway line in Tokyo. From the bus stand outside exit 1 of the station, catch a Toei bus to the Southern Terminal (Minami Taaminaru) of Tokyo ferry harbor (Ariake Futo). This takes about 30 min, but the timing of buses varies so it is best to phone JTB or Japan Travel Phone to ask for up-to-date information. Alternatively, go to Ginza and take a taxi to "Ariake Futo Minami Taaminaru."

The boat for Tomakomai leaves at 23:30 on the first day and arrives at 06:45 on the third day (cheapest fare, ¥11,500); for Kushiro it leaves at 23:00 and arrives at 08:30 (cheapest fare, ¥14,500). The Kushiro ferry terminal is 15 min by bus from Kushiro Station. The return ferry from Tomakomai leaves at 11:45, and the return ferry from Kushiro leaves at 12:30 on the first day and arrives back in Tokyo at 19:40 on the second day. The Tokyo–Tomakomai service operates daily, while that to Kushiro runs two out of three days. Check ferry departures with the Nihon Enkai Ferry (for Tomakomai) ☎(03)574-9561, or Kinkai Yusen (for Kushiro) ☎(03)447-6551.

Two new ferry routes began a couple of years ago from Oarai in Ibaragi Prefecture to Tomakomai, and from Oarai to Muroran. These should be as good as the ferry from Tokyo, but I have not yet tried them.

In August and September (the typhoon season) and during winter storms, boats are sometimes cancelled because of rough seas. If you are making the trip in winter, take plenty of warm clothes, including hats, gloves, and warm footwear. It can get bitterly cold on deck, and with the boat sometimes pushing through brash ice, the trip has a distinctly arctic feel.

Accommodation: Accommodation is available in the form of communal tatami-matted areas with blankets, or in cabins, and a Japanese-style bath is available (an interesting experience on a swaying ship!).

31. Shiretoko Hanto, Northeast Hokkaido 知床

Best birding months: Jan.–March, June–Oct.

Shiretoko Hanto (Shiretoko Peninsula) is a mountainous finger of land protruding into the Okhotsk Sea. The combination of spectacular scenery, deep snow, extensive sea ice, and magnificent birds make this one of the most exciting areas to visit in Japan in winter. The steep-sided river valleys along the coast north from Rausu shelter the roosts of the most magnificent of the eagles, the huge, boldly patterned Steller's Sea Eagle.

Rausu, despite its location almost as far as one can get from Tokyo and still be in Japan, is a surprisingly rich, bustling city. The reason for the wealth of the town, and the wealth of birds, is the concentration of fish in the Nemuro Strait, which separates Hokkaido from the offshore Soviet-occupied island of Kunashiri. The whole region is mountainous with extensive deciduous forests. There are few trails, and in winter anywhere off the main road is inaccessible except to those suitably equipped for winter expeditions. The hills rise steeply from the coast, and thus driving along the section of road north from Rausu is the best way of seeing the area and of finding birds, including eagles.

The 15-km stretch of coast north from Rausu holds over 2,500 eagles at the peak in February, and the majority of these are Steller's— making it the largest concentration of the species in the world. The largest roost and the one to head for is at the Sashiruigawa. Reach the river mouth before dawn, since the spectacular main exodus begins at about 05:15, before it gets light. During the day the eagles fish the channel and perch on the drifting sea ice. When blizzards strike during the day they return quickly to roost in hundreds along the wooded slopes leading down to the sea. But on fine days they begin to return to the roost from about 15:00 onward. The river mouth attracts Harlequin Duck and Common Goldeneye, and there are Brown Dipper on the river itself. Explore the coastline as far as the road is open. More eagles roost at Mosekarubetsugawa, and the scenery all the way along the road is excellent. Watch the road sides for flocks of Rosy Finch. Offshore you will find sea duck and, with luck, sea mammals.

Huge flocks of Jungle Crow and several species of gull are attracted to the harbors and fish-processing factories in Rausu, so once the eagles have left their roosts, it is worth looking through the gull flocks for the occasional rarity. Japan's first Iceland Gull was seen here.

While driving between Rausu and the Sashiruigawa, watch for the flock of Pelagic Cormorant around the cliffs above the tunnel and for Northern Raven both here and at river mouths farther north along the coast. Blakiston's Fish Owl sometimes visit the same river mouths, and

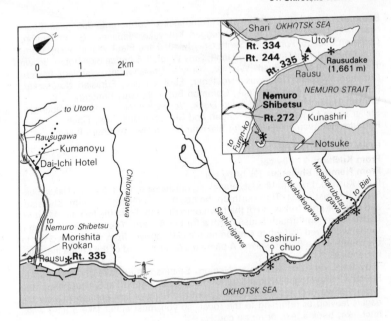

their sonorous duet, "boo-bu, bu," may be heard on windless nights.

In summer, for forest and high-altitude birds, explore the areas beside Shiretoko-toge, the pass from Rausu across the peninsula to Utoro, and up the trail that goes to Rausudake from the camp site just below Kumanoyu. About 1 hr up this trail is an area very good for Gray Bunting.

Shiretoko Hanto is still home to quite a number of Brown Bear, which you may encounter if you hike in the mountains in summer. Hiking is pleasant as late as early September, as at that season it is less popular among Japanese hikers than Daisetsuzan (41). In winter the bears hibernate, so the mammals you are most likely to see are all marine. Steller's Sea Lion winter in Nemuro Strait and can sometimes be seen at the surface on warm days. Harbor Seal occur out among the sea ice and occasionally Ribbon Seal are seen. All species are wary as they are hunted. The best chance to look for them is to join a boat trip out to the sea ice.

BIRDS AND SEASONS
All year: Pelagic Cormorant; White-tailed Eagle; Slaty-backed Gull; Japanese Pygmy Woodpecker; Japanese Wagtail; Brown Dipper; Eurasian Siskin.

Summer: Short-tailed Shearwater; Temminck's Cormorant; Japanese Sparrowhawk; Latham's Snipe; Black-legged Kittiwake; Japanese Green Pigeon; Common Cuckoo; Fork-tailed Swift; Gray-headed and Black Woodpecker; Common House Martin; Olive-backed Pipit; Gray Wagtail; Siberian Blue Robin; Brown Thrush; Stub-tailed Bush Warbler; Gray's Grasshopper Warbler; Eastern Crowned Warbler; Narcissus Flycatcher; Eurasian Jay; Eurasian Nutcracker; Russet Sparrow; Pine Grosbeak; Common Bullfinch; Gray Bunting.
Winter: Harlequin and Long-tailed Duck; Velvet Scoter; Common Goldeneye; Steller's Sea Eagle; Glaucous-winged and Glaucous Gull; Rosy Finch.
Rarities: Hodgson's Hawk Eagle; Blakiston's Fish Owl; Northern Raven.

HOW TO GET THERE

From Kushiro: 4 hr by car.
From Nemuro Shibetsu: 1½ hr by car.
From Kushiro, take Rt. 44 east, branching northeast onto Rt. 272 via Nakashibetsu to the east coast. Turn north up the coast, pass through Nemuro Shibetsu, and take the right fork north of the town onto Rt. 335. From the fork it is 44 km to Rausu. Carry on through Rausu north a further 6.5 km. You will pass through a tunnel with a red and white beacon on the cliffs above, from which it is 3 km to the mouth of the Sashiruigawa. A painted sign at the end of the bridge indicates the eagles.

By train, go from Kushiro to Nemuro Shibetsu, then take an Akan bus to Rausu. Change to a bus bound for Kennebetsu and get off at Sashirui-chuo (the Sashiruigawa river mouth). Buses do not run early or late enough to view the eagles leaving or returning to the roost, so you must either take a long walk, hitchhike, book a taxi, or rent a car.

A boat run by the Morishita Ryokan in Rausu takes visitors out to the sea ice in winter and allows a closer look at eagles, sea lions, and seals. The boat leaves early in the morning on fine days when ice conditions permit. Ask your hotel to book for you. In summer, take the boat from Utoro harbor to the tip of the peninsula for excellent scenery and to see large numbers of Short-tailed Shearwater, Temminck's Cormorant, and Fork-tailed Swift.

The cold here is intense in winter and I thoroughly recommend the outdoor hot spring "Kumanoyu" after a cold day in the field. Go from the Dai-Ichi Hotel west out of Rausu to the closed snow barriers, and cross the river by the footbridge to the pools on the other side.

Accommodation: Comfortable accommodation is available at Rausu Dai-Ichi Hotel ☎(01538)7-2259, which has its own indoor and outdoor hot springs. Or there is Morishita Ryokan ☎(01538)7-2144.

32. Notsuke Hanto and Odaito, East Hokkaido

野付半島/尾袋沼

Good birding months: Jan.–Dec.
Best birding months: Jan.–March, June–Sept.

On hot summer days Notsuke appears to be a chain of low-lying islands with just the roofs of fishermen's houses visible, most of the peninsula disappearing in the haze. On crisp winter days the peninsula stands out sharply across an immense sheet of white ice, while beyond, in the distance, rise the snow-capped mountains of Kunashiri Island.

Notsuke Hanto, a sandy spit extending along the coast and out into the Nemuro Strait, is a fine example, with its series of points, of long-shore drift. The peninsula has extensive flower meadows and conifer stands and, on the inland side, vast salt marshes.

In summer there are carpets of wild roses and irises, and a host of other wild flowers, the most attractive being the wine-colored Kamchatka Fritillary. Siberian Rubythroat sing from the roadside wires and

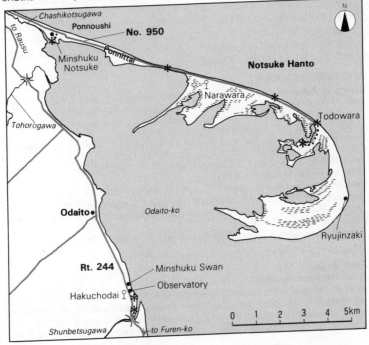

Yellow-breasted Bunting from the rose bushes on the inland side of the peninsula. The area is one of a mere handful where Common Redshank breed in Japan, and several pairs of Japanese Crane breed here too. From the car park at Todowara at the end of the Notsuke road is a well-marked trail across the marshes, including a board walk around an area of inundated pines. Common Redshank are abundant here, and it is a good area to look for other shorebirds, especially in August and September. At these times the small estuary at the mouth of the Shunbetsugawa, just south of the observatory, also attracts shorebirds.

In winter, look here for birds of prey. The first Steller's Sea Eagle usually arrive for the winter at Notsuke during the first week of November. Until the bay freezes over in December/January, it holds large numbers of dabbling duck, while the sea off the peninsula usually harbors several species of sea duck. Shearwaters and alcids are frequently seen too. Frozen or not, the bay near the outflow of the Shunbetsugawa and the sea just off the point are the wintering grounds for the largest concentration of Whooper Swan in Japan (from 3,000 to 5,000 at the peak between January and March). Several hundred of these come in close to shore at Odaito Hakuchodai ("Swan-viewing Point") to be fed, becoming progressively tamer as winter proceeds. In very severe winters, when the river mouth as well as the bay freezes, the swans move south, those that fail to do so sometimes freezing to death.

BIRDS AND SEASONS

Spring & Autumn: Bewick's Swan; Eurasian Wigeon; Falcated and Common Teal; Mallard; Northern Pintail; Kentish and Mongolian Plover; Red-necked Stint; Common Redshank; Gray-tailed Tattler; Ruddy Turnstone; Red-necked Phalarope; Common Black-headed Gull; Common Tern.

Summer: Gray Heron; Eurasian Wigeon; Falcated Teal; Goosander; Japanese Crane; Latham's Snipe; Common Redshank; Common Cuckoo; Siberian Rubythroat; Stonechat; Middendorff's and Lanceolated Warbler; Yellow-breasted and Common Reed Bunting.

Winter: Whooper Swan; Brent Goose (until the bay freezes); Northern Pintail; Common and Velvet Scoter; Common Goldeneye; Goosander; White-tailed and Steller's Sea Eagle; Eurasian Kestrel; Dunlin; Slaty-backed and Glaucous Gull; Rosy Finch; Snow Bunting.

Rarities: White-billed Diver; American Wigeon; Gyrfalcon; Snowy Owl.

HOW TO GET THERE

From Rausu: 1 hr by car.
From the Furen-ko area: 1½ hr by car.
Take Rt. 44 west from Furen-ko to Attoko, then turn north onto Rt. 243, which becomes Rt. 244. After detouring round the inside of Furen-ko, this road runs along the coast for most of the way. From where the road meets the coast, it is about 18 km north to Odaito. The road passes a small estuary, then almost imme-

diately on the right is a large car park, observatory, and restaurant. Take a small side road down from the car park to the shore to observe the swans at close quarters. A further 15 km to the north along Rt. 244, turn sharp right onto prefectural road No. 950, which continues right down Notsuke Hanto. A car park and cluster of souvenir shops and restaurants marks the end of the road at Todowara.

From Nemuro Shibetsu Station: 20 min by bus to Odaito Hakuchodai; or 15 min to Ponnoushi at the base of the peninsula on a bus bound for Todowara. Birdwatch along the road both out to sea and across the marshes.

Accommodation: At the Swan ☎(01538)6-2637, a minshuku just below the observatory at Odaito, you can sleep to the sound of whooping swans; or stay at Minshuku Notsuke ☎(01538)2-3023 at Ponnoushi at the base of the peninsula. Those requiring a little more luxury should stay at Hotel Wakamatsu ☎(01538)2-2151 on the southern outskirts of Nemuro Shibetsu.

33. Furen-ko, Southeast Hokkaido 風連湖

Good birding months: Jan.–Dec.
Best birding months: Jan.–Feb., June

Furen-ko, a huge (52 km²), shallow lagoon nearly 20 km wide, up to 4 km across, and averaging only 1–2 m deep, is surrounded by forests. On higher ground fir, spruce, and yew dominate, on lower ground alder–birch–oak scrub with some maples. The lagoon itself is fringed with reedbeds and tidal mud flats, and opens to the sea at both ends of the long forested island known as Shunkunitai. Birdwatching along the southern shore of the lake, along the coastal marshes and wild rose–covered dunes that separate Shunkunitai from the sea, on Shunkunitai Island itself, and in the forests inland from the lake is some of the finest in Japan. This area easily ranks as my favorite in Japan. It deserves several days and, with several other good sites within easy reach, no trip to Hokkaido, winter or summer, is complete without a lengthy stay here. From January to March the lake and bay are locked in ice and covered with snow, making it a marvellous area to explore on cross-country skis.

The large flocks of waterfowl that pass through Furen-ko in spring and autumn are best seen from the observation area at Hakuchodai. There is a short board walk along the edge of the reeds here and a good trail through the forest on the slope above the lake. Some duck, and occasionally one or two Whooper Swan, remain all summer. For shorebirds, August and September are the best months, although by the end of the July some start passing south again. In September and October several thousand ducks, Bean and Brent Goose, and Whooper

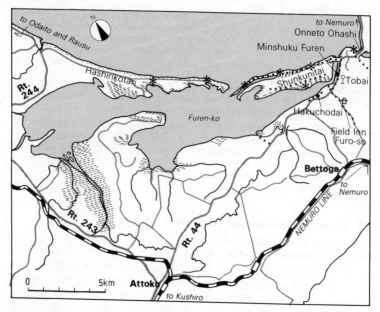

Swan pass through. Up to twenty Japanese Crane can be seen in the area from April to November.

Walk along the shore of Nemuro Bay to the very tip of the sandspit and check the marshes and pools that separate the dunes from Shunkunitai Island for shorebirds. In mid-summer the display calls of Latham's Snipe and the songs of Siberian Rubythroat, Middendorff's Warbler, and Yellow-breasted Bunting dominate the area. In mid-winter, walk around the same area to look for sea duck offshore and Snow and Lapland Bunting and Rosy Finch along the shore.

Just east of Furen-ko is another large lake, Onneto. View this from the bridge for waterfowl, and in spring, particularly May, turn south onto a dirt road just before the bridge to look for forest birds and deer. The small marsh on the seaward side of the bridge is now a WBSJ sanctuary and protects a breeding pair of cranes that can be seen from the road. On summer nights, step outside your minshuku to listen to the songs of three species of *Locustella* warbler and White's Thrush, and to see the huge moon moths that frequent the area. Explore the forest along the road past Field Inn Furo-so for woodland birds.

Mammals frequenting the area include Red Fox, Sika Deer, Flying

Squirrel, Red Squirrel, Asiatic Chipmunk, and Arctic Hare, and at night Long-eared Bat hunt the moths attracted to window lights.

BIRDS AND SEASONS:

All year: Greater Scaup; White-tailed Eagle; Common Buzzard; Hazel Grouse; Ural Owl; Slaty-backed Gull; Gray-headed, Black, Great Spotted, White-backed, Lesser Spotted, and Japanese Pygmy Woodpecker; Northern Wren; Goldcrest; Long-tailed, Marsh, Willow, and Coal Tit; Eurasian Nuthatch; Common Treecreeper; Eurasian Jay; Eurasian Siskin; Common Bullfinch.

Spring & Autumn: Whooper Swan; Bean and Brent Goose; Eurasian Wigeon; Falcated and Common Teal; Mallard; Northern Pintail; Garganey; Northern Shoveler; Common Pochard; Japanese Crane; Kentish, Mongolian, and Gray Plover; Great and Red Knot; Sanderling; Red-necked and Long-toed Stint; Dunlin; Broad-billed Sandpiper; Bar-tailed Godwit; Whimbrel; Common Redshank; Common Greenshank; Wood Sandpiper; Gray-tailed Tattler; Ruddy Turnstone; Red-necked Phalarope; Pomarine and Arctic Skua; Common Blackheaded, Black-tailed, Common, Herring, Glaucous-winged, and Glaucous Gull; Common Tern.

Summer: Gray Heron; Falcated Teal; Tufted Duck; Japanese Sparrowhawk; Northern Hobby; Water Rail; Latham's Snipe; Eurasian Woodcock; Common Redshank; Japanese Green Pigeon; Hodgson's Hawk Cuckoo (uncommon); Common and Oriental Cuckoo; White-throated Needletail; Fork-tailed Swift; Eurasian Wryneck; Sand Martin; Olive-backed Pipit; Japanese Robin; Siberian Rubythroat; Red-flanked Bluetail; Stonechat; White's and Brown Thrush; Middendorff's, Lanceolated, and Gray's Grasshopper Warbler; Black-browed Reed Warbler; Eastern Crowned and Pale-legged Warbler; Sooty, Asian Brown, and Narcissus Flycatcher; Brown Shrike; Red-cheeked Starling; Russet Sparrow; Long-tailed Rosefinch; Yellow-breasted and Common Reed Bunting.

Winter: Whooper Swan; Long-tailed Duck; Common and Velvet Scoter; Common Goldeneye; Steller's Sea Eagle; Glaucous-winged and Glaucous Gull; Ancient Murrelet; Dusky Thrush; Brambling; Common Redpoll; Red Crossbill; Rosy Finch; Snow Bunting.

Rarities: Swinhoe's Egret (May); Lesser White-fronted Goose; Rough-legged Buzzard; Aleutian Tern (September); Blakiston's Fish Owl; Pectoral Sandpiper; Spoon-billed Sandpiper (first half of September); Nordmann's Greenshank (end of August); Lapland Bunting.

HOW TO GET THERE

From Kushiro: 2½ hr by car.
Take Rt. 44 east from Kushiro. On the north side of the road near the 106-km post is an observation area called Hakuchodai that affords views out across the lake. Just after the 108-km post, turn right for Field Inn Furo-so (third house on the left), situated in excellent forest. A further 2 km along Rt. 44 brings you to the mouth of Furen-ko. Fork left off the main road here, pass Minshuku Furen, and cross the lagoon's confluence with the sea by the small bridge to a car park. Walk from here to the point and out to Shunkunitai Island. The trail varies depending on the season, so check with your minshuku host.

Alternatively, take a train from Kushiro to Attoko, then a bus from Attoko Station to Nemuro and get off at Tobai (after 20 min). From there it is a 5-min walk to Shunkunitai-bashi (Shunkunitai Bridge) and a 30-min walk out to Shunkunitai itself. From June to October mosquitoes and horseflies are abundant, so arm yourself with repellent.

Accommodation: While exploring the Furen-ko area and other sites nearby, I thoroughly recommend staying at Field Inn Furo-so ☎(01532)5-3905 with the Takada family. Masaru Takada is an expert on Hokkaido's wildlife, his garden feeders attract many birds, his library is excellent, the food wholesome, and in winter he hires out cross-country skis. Alternatively, stay on the lakeshore at Minshuku Furen ☎(01532)5-3919 with the Matsuo family. Takeyoshi Matsuo is also a knowledgeable naturalist. For those who prefer hotel accommodation, Business Hotel Cairn ☎(01532)3-2826 and the adjacent Beyer Restaurant on the north side of the road on the western outskirts of Nemuro are recommended.

34. Kiritappu, Southeast Hokkaido　霧多布

Good birding months: Jan.–Dec.
Best birding months: Jan.–March, June

The rocky headland beyond the town of Kiritappu, jutting eastward from the southeast coast of Hokkaido, is open and bleak at all seasons except high summer. It lacks trees except in the gulley leading down to a small fishing village and behind windbreaks on the south side of the village. These areas could well harbor interesting migrants but are rarely visited by birdwatchers, who favor the very tip of the cape below the lighthouse. The remainder of the cape is covered with grassland and *sasa*.

The cape (really Tofutsu Misaki, but commonly called Kiritappu Misaki) is an excellent place from which to seawatch, attracts a number of interesting breeding birds, and is well worth a half-day visit. Call in here en route between Kushiro and Nemuro, or make a side trip from the Furen-ko area.

From the lighthouse, take the track down past the foghorn to the tip, which is actually a small island reached by crossing a plank bridge. Just offshore is a small, grass-covered stack where one or two pairs of Tufted Puffin have their burrows amid a Slaty-backed Gull colony. During the breeding season, come here in the early morning for a good chance of seeing them visiting their nesting burrows, and at night stand with your back to the light and scan down the beam for Leach's Petrel. This species breeds in Japan only on islands off southeast Hokkaido. Breeding has not been proven at the cape, although they come regular-

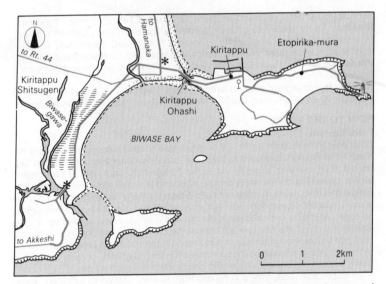

ly. In winter, at the tip of the cape, scan the tide line of the rocks around you, even those below your feet, for Rock Sandpiper. These shorebirds, which are tame and reluctant to fly, are rare in Japan and occur only here and at Choshi (15) in Honshu with any regularity.

Just outside the town of Kiritappu across the bridge on the mainland, a small estuary attracts small numbers of a wide variety of shorebirds in spring and autumn, and Japanese Crane can sometimes be seen here. The beach just beyond the estuary also attracts shorebirds. Just inland of Kiritappu and visible from the road both east and west from the town is a huge marsh, which is home to several breeding pairs of cranes. In June and July it is carpeted with wild flowers and in winter it attracts birds of prey, including Hen Harrier.

Red Fox roam about the area, Kurile Seal are frequently seen off the tip of the cape, and Sea Otter have been sighted again here in recent years, as at Ochiishi (35). In late summer and autumn you will see great strands of kelp put out to dry on the gravel areas adjacent to the marsh and the coast in this area.

BIRDS AND SEASONS

All year: Temminck's and Pelagic Cormorant; Harlequin Duck; Black-tailed and Slaty-backed Gull; Spectacled Guillemot.

Spring & Autumn: Kentish and Mongolian Plover; Red-necked Stint; Curlew

Sandpiper; Dunlin; Common Sandpiper; Gray-tailed Tattler; Ruddy Turnstone.
Summer: Sooty Shearwater; Leach's Petrel; Japanese Crane; Latham's Snipe;
Rhinoceros Auklet; Tufted Puffin; Siberian Rubythroat; Stonechat; Midden-
dorff's and Lanceolated Warbler; Yellow-breasted and Common Reed Bunting.
Winter: Long-tailed Duck; Common and Velvet Scoter; Common and Brunnich's
Guillemot; Ancient Murrelet; Least Auklet; Rosy Finch.
Rarities: Rough-legged Buzzard (winter); Rock Sandpiper; (January to April, and
August); Pigeon Guillemot; Marbled Murrelet (winter); Horned Puffin (summer)

HOW TO GET THERE
From Kushiro: 1½–2 hr by car.
Drive east from Kushiro on Rt. 44. It is possible to take a scenic route along the
coast from Akkeshi eastward to the cape, but in summer this area is often fog-
bound. If so, carry on along Rt. 44 to the 72-km post. Turn right at traffic lights
where there is a coffee shop on the right and a small restaurant on the left.
Follow this road south, turning right at the coast. After a further 5 km you will see
a small mud flat on your left. Turn left at the lights and over the bridge into Kiritappu town. At the far end of town, turn right and wind your way up through a deep
cleft to the top of the hill, turn left here at the crossroads and continue to the car
park just before the lighthouse. Alternatively, turn right at the crossroads and explore the area of planted bushes and trees for tired migrants, or carry straight on
down toward the fishing village and check the trees on the right.

By public transport, take a Toho bus from Kushiro Station to Kiritappu. These
run twice a day and take 2½ hr. There are also buses from Hamanaka Station
(25 min). From the bus stop in Kiritappu it is a 3-km walk to the cape.

Accommodation: Stay near the cape at Minshuku Etopirika-mura ☎(0153)62-
2202, in Hamanaka at Hamanaka Kanko Hotel ☎(0153)64-2311, or in the
Furen-ko area (33).

35. Ochiishi Misaki, Southeast Hokkaido　落石岬
Good birding months: Jan.–Dec.
Best birding months: Jan.–March, June

Ochiishi Misaki (Cape Ochiishi), flat-topped and covered with *sasa*, appears uninteresting from a distance. A closer inspection, however,
reveals attractive coastal scenery, numerous gullies, steep craggy cliffs,
and a shady conifer forest draped with Spanish moss, the haunt of
many birds. The forest floor is carpeted in spring with giant skunk cabbage, and in autumn with mushrooms and more than half a dozen
varieties of edible berries.

My favorite time here is in February and March. Then snow blankets
the cape, the gullies are partially drifted over and great columns of ice
festoon the cliffs; Red Fox forage along the base of these cliffs, and
eagles perch above on exposed crags. It is a harsh landscape in winter

and you need cross-country skis to explore properly and to do the cape justice, but there is a hiking trail to the lighthouse on the cliffs, with a raised boardwalk through the forest of Sakhalin Spruce. Dwarf oaks among the *sasa*, alders in the sheltered gullies, and the spruce forest harbor the few small birds that remain all winter. Coal Tit and Goldcrest are common here, and there is a good chance of observing the more northern wandering species, Common Redpoll and Red Crossbill.

Set up your tripod and telescope just below the lighthouse to look for the resident cormorants and a wide variety of sea duck and alcids in winter. What you see depends very much on the weather and luck, but this cape is the most consistently attractive in southeast Hokkaido to eagles, buzzards, and falcons. For more than fifteen years a single Gyrfalcon (sometimes two) has taken up winter residence, hunting the cape and roosting on the cliffs, often just behind the harbor. For a chance of seeing it return to its roost, visit the harbor in the last half-hour of daylight.

In summer it could hardly be more different. The Pacific coast is often shrouded in fog in the morning, but the sun slowly dissipates it, and then the sea sparkles and Latham's Snipe give their extraordinary diving display flight overhead. Siberian Rubythroat sing from the wooded gullies and Middendorff's Warbler from the *sasa*. Spectacled Guillemot breed, and there are usually a few lingering non-breeding Harlequin Duck. Walk left from the lighthouse, checking the cliffs for breeding cormorants, particularly for the rare Red-faced. This is really a bird of the Aleutian and Kurile Islands, and reaches Japan only in this region.

At any season the cape is a quiet place to walk, a full circuit being easily completed in a day. Most visitors, however, walk more or less straight to and from the lighthouse, so you are unlikely to encounter other people along the cliffs, even in summer. Visit the harbor for close views of duck in autumn and winter and to look for the Gyrfalcon. Take the left turn on top of the cape down into a bay on the east side to look for Rosy Finch and to check the stacks offshore in summer for breeding Red-faced Cormorant.

Mammals include Red Fox, Arctic Hare, and Harbor and Kurile Seal. In recent winters individual Sea Otter have been seen here and elsewhere along the coast. This species was hunted to extinction in Japan toward the end of last century, but now the population on the Kurile Islands may be expanding and one day Hokkaido may be recolonized.

BIRDS AND SEASONS
All year: Temminck's, Pelagic, and Red-faced Cormorant; Harlequin Duck; Spectacled Guillemot; Great Spotted and Japanese Pygmy Woodpecker; Long-tailed,

Marsh, and Coal Tit; Goldcrest; Eurasian Siskin.
Summer: Latham's Snipe; Slaty-backed Gull; Tufted Puffin (non-breeders); Rhinoceros Auklet; Siberian Rubythroat; Stonechat; Middendorff's Warbler; Long-tailed Rosefinch.
Winter: Black-throated Diver; Red-necked and Slavonian Grebe; Long-tailed Duck; Common and Velvet Scoter; Common Goldeneye; White-tailed and Steller's Sea Eagle; Hen Harrier; Common Buzzard; Peregrine; Common and Brunnich's Guillemot; Least Auklet; Common Redpoll; Red Crossbill; Rosy Finch.
Rarities: (winter) Rough-legged Buzzard; Gyrfalcon; Pigeon Guillemot; Marbled Murrelet.

HOW TO GET THERE

From Furen-ko: 45 min by car.
Take Rt. 44 east from Furen-ko. After crossing a large bridge (Onneto Ohāshi) over the mouth of Onneto, take the next right turn at a set of traffic lights. This

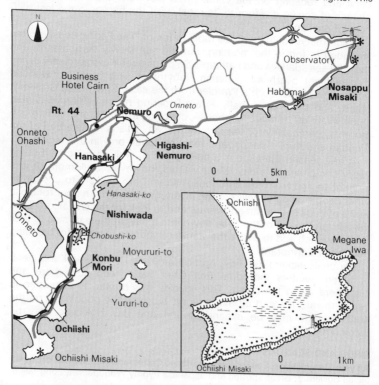

Junction is now signposted in both English and Japanese. After a little over 2 km, turn right and follow this road, which crosses the railway line three times, all the way to Ochiishi village (about 10 km). As you approach the village, the harbor, backed by cliffs, is on your left. At the end of the village the road turns sharply to the right. The entrance to the harbor is to the left just before this turn, and the road to the cape is to the left 150 m after the turn. Turn left to the cape and follow the track that winds uphill. At the top, either turn left and go down a small valley into the bay on the east side of the cape, or carry straight on to the gate that marks the end of the road. From the gate follow the footpath straight on through the forest to the lighthouse.

Alternatively, take a Kotsu bus from Nemuro Station to Ochiishi (30 min); there is one bus in the morning and one in the afternoon. Or take a local train either from Kushiro or Nemuro, get off at Ochiishi Station, and walk 4 km to the cape.

On the way to the cape in summer, visit Chobushi-ko (signposted in English) and walk along the encircling trail for good woodland birding.

Accommodation: This site is best visited on a day trip from a base in the Furen-ko area (33).

36. Nosappu Misaki, Southeast Hokkaido 納沙布岬

Best birding months: Nov.–March

Nosappu Misaki (Cape Nosappu) is the easternmost point on any of the main islands of Japan. The low-lying headland, with its open pastures, tiny valleys, and small wind-blown patches of woodland, is a desolate and cold place in winter. The treetops are covered with drifting snow, the low cliffs are crusted with ice, and the sea along the north coastline is often frozen. At the tip of the cape the channel that separates Japan from four small offshore islands occupied by the Soviet Union is often awash with sea ice drifting south out into the Pacific. The channel and the breaks between the ice floes concentrate the seabirds moving through the channel and, depending on the position of the ice, sea-watching can be excellent here. Small numbers of eagles and other birds of prey are to be found on the headland, and this is the only place in Japan where Steller's Eider winter regularly, albeit in small numbers.

In summer, marshes and pools on the headland attract nesting cranes, while the farmland bird community is typical of much of east Hokkaido.

BIRDS AND SEASONS
Summer: Japanese Crane; Latham's Snipe; Siberian Rubythroat; Stonechat.
Winter: Red-throated and Black-throated Diver; Red-necked Grebe; Northern Fulmar; Temminck's, Pelagic, and Red-faced Cormorant; Harlequin and Long-tailed Duck; Common and Velvet Scoter; Common Goldeneye; Red-breasted

Merganser; White-tailed and Steller's Sea Eagle; Hen Harrier; Common Buzzard; Eurasian Kestrel; Peregrine; Pomarine Skua; Slaty-backed and Glaucous-winged Gull; Black-legged Kittiwake; Common, Brunnich's, and Spectacled Guillemot; Ancient Murrelet; Crested and Least Auklet; Short-eared Owl; Bohemian Waxwing (in Nemuro city); Common Redpoll; Rosy Finch; Snow Bunting.
Rarities: White-billed Diver; Steller's Eider (from late December until March); Pigeon Guillemot; Marbled Murrelet; Whiskered Auklet.

HOW TO GET THERE
From Furen-ko: 1 hr by car.
Take Rt. 44 east to Nemuro. At the T-junction at the far end of town, turn left, then right at the bottom of the hill to follow the northern coastline; alternatively, turn right at the T-junction, then left to follow the southern coastline. Either way it is about 20 km to the cape itself. From Nemuro Station there are buses that take 40 min to reach the cape. Watch from the heated two-story observation center and from the lighthouse.

Accommodation: There is a wide variety of accommodation in Nemuro, but the cape can be reached easily on a day trip from the Furen-ko area (33), so refer to that site for details of accommodation there.

37. Tofutsu-ko, Northeast Hokkaido 涛沸湖
Good birding months: Jan.–Dec.
Best birding months: Feb., June–Sept.

Between Abashiri and Shari on the Okhotsk coast lies the shallow lagoon of Tofutsu-ko, just over 7 km long and up to 2 km wide. Separating it from the sea are low dunes covered with coarse grasses and wild roses where Siberian Rubythroat and Lanceolated Warbler are to be found singing in summer. The northern shore of the lagoon is fringed with reeds, which become more extensive reedbeds at the east end, and beside the road toward the west end is a muddy area attractive to shorebirds in autumn. At the west end itself are woodlands, and inland from the lake roll low wooded hills, with dairy farms, and sugar beet and potato fields. This variety of habitats attracts a large number of birds. The view from the lake to the mountains inland and along Shiretoko Hanto is superb.

From November to March the northern coast of Hokkaido is in the severe grip of winter. The Okhotsk sea is solid with sea ice and most of the lake is frozen. Only near the river outlets, particularly at the west end, is there sufficient open water for a flock of Whooper Swan and Common Goldeneye to survive. This is the season to look for Common Redpoll, Rosy Finch, Snow Bunting, and the rare Lapland Bunting along

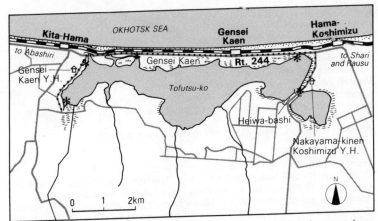

the beaches and dunes, and parties of sea duck on any ice-free patches of water offshore. Winter is also the time when both species of sea eagles may be encountered, although not in such numbers as on the east side of Shiretoko Hanto at Rausu. Exploring the area on cross-country skis is the most enjoyable way of finding birds at this season.

Large numbers of waterfowl pass through on migration, including up to 3,000 Whooper Swan in April (and November). In May the breeding birds begin to arrive, and Gray-headed and Yellow-breasted Bunting are common here. Latham's Snipe, Siberian Rubythroat, and Middendorff's Warbler are next on the scene along with Lanceolated Warbler and Long-tailed Rosefinch. This is the only place where Gadwall are common in Japan in summer. Falcated Teal breed, and both White-tailed Eagle and Northern Hobby nest nearby and hunt the area.

The strip of land between the lagoon and the main road, known as Gensei Kaen, is famous for its profusion of wild flowers from June to August. Red Fox, Sika Deer, Flying Squirrel, Red Squirrel, and Asiatic Chipmunk are common in the area.

BIRDS AND SEASONS

Spring & Autumn: Bean Goose; Eurasian Wigeon; Falcated and Common Teal; Garganey; Northern Shoveler; Common Pochard; Greater Scaup; Mongolian, Pacific Golden, and Gray Plover; Sanderling; Red-necked Stint; Dunlin; Black-tailed and Bar-tailed Godwit; Whimbrel; Spotted Redshank; Wood Sandpiper; Gray-tailed Tattler; Common Black-headed and Black-tailed Gull; Common Tern.

Summer: Gray Heron; Falcated Teal; Gadwall; Mallard; Spot-billed Duck; White-tailed Eagle; Eastern Marsh Harrier; Northern Hobby; Common Moorhen; Common Coot; Latham's Snipe; Common and Oriental Cuckoo; Eurasian Wryneck;

Great Spotted and Japanese Pygmy Woodpecker; Sand Martin; Siberian Rubythroat; Stonechat; Middendorff's, Lanceolated, and Gray's Grasshopper Warbler; Black-browed Reed Warbler; Eastern Crowned Warbler; Narcissus Flycatcher; Coal Tit; Eurasian Nuthatch; Bull-headed and Brown Shrike; Eurasian Jay; Red-cheeked Starling; Long-tailed Rosefinch; Meadow, Gray-headed, Yellow-breasted, and Common Reed Bunting.

Winter: Whooper Swan; Northern Pintail; Common and Velvet Scoter; Common Goldeneye; Smew; Red-breasted Merganser; White-tailed and Steller's Sea Eagle; Short-eared Owl; Brambling; Common Redpoll; Rosy Finch; Snow Bunting.

Rarities: Gyrfalcon; Snowy Owl; Shore Lark; Lapland Bunting.

HOW TO GET THERE

From Kushiro: 4 hr by car or train.

Drive along Rt. 244 from Abashiri to Shari. The road passes within a few hundred meters of Tofutsu-ko. Alternatively, take the train between the same two towns and get off either at Kita-Hama Station and walk east, or at Hama-Koshimizu and walk west. It is a 2-hr walk between these two stations along the lake. Kita-Hama can be reached by train from Kushiro or by bus from Abashiri (40 min). Tofutsu-ko is easily visited by car en route between Shiretoko Hanto (31) and Kawayu (38).

Accommodation: At the east end of the lake is Nakayama-kinen Koshimizu Youth Hostel ☎(0152)64-2011, and at the west end is Gensei Kaen Youth Hostel ☎(0152)46-2630 (cross country skis can be hired here). A wider variety of accommodation is available in nearby Abashiri and Shari.

38. Kawayu, East Hokkaido　川湯

Good birding months: Jan.–Dec.
Best birding months: Jan.–March, June

In the central part of east Hokkaido lies Akan National Park, conspicuous for the steaming peak of Me-Akan-dake (1,499 m) and, a little further to the east, the conical peak of O-Akan-dake (1,371 m). Further east still is Mt. Kamuinupuri (855 m). On clear winter days the view northeast is to the mountainous spine of Shiretoko National Park. Between this group of volcanoes and the Shiretoko mountain range lie two crater lakes, Kussharo-ko and Mashu-ko. Kussharo-ko is reputedly the largest caldera lake in Japan, while the scenery around Mashu-ko ranks with the very best in Japan. For birdwatching I highly recommend the Kawayu area near Kussharo-ko, which is heavily forested with mature conifers.

Rise very early on at least one morning when staying in Kawayu

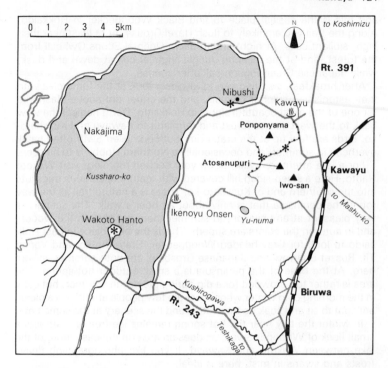

village (this means getting up by 03:00 in summer) and head south out of town. Before reaching the turn-off to the car park at Iwo-san—an area of actively steaming sulphuroles—the road crosses a clearing covered with low shrubs, an area carpeted with azaleas in July. There look for a track off to the right (west). It is wide enough for a vehicle, but is invariably blocked by a gate. Leave your car here and start walking. A 40-min walk will take you through predominantly coniferous forest with an admixture of deciduous trees, over a low ridge and down to a large clearing, almost a bowl between the hills. The trail passes between two almost symmetrical mountains, Ponponyama (Sawanchi-sappu) to the north and Atosanupuri (Makuanchi-sappu) to the south. At one point it forks, but the right fork is little used. Keep left and carry on downhill to a clearing with old dead trees and low scrub. This is an excellent area for early morning bird song in summer and is particularly attractive to woodpeckers. At all seasons I have found all five woodpeckers here, and this is the easiest place to find Black Woodpecker in Hokkaido. Along the trail you are likely to flush Hazel Grouse, or at least hear their high, sibilant calls. At night and at dawn Oriental Scops Owl call from the forest, and at the clearing Jungle Nightjar call at dawn and dusk, while Japanese Green Pigeon call after sunrise.

After breakfast, visit Iwo-san for a closer look at the fumaroles with their astonishing sulphur crystals, and the crater rim above Mashu-ko for one of the most beautiful sights in Hokkaido. Don't neglect the view back to the west across forest and farmland to Kawayu and Kussharo-ko. Birds are few up at the crater rim, but Fork-tailed Swift often hawk overhead in summer, and occasionally a Northern Hobby is to be seen.

For a late afternoon walk, or on your second morning, visit Wakoto Hanto. Here a steep-sided hill covered with mature deciduous trees juts into the southern end of Kussharo-ko. There is a nature trail all the way round the peninsula that is only about an hour's walk. The scenery is very pleasant at any season; in summer there are lilies in the woods, and in autumn the colors are superb. This is the best place in East Hokkaido to look for Gray-headed Woodpecker, Gray Thrush, and Varied Tit. Russet Sparrow and Japanese Grosbeak are both summer visitors here. At the base of the peninsula is a small outdoor hot spring. The area is rather too crowded for a dip during the day in summer, but early in the morning or in winter when there are few people about, it is a pleasant spot to sit and soak up the waters and the scenery at the same time.

In winter the bay near the hot spring remains ice-free and attracts a small flock of Whooper Swan, as does an area on the east shore of the lake between Wakoto and Kawayu. If you like photographing heavy frosts and swans in mist, here is ideal.

While driving between sites in east Hokkaido, always keep an eye open for waxwing flocks in berry-bearing trees in town gardens. En route to Kushiro, stop at Shirarutoro-ko, 26 km north of Kushiro, on the left of Rt. 391. Red-necked Grebe, White-tailed Eagle, Northern Hobby, and Japanese Crane all breed, and in winter Crested Kingfisher is frequently seen.

Droppings and footprints indicate that Brown Bear are present in the Kawayu area, although I have not seen one here. Red Fox, Sika Deer, Red Squirrel, and Asiatic Chipmunk are all common.

BIRDS AND SEASONS
All year: Hazel Grouse; Gray-headed, Black, Great Spotted, White-backed, and Japanese Pygmy Woodpecker; Northern Wren; Goldcrest; Long-tailed, Marsh, Willow, Varied, and Coal Tit; Eurasian Nuthatch; Common Treecreeper; Eurasian Jay; Eurasian Siskin.
Summer: Goosander; Northern Hobby; Eurasian Woodcock; Japanese Green

Pigeon; Hodgson's Hawk Cuckoo; Common and Oriental Cuckoo; Oriental Scops Owl; Jungle Nightjar; White-throated Needletail; Fork-tailed Swift; Olive-backed Pipit; Siberian Blue Robin; Red-flanked Bluetail; White's, Gray, and Brown Thrush; Stub-tailed Bush Warbler; Eastern Crowned and Pale legged Warbler; Asian Brown and Narcissus Flycatcher; Bull-headed and Brown Shrike; Red-cheeked Starling; Russet Sparrow; Japanese Grosbeak; Hawfinch; Meadow Bunting.

Winter: Whooper Swan; Bohemian Waxwing; Pine Grosbeak.
Rarities: Hodgson's Hawk Eagle.

HOW TO GET THERE

From Kushiro: 2 hr by car, or by train and bus.
From Kushiro, take a train to Kawayu Station (1 hr 40 min), then a bus from the station either to Wakoto or to Kawayu (both about 30 min).

By car, Kawayu is 90 km north of Kushiro. Follow signs for Rt. 44 out of Kushiro, but where Rt. 44 branches right after 4.5 km, carry straight on onto Rt. 391. Just before reaching Teshikaga (72 km from Kushiro), turn left onto Rt. 243 and continue on this until 5 km after the town, where you take the right fork onto Rt. 391 again. About 12 km from this junction you will pass Kawayu Station on your right. Take the next turn left to Kawayu passing Iwo-san on your left. The center of Kawayu is a cluster of hotels, a post office, and souvenir shops selling Ainu wood carvings. For a visit to Mashu-ko, turn east just south of Kawayu Station. This road takes you all the way up to the crater rim.

Accommodation: Kawayu is an excellent base, as both Kussharo-ko and Mashu-ko are very close. The hotels all have their own hot spring baths and it is possible to walk out of town in just a few minutes. I can recommend Kawayu Hotel Plaza ☎(01548)3-2211, Grand Hotel ☎(01548)3-2311, and Kawayu Kanko Hotel ☎(01548)3-2121.

39. Kushiro, East Hokkaido 釧路

Best birding months: Nov.–March

The wintering flocks of Japanese Crane in east Hokkaido are one of the four great nature spectacles in the country, the others being the eagles on Shiretoko Hanto (31), the swans at Odaito (32), and the cranes at Arasaki (51) in Kyushu. No visit to Japan is complete without seeing them. In summer the cranes disperse throughout low-lying marshland in eastern Hokkaido, such as at Notsuke Hanto (32), to breed. From late summer onward they begin to congregate at large lakes, such as at the southern end of Furen-ko (33), then move up to farmland and steadily toward Kushiro. In October and November the cranes glean in the maize stubble fields after the harvesting before moving on to the main wintering sites.

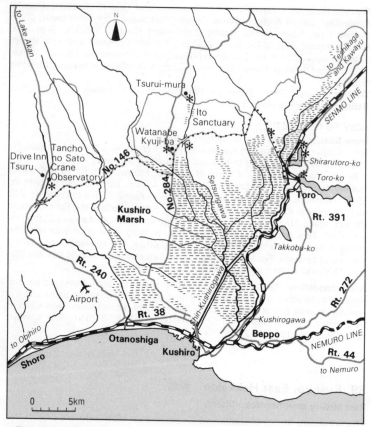

The cranes spend most of the winter in large flocks, visiting certain feeding grounds every day and returning at night to roost in the shallows of fast-flowing, ice-free rivers. To enjoy them at their best, from November onward, allow time for a visit to a roosting site at dawn or dusk and for a visit to one of the main feeding sites at either Tancho no Sato (up to 120 birds) or Tsurui-mura (40–90 birds at Watanabe Kyuji-ba and 40–90 at the Ito Sanctuary).

In January and February just after sunrise (around 06:30 is best), visit the roost at the Setsurigawa. Surrounded by snow and with a thick mist rising from the river into the chill morning air, the cranes cluster in the shallows waiting for the sun. As the sun warms them, they preen a little before flying out between 09:00 and 10:00 to the feeding areas across the low hills to the west. They return about 16:30 onward. View the river from the bridge. However much you want that closer picture, *do not leave the road*, or the cranes will be disturbed.

In February and March crane pairs indulge in dancing and bugling displays. Dancing is contagious, often spreading throughout the flock. The sight of a whole flock of black and white, red-crowned cranes dancing gracefully in deep snow against a backdrop of stark wintry hills is the most beautiful wildlife spectacle to be seen in Japan.

At Tancho no Sato, the most famous wintering area, the food put out daily for the cranes attracts scavengers. Eurasian Tree Sparrow, Carrion and Jungle Crow, and Rock Dove filch the maize that is put out in the morning. The afternoon feed around 15:00 is of fish, which attracts Red Fox that avoid stabbing beaks to dodge in and out among the flock to pilfer. White-tailed Eagle sometimes put in an appearance too, and with luck you may see cranes, foxes, and eagles competing together for the food.

Most small birds leave Hokkaido in winter, but in the area between the crane sites and along the river valleys, you may find various woodpeckers and other woodland birds. At the Setsurigawa roost you may also find Whooper Swan and Rosy Finch, and when crossing the hills and marshlands to Tsurui-mura, look out for Great Gray Shrike and Pallas's Rosefinch.

The crane areas are generally good for Red Fox and Sika Deer. Keep a look out for deer along woodland edges and crossing fields in the early morning.

BIRDS AND SEASONS
Winter: Whooper Swan; White-tailed Eagle; Northern Goshawk; Northern Sparrowhawk; Japanese Crane; Japanese Pygmy Woodpecker; Eurasian Nuthatch; Eurasian Siskin; Rosy Finch; Hawfinch.
Rarities: Great Gray Shrike; Pallas's Rosefinch.

HOW TO GET THERE
From Kushiro: 1 hr 10 min by car to Tancho no Sato.
For Tancho no Sato (35 km from Kushiro), leave Kushiro going west on Rt. 38. After 12 km, follow the sign for the airport and turn north onto Rt. 240. Continue past the airport north along Rt. 240 toward Akan National Park. Just after the 22-km post is a large round sign on the left depicting a crane and indicating the crane observatory. Also on the left is a car park, a restaurant, and Drive Inn Tsuru. Park here and walk across the main road and about 100 m down the track to the observatory, which is open daily from 08:30 to 16:30.

For Tsurui-mura, either take prefectural road No. 284 out of Kushiro, or cross east from Tancho no Sato on prefectural road No. 146. Feeding grounds are at Watanabe Kyuji-ba and the Ito farm; the latter is now a WBSJ sanctuary. Turn right just before Watanabe Kyuji-ba and continue until the road crosses the Setsurigawa, where the cranes roost.

In October and November, visit Segawa Bokujo (Segawa Ranch) to look for cranes on the maize stubble there. Cross the bridge at the Setsurigawa and take the next fork right. The cranes should be in the fields alongside the road.

Accommodation: Stay either just opposite the Tancho no Sato observatory at Drive Inn Tsuru ☎(0154)66-3073, managed by Mr. Nishioka, or at Drive Inn Taito ☎(0154)64-2010 in Tsurui-mura, managed by Mr. Wada. Both men are keen crane photographers and will be able to help you find the flight lines and roosts that are currently being used. Those willing to make a longer early morning drive will find hotel accommodation, such as the Tokyu Inn ☎(0154)22-0109, near Kushiro Station.

40. Sarobetsu and Kucharo-ko, North Hokkaido

サロベツ / クッチャロ湖

Good birding months: Jan.–Dec.
Best birding months: June–Aug.

If you enjoy wide vistas of rolling hills, make the trip to northern Hokkaido. With an airport near Wakkanai, connected to Sapporo, and direct flights from Tokyo, this far-flung outpost of Japan is surprisingly only a well-planned long morning or afternoon from Tokyo.

In autumn and early spring large flocks of geese and swans pause to rest and feed at the Sarobetsu marshes or at Kucharo-ko. As the last of the swans leave, the first summer migrant duck, waders, warblers, and flycatchers arrive. Once the summer birds have bred and fled south again and the returning waterfowl have passed through, a kind of bleak beauty settles over the land, with cold winds, sea ice, and snow creating an arctic landscape. Yet on clear winter days at river mouths and in ice-free areas just offshore there are Long-tailed and Harlequin Duck, and they look all the more spectacular in the low winter light. A few White-tailed and Steller's Sea Eagle winter here, and Rough-legged Buzzard and Gyrfalcon occur each winter.

For a wide variety of birds and marsh flowers, plus warm or sunny weather, from June to August is the best time for a visit. Starting from the airport, drive east along Rt. 238, which follows the coastline, for nearly 20 km to Soya Misaki, the northernmost tip of Hokkaido. Offshore are many gulls, mostly Black-tailed, and flocks of feeding Rhinoceros Auklet with an occasional Ancient Murrelet among them.

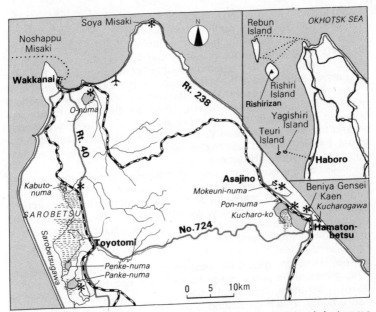

The nearest breeding colonies are probably on Rishiri Island, but some may come from as far away as Sakhalin—which on clear days can be seen as a beautiful, mountainous land along the northern horizon.

From Soya Misaki, carry on south down Rt. 238, which follows the east coast passing through wonderful scenery—forested hillsides with patchworks of dark green conifers, paler green birches and oaks, and a wide variety of wild flowers. Away to the south, the northern flanks of the Teshio mountains can be seen. Along this road are plenty of Stonechat, and look out for Gray-headed Bunting, which often sing from roadside fence posts. Approximately 4 km south of Asajino Station, fork left, take the next fork left, and after 1 km turn left to Mokeuni-numa.

This reed-fringed lagoon is the most beautiful I have visited in Japan. A border of mixed woodland covers the slopes down to it, and the scattered trees and bushes between the woods and reedbed provide exactly the habitat liked by Yellow-breasted Bunting. The attractive yellow and chocolate-brown males sing their short songs from low treetops. Black-browed Reed Warbler is here too, as are Common and Oriental Cuckoo, Gray's Grasshopper Warbler, and Siberian Rubythroat. Next head toward Kucharo-ko, pausing en route to take a quick look at Pon-numa, another lovely lagoon just north of the main lake, to see the Red-necked Grebe that breed there. Kucharo-ko is famous for the large flocks of Bewick's Swan and the geese that visit in April on their way north to breed. Throughout May the summer visitors continue to arrive, but only after about June 10 have the last arrived, the three *Locustella* warblers.

The reedbeds on the west side of the lake are one of the few breeding grounds in Japan of Great Bittern. Listen for their deep foghornlike booming calls early in the morning or at night. In the reeds and woods around the lake are Eurasian Wryneck, Brown Thrush, Siberian Ruby-throat, Pale-legged and Eastern Crowned Warbler, Yellow-breasted Bunting, and Long-tailed Rosefinch.

Finally, before leaving the area, visit Beniya Gensei Kaen, between the main road and the Okhotsk Sea. This area of mixed grassland, reed-bed, and scrubland is carpeted with blue irises and yellow lilies in early summer, with plenty of Yellow-breasted Bunting, Black-browed Reed Warbler, and *Locustella* warblers. Brown Shrike hunt the scrub areas, and Yellow Wagtail breed here, while offshore are Black-tailed Gull and Rhinoceros Auklet.

From Hamatonbetsu, drive west for 58 km on prefectural road No. 724, a marvelous scenic route through hills and forest to Toyotomi. Join Rt. 40 there, turn south, travel for 7–8 km, then turn west to Panke-numa. This huge lagoon is situated in Sarobetsu marsh, a vast peat bog along the west coast of northernmost Hokkaido. It is surrounded by reeds and holds many of the same birds as Kucharo-ko, but in addition Gray Heron are common and Eastern Marsh Harrier drift lazily back and forth over the reeds. Latham's Snipe display overhead, and woodland patches have singing Brown Thrush, with Gray's Grasshopper Warbler in the damper wooded areas.

To complete your circuit around northernmost Hokkaido, travel to Wakkanai (just under 50 km further north), Noshappu Misaki, and O-numa by way of Kabuto-numa. Red-necked Grebe, Falcated Teal, and Tufted Duck are here, as are several species of warbler. Sand Martin hawk low over the water, and are sometimes joined by Fork-tailed Swift. The parklike area and camp site by the shore of Kabuto-numa are frequented by Red-cheeked and Gray Starling and Russet Sparrow, and are very good for early morning birdwatching. Out to sea the huge cone of Rishiri Fuji is an impressive sight from here.

If you have time, visit the islands of Rebun and Rishiri off the west coast, both of which can be reached by daily ferries from Wakkanai. Rebun is renowned for its flowers, but Rishiri is better for birds, with Japanese Robin, Gray Bunting, plentiful Common Treecreeper, and the pink form of Common Bullfinch among many other species. During spring migration, rarities turn up here, as they do on Teuri (an island further down the coast), and seabirds should be looked for on the crossing. On the cliffs at the south end of Teuri are large gull colonies and breeding Common and Spectacled Guillemot. Japan's first record of Common Jackdaw was on Teuri.

Mammals that may be encountered in northernmost Hokkaido include Red Fox, Brown Bear, Sable, Harbor Seal, Sika Deer, Red Squirrel, Asiatic Chipmunk, and Arctic Hare.

BIRDS AND SEASONS

All year: Temminck's and Pelagic Cormorant; Harlequin Duck; Spectacled Guillemot; Ancient Murrelet; Long-tailed, Marsh, Willow, and Coal Tit; Eurasian Nuthatch.

Spring & Autumn: Bewick's Swan; Bean Goose; Eurasian Wigeon; Falcated and Common Teal; Mallard; Northern Pintail; Common Pochard; Tufted Duck; Dunlin; Spotted Redshank; Wood Sandpiper.

Summer: Red-necked Grebe; Gray Heron; Falcated Teal; Mallard; Tufted Duck; Eastern Marsh Harrier; Osprey; Northern Hobby; Little Ringed and Kentish Plover; Latham's Snipe; Common Sandpiper; Black-tailed Gull; Common Guillemot; Rhinoceros Auklet; Common Cuckoo; Jungle Nightjar; White-throated Needletail; Fork-tailed Swift; Common Kingfisher; Eurasian Wryneck; Great Spotted and Japanese Pygmy Woodpecker; Sand Martin; Olive-backed Pipit; Yellow Wagtail; Stonechat; Brown Thrush; Middendorff's, Lanceolated, and Gray's Grasshopper Warbler; Black-browed Reed Warbler; Eastern Crowned Warbler; Asian Brown Flycatcher; Bull-headed and Brown Shrike; Red-cheeked Starling; Russet Sparrow; Long-tailed Rosefinch; Gray-headed, Yellow-breasted, and Common Reed Bunting.

Winter: Greater Scaup; Long-tailed Duck; Common and Velvet Scoter; Common Goldeneye; Red-breasted Merganser; Goosander; White-tailed and Steller's Sea Eagle; Snow Bunting.

Rarities: (winter) Rough-legged Buzzard; Gyrfalcon; Snowy Owl.

HOW TO GET THERE

From Tokyo: 2 hr by plane to Sapporo.
From Sapporo: 8 hr by car.
Many flights operate daily between Tokyo's Haneda Airport and Sapporo's Chitose Airport, taking less than two hours for the journey. From Sapporo it is a further 1 hr by plane to Wakkanai. At Wakkanai Airport, rent a car and drive the route outlined above. Alternatively, drive from Sapporo taking Rt. 231 northward out of the city (this becomes Rt. 232 and eventually Rt. 40) to Wakkanai. About 11 km north of the junction between Rt. 232 and Rt. 239 you pass through a town called Haboro. If you have time, stop over and take a trip out to Teuri Island. There are minshuku and a youth hostel on this small island, which is a very pleasant place to visit in late spring or early summer.

Accommodation: A wide variety of minshuku, ryokan, and hotels is available in Wakkanai, Toyotomi Onsen, and Hamatonbetsu, or else you can camp at Kabuto-numa.

41. Daisetsuzan, Central Hokkaido 大雪山
Best birding months: June–Nov.

Daisetsuzan National Park, a huge mountainous area in the middle of Hokkaido known as the "roof of Hokkaido," is the largest national park in Japan (231,000 ha) and encompasses more than ten volcanoes over 2,000 m high. It is a fine area for hiking, with beautiful gorges, ravines, and dramatic volcanic scenery including active, extinct, and shield volcanoes, lava streams, and fumaroles. It also has high-altitude marshes and vast stretches of forest. Numerous long trails make this an excellent destination for those with a week to spare, but for those with limited time I recommend the easy hike across the mountaintops from Kurodake (1,984 m), perhaps as far as Hokkaido's highest peak, Asahidake (2,290 m).

In summer the forests of the lower and middle slopes are alive with birds, and in late July the tops are covered with alpine flowers. In autumn the slopes are ablaze with color, the dark dwarf pine contrasting with the bright reds and oranges of Mountain Ash. Early in the season the birds will be up on the tops, and the most sought-after species—Japanese Accentor, Eurasian Nutcracker, and Pine Grosbeak—are usually in evidence around the clumps of dwarf pine. Between mid-October and mid-November you will encounter flocks of up to twenty Pine Grosbeak before you even reach the summit of Kurodake, and accentors and nutcrackers will have also moved down. Look also at the Ishikarigawa running through the Sounkyo gorge for wagtails and Brown Dipper. Allow at least one full day for exploring the area. If you have time, the areas around Aizanke and Asahidake are well worth exploring. Daisetsu means "great snow" and winter snows here are deep, with some snow fields lasting throughout the summer up on the tops. Do not attempt winter hiking here unless you are well equipped and experienced.

The Daisetsuzan area is one of the few remaining strongholds in Hokkaido of Brown Bear, particularly between Kogen Onsen and Takanegahara. Keep a wary eye open for them, although your chance of seeing one before they flee is slim. Red Fox are reasonably common, as are Asiatic Chipmunk, and in areas of loose rock piles, look for Asiatic Pika.

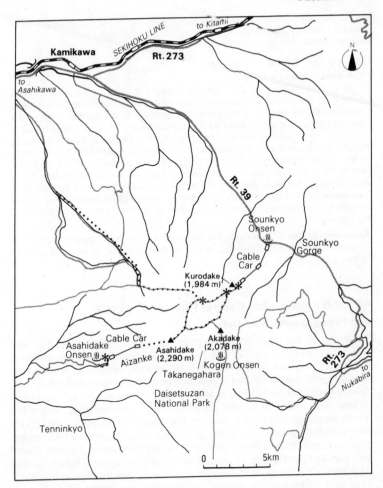

BIRDS AND SEASONS

Summer Japanese and Northern Sparrowhawk; Common Buzzard; Hodgson's Hawk Cuckoo (uncommon); Common Cuckoo; White-throated Needletail; Fork-tailed Swift; Common House Martin; Olive-backed Pipit; Gray and Japanese Wagtail; Brown Dipper; Northern Wren; Japanese Accentor; Japanese Robin; Siberian Rubythroat; Red-flanked Bluetail; Siberian and Brown Thrush; Pale-

legged Warbler; Goldcrest; Asian Brown Flycatcher; Coal Tit; Eurasian Nutcracker; Eurasian Siskin; Pine Grosbeak; Common Bullfinch.
Rarities: Three-toed Woodpecker.

HOW TO GET THERE

From Asahikawa: 1½ hr by car.
Rt. 39 works its way northeast from Asahikawa to Kamikawa around the northern limit of the Daisetsu mountain range and eventually heads southeast to Sounkyo (65 km) and on to Nukabira. The gateway to the northern part of the Daisetsu range is Sounkyo, a hot spring and ski resort with several large hotels in the 13-km-long Sounkyo gorge. The gorge itself is flanked by rock walls rising 150 m, with several attractive waterfalls. A cable car and chair lift run partway up the flank of Kurodake to the south of Sounkyo. From the top of the cable car, hike to the peak, then explore southward across the open mountaintops. If you want to tackle the long hike from the other end, take a bus (1 hr 40 min) from Asahikawa to Asahidake Onsen (formerly Yukomambetsu). From there, a good trail goes to the top, or take the cable car that goes most of the way and just hike the last section.

Accommodation: At Sounkyo, try Sounkyo Kanko Hotel ☎(01658)5-3101, Tabi no Hausu ☎(01658)5-3402, or stay at the camp site; or stay at Asahidake Onsen.

42. Shikaribetsu-ko, Central Hokkaido   然別湖

Best birding months: May–Oct.

Southeast of the main Daisetsu range lies Shikaribetsu-ko, a large lake with a circumference of 16 km, formed after volcanic activity dammed the Yanbetsugawa. It is situated at an altitude of 800 m among hills wooded with mature mixed coniferous and deciduous forests that have a wide variety of birds. This is another beautiful area for autumn colors in late September and early October. The northern end, where the Yanbetsugawa enters the lake, is the best birding area since Black Woodpecker usually nest at the north end of the camp site here and at night a lone Fish Owl (there used to be a pair) frequents the river mouth and can be heard giving its deep double hoot. Hodgson's Hawk Cuckoo and White's Thrush both sing at night here, the former with a shrill, repeated, rising "ju-ichi, ju-ichi" call and the latter a mournful two-note whistle.

The best season is from May onward when it is getting warmer and when birds are breeding. In winter the snow is very deep and prefectural road No. 726 from Nukabira is closed from November until early May.

There are many Sika Deer, Asiatic Chipmunk, and Arctic Hare in the

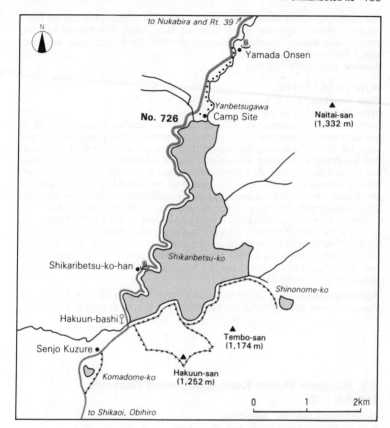

forests here. Just beyond the south end of the lake a hiking trail leads south to Komadome-ko. A 30-min walk from Shikaribetsu-ko-han will bring you to a rock-strewn slope where Asiatic Pika is quite common. It produces very high-pitched calls, and can thus be tracked down relatively easily.

BIRDS AND SEASONS

Summer: Mallard; Goosander; Common Buzzard; Osprey; Hazel Grouse; Eurasian Woodcock; Japanese Green Pigeon; Hodgson's Hawk Cuckoo; Common Cuckoo; Oriental Scops Owl; White-throated Needletail; Black, Lesser Spotted,

and Japanese Pygmy Woodpecker; Common House Martin; Olive-backed Pipit; Northern Wren; Japanese Robin; Siberian Blue Robin; Red-flanked Bluetail; White's and Brown Thrush; Pale-legged Warbler; Goldcrest; Sooty and Narcissus Flycatcher; Coal Tit.
Rarities: Blakiston's Fish Owl.

HOW TO GET THERE
From Sounkyo: 3–4 hr by car.
From Obihiro: 2 hr by car.
From Sounkyo (Daisetsuzan, 41), drive 90 km southeast along Rt. 39 to Nukabira and turn southwest onto prefectural road No. 726, a winding mountain road, for 15 km. As it nears the lake the road runs alongside the Yanbetsugawa. The camp site is beside the river mouth, east of the road. From Obihiro, it is 60 km to the lake. Take Rt. 241 north and turn left across the railway lines 4 km after it crosses the main river. This area has innumerable sideroads, and for those who cannot read Japanese, it may be easier to continue north along Rt. 241, fork left onto Rt. 273 to Nukabira, and turn south there to the lake.

By bus, take a Takushoku bus from Obihiro Station to Shikaribetsu-ko-han and get off at the last but one stop (Hakuun-bashi) to walk to Hakkuun-san and Tembo-san. The trails to these mountains take 3–4 hr and pass through attractive forest. Alpine flowers are at their best during May/June. From Shikaribetsu-kohan there is a Kohan Onsen bus for Nukabira, which takes 15 min to the Shikaribetsu-ko camp site.

Accommodation: Stay at Shikaribetsu-ko-han Hotel ☎(01566)7-2211, at Yamada Onsen ☎(01566)7-2301 near the camp site, or at the camp site itself.

43. Nopporo Shinrin Koen, Southwest Hokkaido
野幌森林公園

Good birding months: Jan.–Dec.
Best birding months: April–July, Oct.–Feb.

Nopporo Shinrin Koen (Forest Park) was designated a Hokkaido prefectural nature park in 1968 in commemoration of the centennial of the initiation of Hokkaido's development. The park boasts a museum, an historical village, and a memorial tower which, with its huge jagged top, can be seen from almost anywhere on Ishikari Plain. Much of the park is a well-wooded forest conservation area. Despite the local name for the area, which means "primeval forest," a large proportion of it is planted with conifers. The natural areas of mature mixed woodland of spruce, fir, maple, basswood, katsura, and kalopanax have some 500 plant species, and nearly 140 bird species have been recorded.

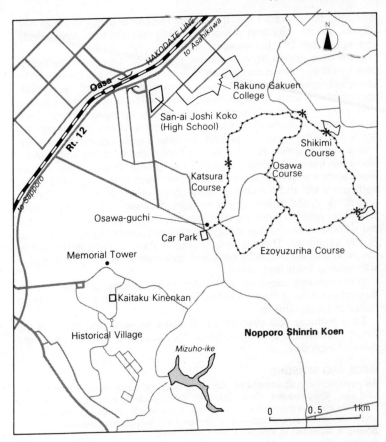

Most visitors head for the park center with its museums, but I recommend birders to hike into the forest straightaway, or to enter by way of one of the smaller entrances. The best areas for birding are the Katsura, Osawa, Ezoyuzuriha, and Shikimi courses, which start from a car park approximately 3 km from Oasa Station. Walks vary in length, and if a 6-km hike is not too long, enter the forest, then turn left after about 100 m, where the trails cross, onto the Katsura course. Follow the trail down to a stream, past two small ponds on the Shikimi course, then complete the circuit back to the crossroads. Having lived right next to this forest for nearly three years I can thoroughly recommend this route at any season, but the very best seasons for birds here are from April to July and again from October onward.

In the deep snows from December to early April the trails are cross-country skiing courses and birding is easier on skis. This is the season to see woodpeckers easily and to have a very good chance of seeing both species of waxwing. Spring is heralded by the first flowers of the year, a kind of umbellifer known locally as *fuki*, quickly followed by large white skunk cabbage along streamsides and in damp areas around melting snow. Once these have appeared, summer visitors are not far behind.

In summer, arrive as early as you can in the morning and wander along the trails very slowly while bird song is at its peak. The mature woodlands attract numerous woodpeckers and other woodland birds, particularly tits and nuthatches, although in recent years Hazel Grouse and Black Woodpecker appear to have declined, if not disappeared. From May onward there are cuckoos, thrushes, and flycatchers, and in the woodland around the pond you may encounter Mandarin Duck or Ruddy Kingfisher. There is quite a large heronry in the eastern part of the park, and the adults fly back and forth from their nests to forage in surrounding fields and rivers.

In the autumn, especially in October, large numbers of thrushes pass through, and this is the time to find Eye-browed Thrush among the large flocks of Dusky Thrush.

Early morning and evening are the best times to see some of the forest mammals, including Red Fox, Flying Squirrel, Red Squirrel, and Asiatic Chipmunk.

BIRDS AND SEASONS

All year: Northern Sparrowhawk; Common Buzzard; Hazel Grouse (uncommon); Ural Owl; Gray-headed, Great Spotted, White-backed, and Japanese Pygmy Woodpecker; Northern Wren; Goldcrest; Long-tailed, Marsh, Willow, Varied, and Coal Tit; Eurasian Nuthatch; Common Treecreeper; Eurasian Jay.

Spring & Autumn: Eye-browed and Dusky Thrush.

Summer: Gray Heron; Mandarin Duck; Common Teal; Mallard; Northern Hobby; Latham's Snipe; Eurasian Woodcock; Japanese Green Pigeon; Common and Oriental Cuckoo; Jungle Nightjar; White-throated Needletail; Ruddy Kingfisher; Olive-backed Pipit; Siberian Blue Robin; Stonechat; White's, Gray, and Brown Thrush; Stub-tailed Bush Warbler; Eastern Crowned Warbler; Blue-and-White, Asian Brown, and Narcissus Flycatcher; Brown Shrike; Red-cheeked Starling; Russet Sparrow; Japanese Grosbeak; Hawfinch; Meadow Bunting.

Winter: Japanese and Bohemian Waxwing; Dusky Thrush; Brambling; Eurasian Siskin; Common Redpoll; Common Bullfinch.

Rarities: White-tailed Eagle; Black Woodpecker; Pine Grosbeak.

HOW TO GET THERE

From Sapporo: 1 hr by train and on foot.

From Sapporo Bus Terminal (next to the main station), take a JR bus to Shinrin-koen-mae for the museum and historical village. Or take the subway to Shin-Sapporo, then a bus toward Ebetsu, and get off at San-ai Joshi Koko-mae. From the bus stop, walk up the hill from Rt. 12, turn left at the top, skirting the edge of the woodland and a housing estate, until you reach the car park and forest entrance. Turn left into the forest onto a broad trail. Alternatively, take a train on the JR line for Ebetsu and Asahikawa, get off at Oasa, cross the tracks and Rt. 12 by the pedestrian walkway, turn left up Rt. 12 (in the direction your train was heading), turn right at the traffic lights after about 300–400 m, just before San-ai Joshi Koko (a girl's high school), and walk up the hill (see above). There are usually plenty of taxis at Oasa Station, so if you don't want to walk to the forest, show the driver your map.

Accommodation: Nopporo Forest is best visited from Sapporo where abundant accommodation of all types is available.

44. Shikotsu-ko, Southwest Hokkaido   支笏湖

Best birding months: May–June

Shikotsu-ko, one of the most beautiful lakes in Hokkaido, lies 30 km south of Sapporo and 20 km west of Chitose, the airport that serves Sapporo. It is a caldera lake 41 km in circumference, and, being 360 m deep, is the second deepest lake in Japan. The lake remains ice-free all winter, but because of its depth is relatively lifeless. The surrounding forests, however, contain abundant bird life. The mountainous and volcanic scenery around the lake, the deciduous forests, the outdoor hot springs, and the abundance of woodland birds in summer make this a pleasant place to combine with a visit to Utonai-ko (45). The scenery is dominated by Eniwadake (1,320 m), a steaming cone-shaped volcano just to the northwest, by Fuppushidake (1,103 m) and by the gentle slopes of Tarumae-san (1,038 m) to the south.

On early summer mornings (May and June are best), start from the car park on the east side of the lake at about 03:00 since bird activity peaks soon after dawn. Cross the river mouth by the footbridge to the parklike area on the other side, which is very good for woodpeckers and flycatchers, and explore the 1.5-km nature trail along the wooded slopes above the lake shore. Although best for birds in early summer, the autumn colors are superb in September and the hiking is good all year round.

If you have time, hike up Eniwadake for superb views of the whole

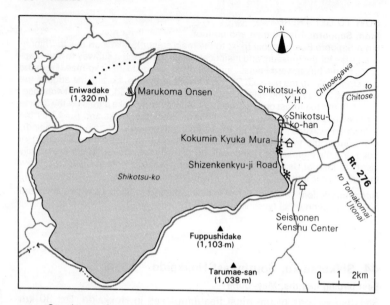

area. Starting at the gate near the Poropinai camping area, it takes 5½ hr to the top and back. At the foot of the mountain, on the lake shore, is the Marukoma outdoor hot spring. A hot soak is an ideal way to end a long day in the field and is especially stimulating in winter.

Mammals here include Yellow Marten, Red Squirrel, Asiatic Chipmunk, and very occasionally Brown Bear.

BIRDS AND SEASONS
Summer: Common Buzzard; Japanese Green Pigeon; Oriental Cuckoo; Oriental Scops Owl; Crested Kingfisher; Gray-headed, Black, Great Spotted, and Japanese Pygmy Woodpecker; Common House Martin; White's, Brown, and Gray Thrush; Siberian Blue Robin; Stub-tailed Bush Warbler; Eastern Crowned and Pale-legged Warbler; Blue-and-White, Asian Brown, and Narcissus Flycatcher; Marsh and Varied Tit; Eurasian Nuthatch; Russet Sparrow; Japanese Grosbeak.
Winter: Whooper Swan; Tufted Duck; Common Goldeneye; White-tailed Eagle (sometimes).
Rarities: Harlequin Duck.

HOW TO GET THERE
From Sapporo: 1 hr 20 min by bus.
From Sapporo bus terminal, take a Chuo bus for Shikotsu-ko, and get off at

Shikotsu-ko-han. Or take a Chuo bus from either Chitose Airport or Chitose Station to the same bus stop. In winter only the buses from Chitose run.

From Lake Utonai: 40 min by car.

Follow Rt. 36 southwest 10 km into Tomakomai City, then turn northwest onto Rt. 276. After 20 km the main road takes a sharp left. Go straight on here and turn left at the next junction, following the road down to the lake shore. Park on the left by the cluster of shops and hotels and walk south along the shore.

Accommodation: Stay either at Shikotsu-ko Youth Hostel ☎(0123)25-2311, at one of the many hotels in the area, or at Marukoma Onsen ☎(01232)5-2341.

45. Utonai-ko, Southwest Hokkaido　ウトナイ湖

Good birding months: Jan.–Dec.
Best birding months: March–June, Aug.–Nov.

Address: Utonai-ko Sanctuary Nature Center, 150-3 Uenae, Tomakomai-shi, Hokkaido 059-13; ☎(0144)58-2505. Open 09:00–17:00, Thursday to Monday.

Utonai-ko, near the southwest coast of Hokkaido, is a shallow lagoon, 230 ha in extent, with an average water depth of just 60 cm, surrounded by marshes, reedbeds, grassland, thickets of alder, birch, and oak, and mature woodland. It lies on the migration route of many of Japan's wintering waterfowl, and spectacular concentrations occur here in both spring and autumn, with some remaining until the lake freezes in early winter before moving south.

In 1981, an agreement between the WBSJ and the local government established Utonai-ko as Japan's very first bird sanctuary. While the total area of the sanctuary is 511 ha, only 50 ha along the north shore are open to the public. The sanctuary headquarters and nature center on the shore has two full-time English-speaking wardens, an exhibition area, a library, and an observation area with telescopes. Bird tables close to the center attract many birds, especially in winter when Northern Sparrowhawk, Gray-headed, White-backed, and Great Spotted Woodpecker, Marsh Tit, and Brambling are all regular visitors. There are nature trails through the woodland and along the lake shore, two small hides on the shore and a larger one at the forest edge. After a walk through the woodland, walk along the shoreline from the center east toward the Bibigawa river mouth and west past the youth hostel and Utonai Lake Hotel to the bay at the west end of the lake, which attracts geese and waders. The grassland along the north shore harbors several species of bunting. Birds are most in evidence from late March to June and again from August to November.

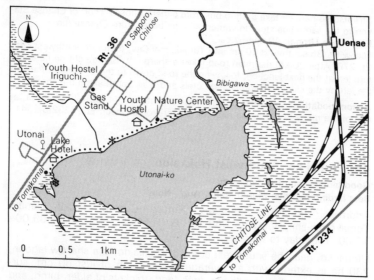

After the breeding season migrants appear in August with the return of the Sand Martin and White-throated Needletail. In August and September shorebirds pass through, by mid-September the geese are arriving again, in October Bewick's Swan pass through, and in November come most of the Whooper Swan. Some 200 Whooper Swan and a small flock of Pintail winter here, and can be seen close to the sanctuary headquarters, particularly in January and February when the lake is covered with ice. At this time the two species of sea eagle reach their peak of 20–50 birds. By late March up to 1,000 swans and several thousand geese and duck are present, with more than 20 waterfowl species represented. More than 200 bird species have been seen around the lake.

From August onward Sweet Brier is in bloom, and by October the autumn colors are ablaze.

Mammals to look for are Red Fox, Red Squirrel, and Asiatic Chipmunk. The latter are attracted to sunflower seeds on the bird tables in autumn, which they store up for the winter.

BIRDS AND SEASONS

All year: Gray Heron; Mute Swan; Mallard; Northern Goshawk; Northern Sparrowhawk; Common Buzzard; Gray-headed, Great Spotted, White-backed, and Japanese Pygmy Woodpecker; Marsh Tit.

Spring & Autumn: Bewick's and Whooper Swan; Bean and Greater White-fronted Goose; Eurasian Wigeon; Falcated and Common Teal; Spot-billed Duck; Northern Pintail; Garganey; Common Pochard; Tufted Duck; Greater Scaup; Smew; Goosander; Red-necked Stint; Sharp-tailed Sandpiper; Ruff; Spotted Redshank; Common Greenshank; Wood and Common Sandpiper; Common Black-headed Gull; Common Tern.

Summer: Red-necked Grebe; Falcated Teal; Spot-billed Duck; Eastern Marsh Harrier; Latham's Snipe; Eurasian Woodcock; Common Cuckoo; Eurasian Wryneck; Sand Martin; Siberian Rubythroat; Stonechat; Brown Thrush; Gray's Grasshopper Warbler; Black-browed Reed Warbler; Narcissus Flycatcher; Brown Shrike; Red-cheeked Starling; Russet Sparrow; Hawfinch; Gray-headed, Yellow-breasted, and Common Reed Bunting.

Winter: Whooper Swan; Eurasian Wigeon; Northern Pintail; Goosander; White-tailed and Steller's Sea Eagle; Brambling.

Rarities: Slavonian and Black-necked Grebe (late autumn); Little and Great Egret; White Spoonbill (sometimes in spring); Graylag, Snow, and Canada, or even the very rare Swan Goose occasionally join the goose flocks in spring and autumn; American Wigeon (most autumns with the large Eurasian Wigeon flocks).

HOW TO GET THERE

From Tomakomai Ferry Terminal: 45 min to 1 hr by bus.
Utonai-ko is 10 km from Tomakomai. Catch the bus that meets the ferry (30) to Tomakomai Station and change there to a bus bound for Chitose Station or Chitose Airport. Get off at the Yusu Hosteru Iriguchi (Youth Hostel Entrance) bus stop, or at the Utonai Reikurando-mae bus stop if you catch an express bus. You will see the lake and the large Utonai Lake Hotel on your right before the bus stop.

From Chitose Airport: 20 min by bus.
Take a bus going toward Tomakomai or Noboribetsu and get off at the bus stops listed above.

By car, Utonai-ko is just off Rt. 36, which connects Sapporo to Tomakomai. The best landmark to look for is a red, pyramid-shaped coffee shop, called the "Chicken House," on the east side of the road (left, if you are driving from Sapporo); next to it is a garage and just to the south of that a narrow road that leads to the sanctuary and the youth hostel. There is a rather hard-to-see wooden signboard on the main road with a Gray Heron painted on it, indicating the sanctuary. If you miss the turn you will reach the hotel after 1 km, also on your left.

Accommodation: Both Utonai Lake Hotel ☎(0144)58-2111 and Utonai Lake Youth Hostel ☎(0144)58-2153 are on the lake shore, and the latter is within two minutes of the nature center. A wide range of minshuku, ryokan, and hotels is available in Tomakomai or Chitose, but for early morning birdwatching, visitors should stay at the lake.

46. Ogawara-ko Shogun, Aomori Prefecture 小川原湖

Good birding months: Jan.–Dec.
Best birding months: May–June

Ogawara-ko shogun is a series of reed-fringed shallow lagoons surrounded by reedbeds at the base of Shimokita Hanto. This is one of the few places in Japan where Great Crested Grebe breed. This bird is a regular winter visitor, in small numbers, to reservoirs in the Tokyo area, and, in larger numbers, to western Japan, especially Biwa-ko in Shiga Prefecture and Hakata Bay in northern Kyushu. The majority of the wintering population in Japan come from the Asian continent. A few pairs do breed at Ogawara-ko, however. The other specialties here are Schrenck's Bittern and Japanese Marsh Warbler. The latter has a very restricted range in Honshu and China and is a difficult bird to find. Here and at Tonegawa (14) it is possible to watch them singing from the reedbeds from late May until August or September. Their wintering grounds are poorly known in Japan with birds appearing irregularly at sites in the south in very small numbers.

In early spring lingering snow and ice mean there are few birds here, although in March flocks of geese visit on their way back north. From late April sandpipers and plovers visit Obuchi-numa, and in May Great Crested Grebe display at Ichiyanagi-numa and Tamogi-numa. Garganey are early spring visitors and occasionally remain, possibly to breed. The Takasegawa river mouth is a good place to find them, and in the same area look for migratory phalaropes. In summer the area around Obuchi-numa is generally good for small birds. Around Takahoko-numa and between Ichiyanagi-numa and the coast there are Japanese Marsh

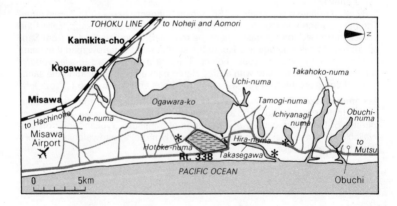

Warbler and Japanese Reed Bunting, while in the area of the reclaimed Hotoke-numa there are both these species, Schrenck's Bittern, Black-browed and Oriental Reed Warbler, and in June and July Ruddy Crake. There is a colony of Common Cormorant in this area as well.

In August and September, look for shorebirds again, particularly the rarer Asian species, around Obuchi-numa and at the Takasegawa river mouth. From September the geese visit again on their way south to Izu-numa (47). Flocks of duck, geese, and swan visit Obuchi-numa and Ogawara-ko, and small numbers of sea eagles and other raptors can be seen in the same area. In mid-winter small birds are very few, but you may find Snow and Lapland Bunting around Ogawara-ko and along the beach.

BIRDS AND SEASONS
Spring & Autumn: Bewick's and Whooper Swan; Bean, Greater White-fronted, and Brent Goose; Garganey; Mongolian and Pacific Golden Plover; Red-necked Stint; Sharp-tailed Sandpiper; Ruff; Spotted Redshank; Red-necked and Gray Phalarope.
Summer: Little and Great Crested Grebe; Great Cormorant; Yellow and Schrenck's Bittern; Ruddy Crake; Common Coot; Latham's Snipe; Japanese Marsh Warbler; Black-browed and Oriental Reed Warbler; Common and Japanese Reed Bunting.
Winter: White-tailed and Steller's Sea Eagle; Eastern Marsh and Hen Harrier; Rough-legged Buzzard; Glaucous Gull; Common Redpoll; Lapland, Snow, and Yellow-throated Bunting.
Rarities: Whistling Swan (*C. c. columbianus*); American Wigeon; Nordmann's Greenshank.

HOW TO GET THERE
From Aomori: 1 hr 15 min by train.
Take the JR Tohoku Line from Aomori to Noheji Station (35 min by *tokkyu* express). From Noheji, board a Shimokita bus for Tomari (30 min), or a Jutetsu bus for Obuchi, and get off at Obuchi bus stop (30 min), or Obuchi-numa. Alternatively, take a train from Aomori to Misawa (the same line as above), then a Jutetsu bus from Misawa for Hira-numa and get off at Amagamori, Ogawara-ko. There are daily flights from Tokyo to Misawa, and cars can be rented at the airport or near the station. By car it is possible to visit the whole area in one day. If you are on foot, allow two days.

Accommodation: Minshuku accommodation is available in the area. In particular, try Inaho Ryokan ☎(0175)75-2532 at Tamogi-numa.

47. Izu-numa and Uchi-numa, Miyagi Prefecture 伊豆沼/内沼

Good birding months: Jan.–Dec.
Best birding months: Nov.–March

Izu-numa, 60 km north of Sendai, is an excellent place for winter birding. There are large flocks of swans and ducks, and one of the largest wintering flocks of geese in Japan. The geese are the most spectacular since they make dusk and dawn flights between the lake where they roost and the fields where they feed.

Izu-numa and nearby Uchi-numa, both now protected under the Ramsar Convention, are both shallow, reed-fringed lakes with abundant aquatic vegetation, surrounded by rice paddies and small patches of woodland. With an early start it is possible to walk round Izu-numa (16 km in circumference) and visit nearby Uchi-numa in one day. The south side of Izu-numa is much better than the north, which has a busy road along part of it.

In early autumn large flocks of Sand Martin pause here to roost and feed, while a little later the ducks begin to arrive for the winter. The geese begin to arrive in late September, with the peak in October. By late October some ten thousand Greater White-fronted Goose (more than eighty percent of the Japanese wintering population) and Bean Goose have arrived. The geese remain during mid-winter, then gradually decline in number from the end of February onward as they move back north. Small birds and shorebirds also pass through, and in November the swans arrive. These, mostly Whooper Swan, remain throughout the winter, leaving again toward the end of March.

Morning flight, when the mist is rising off the water and the reeds and surrounding fields are coated with rime or have a sprinkling of snow, is not to be missed. It begins soon after dawn and may continue for an hour or more, depending on the weather. Even before dawn, calling geese can be heard: the high "kyow-yow" of the White-fronted and the lower "ang-ank" of the Bean Goose. Bean Goose depart before dawn, and soon after first light small flocks of White-fronted rise and head out to the fields to feed. The calling crescendos, and there is a sudden roar as most of the remaining birds take wing and the sky is filled with a huge flock of geese. The flock gradually breaks up and the birds move off in straggling lines and groups. Bean Goose prefer to roost near the eastern end of the lake and fly out mainly to the east and the south, while White-fronted roost mainly at the west end and fly out in various directions. There is, of course, some mixing, depending on the feeding areas being used. The goose flocks often attract rare winter stragglers such as Lesser White-fronted Goose and Snow Goose. Swan Goose, now an

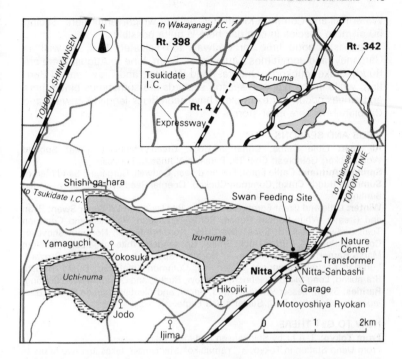

extremely rare vagrant to Japan, has also been seen here on several occasions, and Japan's only record of an Emperor Goose was here.

By about 10:00 the geese have all left, and the day can be spent wandering the lake shore in search of other birds until the evening flight back from the feeding grounds. Among the many species of duck occurring at both Izu-numa and Uchi-numa, particularly in January and February, are the delicate, diminutive Smew, and Falcated Teal. I have seen up to 60 Falcated Teal at Uchi-numa in March, while Smew (sometimes up to 600) prefer Izu-numa. Goosander also occur in large flocks. The lakes also attract a variety of wintering birds of prey, and a small number of White-tailed Eagle are usually present.

Buntings and finches are the commonest small birds in the reedbeds and surrounding countryside in winter, and Long-tailed Rosefinch, which in summer breed in Hokkaido, winter here in small numbers and can be seen in rough vegetation along woodland edges. Listen for their soft, whistled calls. Along the water's edge and in dykes, look out for

Water Rail and Common Kingfisher, both of which winter here. Seeing 50 or more species in one day here is quite possible.

April is a good time for Gadwall and Falcated Teal, as well as Garganey, and sometimes Cattle Egret. From June to August there are Ruddy Crake, cuckoos, Oriental Reed Warbler, and Gray-headed Bunting, while in the typhoon season seabirds are sometimes blown here and rarities occur. For example, I have seen Black-legged Kittiwake and Caspian Tern here after storms.

BIRDS AND SEASONS

All year: Little Grebe; Common Coot; Green Pheasant; Great Spotted Woodpecker; Goldcrest; Coal Tit; Eurasian Nuthàtch; Eurasian Jay.

Spring & Autumn: Cattle Egret; Falcated Teal; Gadwall; Garganey; Sand Martin.

Summer: Ruddy Crake; Common Cuckoo; Oriental Reed Warbler; Gray-headed Bunting.

Winter: Little and Great Egret; Gray Heron; Bewick's and Whooper Swan; Bean and Greater White-fronted Goose; Eurasian Wigeon; Falcated and Common Teal; Gadwall; Mallard; Spot-billed Duck; Northern Pintail; Northern Shoveler; Common Pochard; Tufted Duck; Smew; Goosander; White-tailed Eagle; Eastern Marsh Harrier; Northern Goshawk; Northern Sparrowhawk; Common Buzzard; Eurasian Kestrel; Peregrine; Water Rail; Common Kingfisher; Dusky Thrush; Brambling; Long-tailed Rosefinch; Meadow, Rustic, and Common Reed Bunting.

Rarities: Swan, Lesser White-fronted, Snow, and Aleutian Canada Goose (*B. c. leucopareia*); Baikal Teal; Steller's Sea Eagle.

HOW TO GET THERE

From Tokyo: 3–4 hr by Shinkansen and local train.

From Ueno Station in Tokyo, a "Yamabiko" Shinkansen takes just two hours to Sendai, and from there it is one hour farther north by the Tohoku Line to Nitta Station. Thus a weekend trip from the capital is quite possibie. The lake is visible from Nitta Station and a 15-min walk will take you to the shore.

Turn left out of the station and walk up the village main street until you pass a small garage on your left. Soon after the garage and immediately before an electrical transformer supplying the railway, there is a narrow road off to the left. Follow this across the railway tracks and along the south shore of the lake. About 300 m after the railway crossing, there is a car park, a nature center, and a feeding site where hundreds of ducks and swans gather to be fed. Spend a day walking along the south shore and around Uchi-numa.

By car, take the Tohoku Expressway, get off at the Tsukidate Intersection (No. 32), join Rt. 4 to Tsukidate, then carry on east to the lake.

Accommodation: In Nitta, Motoyoshiya Ryokan ☎(02202)8-2010 caters for many birdwatching/naturalist visitors.

Kyushu and the Nansei Shoto

48. Tsushima, Nagasaki Prefecture 対馬

Best birding months: April–June, Sept.–Oct.

Tsushima and Hegurajima (23) are the two Japanese offshore islands most famous for birdwatching, adding new birds almost annually to the Japanese list. Tsushima is an island, or rather two islands separated only by an 80-m-wide channel, lying between Kyushu and South Korea. Travel books virtually ignore it, but it is perfectly situated for watching migratory birds, although being so much larger it is not so easy to work as Hegurajima.

Izuhara, the main town situated in southeast Tsushima, is a five-hour ferry trip from Hakata, via Ikijima. In spring the boat passes through flocks of Streaked Shearwater and Red-necked Phalarope, and when birds are not in view there are usually dolphins to watch.

Izuhara, with its pachinko halls, bars, and coffee shops, seems at first sight just like a smaller version of any Japanese city, and is not the best introduction to Tsushima. However, after you have explored the islands, the out-of-the-way villages with small streets, wooden houses, unique long-legged storage barns (some with their original stone-slab roofs), have met the friendly local people, and have seen the forested mountain scenery, I think you will agree that this is an attractive place to stay a few days. The island's industries are forestry, fishing, and cultivating delicious *shiitake* mushrooms and other market-garden crops.

Situated in the Korea Strait only 50 km south of South Korea, these islands lie on the migration route of birds traveling up the Japan Sea from Southeast Asia to Korea, China, and the USSR as well as to Japan. Many birds here are blown off course from routes further west, adding

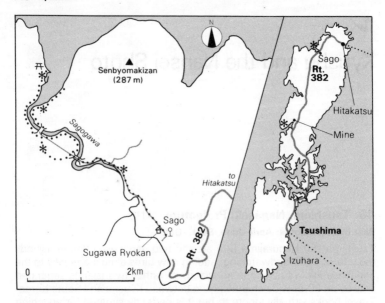

spice to the daily bird list, especially during the peak of the migration in early May.

The Kisaka Yacho no Mori near Mine and the Sagogawa valley in the northwest are the best places to explore for birds, unless you make a midsummer visit for the elusive Japanese Night Heron and Fairy Pitta in the forests of the central mountains.

At any season the islands have plenty of common birds. In the morning and evening, the loud "hok-a-kok" calls of Common Pheasant (introduced from South Korea) echo from one steep forested hillside to another. And in the forest Varied Tit seem even commoner than Great Tit. In winter there are flocks of thrushes, but it is the buntings that are the most interesting. Along with the commoner species are flocks of Yellow-throated Bunting (Tsushima is the only breeding area in Japan for this species) and small numbers of Gray Bunting. These two species are usually shy and hard to see, but on Tsushima they are common and confiding.

In spring and autumn migrants are evident, their numbers changing daily. Even though locals insist that there are only birds in the Golden Week holiday in late April and early May, you will find birds almost whenever you visit.

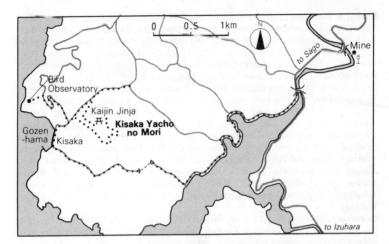

Out of the flocks of hundreds of White-naped Crane that pass through in late February and early March on their way north from their wintering grounds at Arasaki (51), some linger on into early April. The last winter flocks of Rook are still present then, and are augmented by migrants moving north from Kyushu, while swallows, swifts, ducks, and a few shorebirds are already on the move.

Early migrants in April include Hoopoe, Red-throated Pipit, and Scarlet Rosefinch, then later Blue-and-White, Japanese Paradise and other flycatchers pass through along with many more typical summer birds and a whole host of rare migrant warblers, buntings, and so on.

Concentrate on the winding Sagogawa valley, the rice paddies (for shorebirds), field edges, forests, and the river itself, in fact any place sheltered from the wind, with a mixture of habitats, is good. Also make a side trip or two to the Kisaka Yacho no Mori. During Golden Week these places also attract many birders, so it is best to take a leisurely trip either before or after the peak season.

Tsushima was home to Japan's only population of White-bellied Woodpecker until the 1920s, but can still boast Japan's only Small-eared Cat population. The latter is nocturnal and secretive, but occurs even in the Sago area.

BIRDS AND SEASONS
All year: Eastern Reef Egret; Gray Heron; Hodgson's Hawk Eagle (uncommon); Common Pheasant; Collared Scops Owl; Long-tailed, Willow, Varied, and Coal Tit; Yellow-throated Bunting.

Spring & Autumn: Streaked Shearwater; Crested Honey Buzzard; Northern and Japanese Sparrowhawk; Chinese Sparrowhawk; Gray-faced and Common Buzzard; Oriental Pratincole; Little Ringed and Mongolian Plover; Gray-headed Lapwing; Red-necked and Long-toed Stint; Sharp-tailed Sandpiper; Spotted Redshank; Common Greenshank; Green and Wood Sandpiper; Gray-tailed Tattler; Red-necked Phalarope; Japanese Green Pigeon; Hodgson's Hawk Cuckoo; Common, Oriental, and Little Cuckoo; Oriental Scops Owl; White-throated Needletail; Fork-tailed Swift; Dollarbird; Hoopoe; Richard's, Olive-backed, and Red-throated Pipit; Forest, Yellow, and White Wagtail; Ashy Minivet; Japanese Robin; Siberian Rubythroat; Siberian Blue Robin; Stonechat; White's, Siberian, Pale, Eye-browed, and Dusky Thrush; Stub-tailed Bush Warbler; Black-browed and Oriental Reed Warbler; Eastern Crowned Warbler; Pale-legged Warbler; Arctic Warbler; Blue-and-White, Sooty, Asian Brown, Mugimaki, Tricolored, Narcissus, and Japanese Paradise Flycatcher; Tiger, Bull-headed, and Brown Shrike; Rook; Red-cheeked Starling; Chinese and Japanese Grosbeak; Hawfinch; Meadow, Gray-headed, Rustic, Little, Chestnut, and Yellow-breasted Bunting.

Summer: Japanese Night Heron; Brown Hawk Owl; Ruddy Kingfisher; Fairy Pitta; Stub-tailed Bush Warbler; Eastern Crowned Warbler; Blue-and-White, Narcissus, and Japanese Paradise Flycatcher.

Winter: Black-throated Diver; Red-necked Grebe; White-naped Crane; Black-tailed and Slaty-backed Gull; Olive-backed Pipit; Daurian Redstart; Brown, Pale, and Dusky Thrush; Rook; Chinese Grosbeak; Gray, Meadow, and Rustic Bunting.

Rarities: Chinese Pond Heron; White-tailed, and Steller's Sea Eagle; Golden Eagle; Black-capped Kingfisher; Siberian Accentor; Rufous-tailed Robin; Yellow-browed Warbler; Black-naped Oriole; Common Rosefinch; Yellow-browed and Tristram's Bunting.

HOW TO GET THERE

From Hakata: 5 hr by ferry to Izuhara.

Tsushima is easily reached by ferry from Kokura or Hakata (both stations on the Shinkansen line). Two boats a day run each way from Hakata to Izuhara (5 hr), and one a day each way from Kokura to Hitakatsu (4 hr). Alternatively, it is possible to fly from Fukuoka (40 min, six times a day) or from Nagasaki (45 min, twice a day). From Izuhara, take a bus for Hitakatsu and get off at Sago (1½ hr), or at Mine bus stop for Kisaka Yacho no Mori. It is 1½ hr on foot to the latter from Mine. Cars can be rented at the airport, in Izuhara, or in Sasuna (in the north).

Accommodation:

Minshuku, ryokan, and hotels are scattered around the island. Sugawa Ryokan ☎(09208)4-5175 in Sago village is the most convenient, but is likely to be fully booked during the busy holiday season, so phone ahead. During my stay a Collared Scops Owl spent each evening calling from trees just outside the inn. There is also a camp site at the river mouth.

49. Zuibaijigawa, Fukuoka Prefecture   瑞梅寺川
Good birding months: Sept.–April

At the west end of Hakata Bay, the famed site where the divine Kamikaze wind destroyed the invading Mongol hordes in 1274 and 1281, is the smaller Imazu Bay, which, along with the estuary of the Zuibaijigawa, is one of the best sites for migrating shorebirds in north Kyushu. It regularly attracts several of the east Asian rarities, particularly Spoon-billed Sandpiper and Nordmann's Greenshank in September, and Saunders's Gull in winter. Japan's first Slender-billed Gull was seen here in the winters of 1983 and 1984.

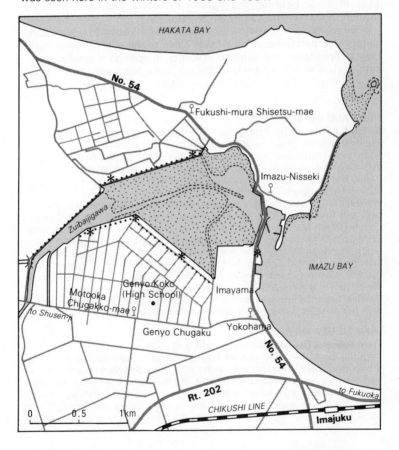

Hakata Bay itself is the major wintering ground in Japan for Great Crested Grebe and Common Black-headed Gull, while the Zuibaijigawa estuary, reedbeds, and nearby fields are very good for birding in winter and attract a wide variety of shorebirds in spring and autumn. Roads border the estuary to the north and south, making this a very easy area to watch, but remember also to watch Imazu Bay from beyond the road bridge. Herons and egrets fish the shoreline of the estuary, Temminck's Cormorant and gulls roost on the sandbar, and the small island in the river feeding the estuary is a roosting site for egrets and ducks in winter, and shorebirds in spring and autumn. This area is also on the migration route of Rook between the Korean Peninsula and their wintering grounds in central and southwest Kyushu.

In winter flocks of waterfowl are occasionally flushed by a wandering raptor. Rice paddies and lotus fields close to the estuary have Dusky Thrush, Brambling, and buntings in winter, in addition to resident Common Skylark and Black-backed Wagtail. Adjacent reedbeds, although small, are attractive to Water Rail, Penduline Tit, and Common Reed Bunting.

BIRDS AND SEASONS

Spring & Autumn: Little Ringed, Kentish, Mongolian, and Pacific Golden Plover; Red-necked Stint; Sharp-tailed Sandpiper; Dunlin; Broad-billed Sandpiper; Bar-tailed Godwit; Whimbrel; Eurasian and Eastern Curlew; Spotted Redshank; Common Greenshank; Wood, Terek, and Common Sandpiper; Gray-tailed Tattler; Yellow and Gray Wagtail; Stonechat; Black-browed and Oriental Reed Warbler; Black-billed Magpie (wanderers); Rook.

Winter: Little, Great Crested, and Black-necked Grebe; Temminck's Cormorant; Little and Great Egret; Gray Heron; Eurasian Wigeon; Falcated Teal; Gadwall; Common Teal; Mallard; Spot-billed Duck; Northern Pintail; Northern Shoveler; Red-breasted Merganser; Eastern Marsh and Hen Harrier; Common Buzzard; Osprey; Eurasian Kestrel; Water Rail; Common Moorhen; Little Ringed and Kentish Plover; Dunlin; Spotted Redshank; Wood Sandpiper; Common Black-headed, Common, and Herring Gull; Common Kingfisher; Dusky Thrush; Penduline Tit; Bull-headed Shrike; Meadow and Common Reed Bunting.

Rarities: Common Shelduck; Baikal Teal; Common Oystercatcher; Black-winged Stilt; Spoon-billed Sandpiper; Nordmann's Greenshank; Saunders's Gull.

HOW TO GET THERE

From Fukuoka (Hakata): 40 min by train and bus.

Take the local Chikushi Line from Hakata Station in Fukuoka (the end of the Shinkansen line) for Karatsu and get off at Imajuku Station. Leave the station, turn left, right, and left again onto Rt. 202. The bus terminal is then on your right. Buses run to Imayama, which is very close to the estuary. For those willing to take a 30–40-min walk, pass the bus station and take the next fork right onto prefectural road No. 54 (there is a sign to the Mongolian invasion site over the road at this point), and keep straight on to Imayama. Once at Imayama, pass both the 7-11 store and a shop called Ueno, then turn left through a housing estate; a right, then a left brings you to a small bridge across a river running into the estuary and onto the south perimeter road. Alternatively, carry on along prefectural road No. 54, cross the main bridge, then turn left along the north perimeter road.

This site is easily visited by public transport and taxi. Driving in this area can be fraught with difficulties because the roads tend to be crowded.

Accommodation: Stay in one of the many hotels, minshuku, and ryokan in Fukuoka.

50. Ariake-kai (Saga and Isahaya), Saga Prefecture 有明海
Good birding months: Sept.–April

Huge Ariake-kai (1,500 km^2), virtually an inland sea, in central western Kyushu, is a must for anyone visiting the island from autumn to spring. The bay is a major wintering ground for shorebirds (two species of curlew can be seen), the only wintering ground for Common Shelduck in Japan (there are several hundred), and the best site to look for Black-faced Spoonbill. Saunders's Gull are annual, and Penduline Tit winter in reedbeds around the bay.

Black-billed Magpie, which are restricted to northern and western Kyushu, have their center of distribution in the Saga area at the north end of the bay. Here magpies are particularly common, with winter roosts attracting more than a hundred birds.

For those with a car there are many points around the bay worth stopping at, such as rivers, mud flats, and the reclaimed land at the north end. For the less mobile, two areas—Daijugarami at the north end, just south of Saga, and Isahaya at the southwest corner—should not be missed. Reclaimed land at Daijugarami attracts raptors, shrikes, starlings, finches, and buntings in winter, while the mud flats have duck, shorebirds, and gulls. In late August and early September, look for Spoon-billed Sandpiper, Asian Dowitcher, and Nordmann's Greenshank at Isahaya, and in winter spoonbills, shelduck, and shorebirds. The tide here rises and falls 5 m, leaving immense mud flats at low tide. Four or five hours before high tide is best as the rising tide moves the birds closer to shore. At high tide they roost on the marshland and paddies.

BIRDS AND SEASONS
All year: Little Ringed and Kentish Plover; Fan-tailed Warbler; Black-billed Magpie.
Spring & Autumn: Cattle Egret; Black-winged Stilt; Oriental Pratincole;

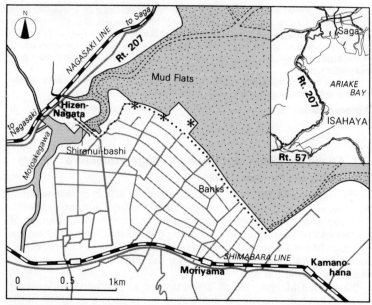

Mongolian, Large Sand, Pacific Golden, and Gray Plover; Great Knot; Red-necked and Long-toed Stint; Sharp-tailed and Curlew Sandpiper; Dunlin; Broad-billed Sandpiper; Black-tailed and Bar-tailed Godwit; Whimbrel; Eurasian and Eastern Curlew; Spotted Redshank; Common Greenshank; Wood Sandpiper; Terek Sandpiper; Gray-tailed Tattler; Ruddy Turnstone.

Winter: Black-crowned Night Heron; Little and Great Egret; Gray Heron; Common Shelduck; Eurasian Wigeon; Falcated and Common Teal; Mallard; Spot-billed Duck; Northern Pintail; Northern Shoveler; Eastern Marsh and Hen Harrier; Eurasian Kestrel; Peregrine; Ruddy Crake; Common Moorhen; Gray Plover; Northern Lapwing; Dunlin; Common Snipe; Bar-tailed Godwit; Eurasian and Eastern Curlew; Common Sandpiper; Saunders's Gull; Common Black-headed, Herring, and Slaty-backed Gull; Water Pipit; Daurian Redstart; Dusky Thrush; Penduline Tit; Bull-headed Shrike; Rook; Meadow, Gray-headed, Rustic, and Common Reed Bunting.

Rarities: White and Black-faced Spoonbill; Merlin; Spoon-billed Sandpiper; Asian Dowitcher; Nordmann's Greenshank; Common Starling; Pallas's Reed Bunting.

HOW TO GET THERE

From Fukuoka (Hakata): 40 min by train to Saga.
From Saga Station it is a 10-km walk south to the shoreline of Daijugarami. Go west from the station a few hundred meters to Rt. 263. Take this south for just

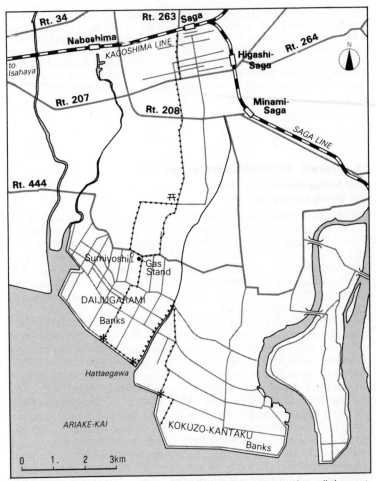

over 1 km to the main street in town (Rt. 264). Turn west again until the next road south and continue south out of town through open farmland for about 5 km. When you meet Rt. 444, turn west again, then take the next road south. Explore the fields and tracks here, heading steadily south toward the northern shoreline of the bay. Alternatively, take a Shie bus from Saga Station to Saga Daigaku Keiyu Higashi Yoga and get off after 35 min at Sumiyoshi bus stop. From there it is a walk of 1 hr 20 min to Daijugarami.

For the Isahaya mud flats, take either Rt. 207 down the west side of the bay from Saga or take a train toward Nagasaki, but get off two stops before Isahaya at Hizen-Nagata. From the station, cross Rt. 207 and cross the bridge over the Motoakegawa. Turn left at the far end of the bridge and walk north up the east bank of the river to look out across the mud flats. Also explore the reclaimed land in this area. Isahaya is 30 min from Nagasaki Airport by car and is thus very convenient for birders en route to Tokyo or Okinawa.

Accommodation: Business hotels, ryokan, and minshuku are available in both Saga and Isahaya.

51. Arasaki, Kagoshima Prefecture　荒崎
Good birding months: Nov.–March
Best birding months: Dec.–Feb.

The rice fields around Arasaki are the roosting and feeding site for up to 8,000 cranes every winter, the largest concentration in Asia. The spectacle of this huge flock of birds makes Arasaki one of the most exciting sites to visit in Japan. Two species of crane are common here; over 6,000 Hooded Crane occur each winter (the only other regular wintering site in Japan is at Yashiro in Yamaguchi Prefecture, with fewer than 100 birds), and with them are 1,000 or more White-naped Crane, the only wintering flock in Japan.

The cranes begin to arrive in small numbers in the last ten days of October and usually stay until the last week of February. This large flock and its locality at the end of a flyway beginning in China and passing down peninsular Korea often attracts stragglers. For example, in 1982 I saw six of Japan's seven species of crane here. The Common Crane, a very rare bird elsewhere in Japan, is an almost annual visitor, with up to four present in recent years, while the rare Sandhill Crane has also been wintering regularly since the early 1980s. Demoiselle and Siberian Crane are, however, great rarities in Japan, even at Arasaki. In addition to rare cranes, the flock attracts other rarities, sometimes a spoonbill, a stork, or a Ruddy Shelduck, and, to test the unwary, a family of hybrid Hooded x Common Crane have also been wintering regularly.

The area where the cranes roost has been designated a special national monument by the Ministry of Culture, although the land has not been purchased as a reserve. Instead, the area is rented from local farmers during the winter to provide a measure of safety for the cranes. A warden (a local farmer and minshuku owner) feeds the cranes daily.

Although widely known for its cranes, Arasaki deserves wider recognition as one of the finest areas for winter birding in Japan. I rank this

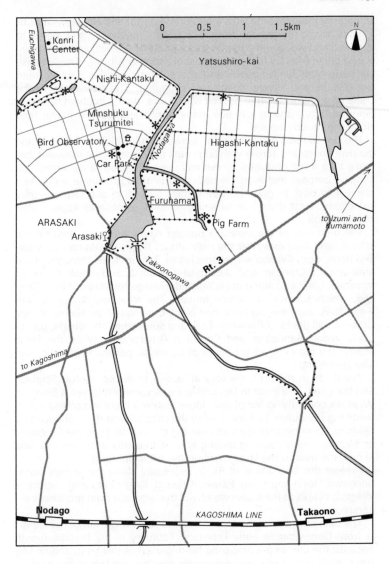

among my three favorite sites after Furen-ko (33) and Hegurajima (23). A wide range of habitat from sea coast, reedbeds, and pools to farmland and woodland attract a great variety of species, and seeing sixty or more in one day (difficult in most of Japan in winter), is quite possible here. Wet fields, pools, and rivers attract various dabbling and diving duck and several species of shorebird. The river close to the crane observatory is often packed with ducks (Baer's Pochard has been reported here), and at low tide many Dunlin and Kentish Plover feed along the muddy edges.

The bay is used extensively for seaweed cultivation and both it and the river are strung across with large nets to "protect" the seaweed, but these take a toll of ducks, crows and even Streaked Shearwater. The hanging corpses and even live netted birds are a gruesome sight. As a result it is best to give the bay a miss except to see Osprey—they sometimes hunt there—or to see gulls that sometimes appear after strong winds.

The area east of the river is a popular daytime feeding area for the cranes, and the fields near the river attract flocks of Daurian Jackdaw and Rook, both Kyushu winter specialties. Mature trees throughout the area attract Chinese and Japanese Grosbeak and small flocks of thrushes. Look also along the wires and treetops for flocks of Gray Starling, which sometimes include rarities. The small marshy pond with water lilies, near the pig farm, has Black-crowned Night Heron, Ruddy Crake, small flocks of Common Teal, and sometimes shorebirds, particularly Wood Sandpiper and Common Greenshank, while the fields around the pig farm attract flocks of buntings, particularly Rustic, and also Brambling.

Reedbeds in the area are very attractive to ducks, raptors, crakes, and buntings, and once in December I was surprised to see a Eurasian Wryneck come flying out of one. More regularly there is a small flock of wintering Penduline Tit here. Follow the road around the crane feeding fields to the pools and reedbed near the chicken farm on the far side— an excellent early morning birding area, with plenty of passerines, and across the river in the large trees on the hill is an egret roost.

Explore the area south of Rt. 3, especially along the shingly Takaonogawa, for Long-billed Plover, Crested Kingfisher, and Japanese Wagtail. Flocks of Rook also wander in this area and both grosbeaks are common.

The best time to visit the area in order to see a large number of cranes is from December to early February. February is my favorite month because the cranes are preparing for migration at this time, and on fine days small groups soar up on thermals over the low hills to the north of

Arasaki. If the weather continues fair they head off, although in the early days of the migration they are as likely to be back within half an hour as to continue north. In spring or autumn, when the cranes are not present, look out for shorebirds, particularly tattlers and Whimbrel on wet fields. Oriental Plover and Little Curlew are occasionally seen here.

BIRDS AND SEASONS
Winter: Little Grebe; Black-crowned Night Heron; Striated Heron; Cattle, Little, Intermediate, and Great Egret; Gray Heron; Eurasian Wigeon; Falcated Teal; Gadwall; Common Teal; Mallard; Spot-billed Duck; Northern Pintail; Northern Shoveler; Common Pochard; Tufted Duck; Greater Scaup; Eastern Marsh and Hen Harrier; Common Buzzard; Osprey; Eurasian Kestrel; Northern Hobby; Peregrine; Japanese Quail; Chinese Bamboo Partridge; Green Pheasant; Water Rail; Ruddy Crake; Hooded and White-naped Crane; Greater Painted Snipe; Little Ringed, Long-billed, Kentish, Mongolian, Pacific Golden, and Gray Plover; Northern Lapwing; Dunlin; Common Snipe; Eurasian Woodcock; Common Greenshank; Green and Wood Sandpiper; Short-eared Owl; Common and Crested Kingfisher; Red-throated and Water Pipit; Gray and Japanese Wagtail; Daurian Redstart; Blue Rock Thrush; Pale and Dusky Thrush; Fan-tailed Warbler; Penduline Tit; Bull-headed Shrike; Daurian Jackdaw; Rook; Russet Sparrow; Brambling; Chinese and Japanese Grosbeak; Hawfinch; Meadow, Gray-headed, Yellow-throated, Rustic, and Common Reed Bunting.
Rarities: Eastern White Stork; Black-faced Spoonbill; Ruddy Shelduck; Common, Sandhill, Siberian White, and Demoiselle Crane; Japanese Waxwing; Chinese and Common Starling; Pallas's Reed Bunting.

HOW TO GET THERE
From Kagoshima Airport: 2 hr by car.
Izumi, the nearest town to Arasaki, can be reached by train from either Kagoshima or Kumamoto, both of which have airports. From Izumi Station take a taxi. Outside the station there is a large map of the local area showing Arasaki and a picture of the cranes, which are popular with Sunday visitors. If language is a problem, simply show your taxi driver the picture of the cranes and mention Arasaki and you will reach the crane observatory without any problem.

Alternatively, fly to Kagoshima Airport from Tokyo or Okinawa and rent a car. The shortest route to Arasaki is 83 km and takes about 2 hr. The route is as follows: head north from the airport (i.e., turn right out of the airport exit, or left from the car rental companies). Two lanes of traffic turn right; but to drive north, keep left and follow Rt. 447. It isn't well signposted, but when you have driven 3.2 km you should see a 19-km marker. When you have driven 6 km from the airport, there is a poorly signposted crossroads with traffic lights, at which you turn right onto prefectural road No. 55. After 8 km on road No. 55 (14 km from the airport), you'll see a sign over the road that says Okuchi, 22.7 km and Kurino, 6.7 km. Carry straight on until you reach a crossroads with a red rail bridge over the road ahead (16 km from airport). Turn left here to Okuchi and you will be on prefectural road No. 53. This is a pleasant drive through some very attractive countryside of low sandstone hills, with persimmon trees, bamboo, rice fields, and crytomerias. If you have time, explore some of the side roads and look out for Copper Pheasant, Japanese Grosbeak, and Yellow-throated Bunting.

You will join Rt. 268 where a sign says Okuchi, 10 km, then in Okuchi, look for a sign onto Rt. 267. At a large road sign above the road, turn left and after about 1.5 km turn right to Izumi.

From Izumi Station drive 4 km north on Rt. 328, turn sharply left onto Rt. 3, travel 7.5 km south down Rt. 3, then turn right where a sign with a crane hangs above the road. From there it is another 3 km to the observatory.

Accommodation: The crane warden Matano-san and his family run a minshuku at Arasaki. This is by far the best place to stay in the area since you can sleep to the sound of the roosting cranes and watch them flying back in for their morning feed while you eat your own breakfast. For reservations, phone Minshuku Tsurumitei ☎(09968)3-3944. The next nearest accommodation is in Izumi itself, where a variety of ryokan, minshuku, and business hotels is available. Stay at Business Hotel Tsuru ☎(0996)62-5353, or Hotel Shin-kame-ya ☎(0996)62-1615.

52. Mi-ike, Miyazaki Prefecture 御池
Good birding months: Jan.–Dec.
Best birding months: May–June

Mi-ike, Ebino-kogen (Ebino Plateau), and Kirishimayama form part of the Kirishima-Yaku National Park, an intensely volcanic area, and a welcome change after the coastal flatlands if you have been visiting Arasaki (51). The area has a variety of habitats, from fast-flowing rivers, freshwater lakes, and lowland broadleaf forests to higher-altitude forests and mountains. Here you will find most of the common woodland birds, including both pheasants endemic to Japan, as well as the endemic Japanese Green Woodpecker.

Mi-ike, nestled low on the eastern flank of Takachihonomine (1,574 m), is an almost circular lake 970 m across that attracts up to 5,000 duck in winter. The forest to the west of the lake, mostly composed of broad-leaved evergreens, the taller trees hung with lianas and epiphytes, has nature trails from which birding is both easy and rewarding, although in summer be sure to be out early, before it gets too hot. Red-billed Leiothrix, presumably escapees, have been seen here recently and may be resident. From late May to mid-August Mi-ike takes on a greater significance as a regular breeding site for the gorgeous Fairy Pitta, aptly called the eight-colored bird (*yairocho*) in Japanese. Up to twenty occur here in most years, and calling activity is at its peak between May 25 and June 10. Look for it just after dawn in shady areas

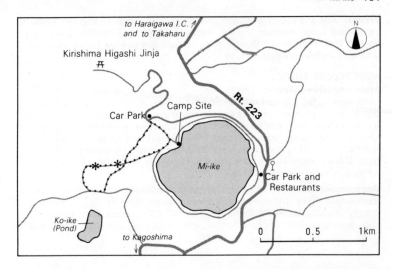

near streams. Follow the signs to the Wild Bird Forest and park at the end of the road. Take the broad track down left (to the lake shore), turning off to the right into the forest at the bottom of the hill. Explore the forest trails. The trails near small streams close to an observation hut are good for the Pitta.

The route up to Mt. Kirishima passes through forest with some large old pines. Birdwatching from the roadside in winter is good for common woodland birds and tit flocks. In spring the area is famous for its lilies and in autumn for the forest colors.

Mammals in the Mi-ike area include Racoon Dog, Badger, Wild Boar, Sika Deer, and Giant Flying Squirrel. For a chance of seeing them, walk along the forest trails at night with a flashlight.

BIRDS AND SEASONS

All year: Copper and Green Pheasant; Japanese Green Pigeon; Common and Crested Kingfisher; Japanese Green, White-backed, and Japanese Pygmy Woodpecker; Gray and Japanese Wagtail; Ashy Minivet; Northern Wren; Long-tailed, Willow, Varied, and Coal Tit; Eurasian Nuthatch; Common Treecreeper; Eurasian Jay; Japanese Grosbeak; Meadow Bunting.

Summer: Striated Heron; Little Egret; Gray-faced Buzzard; Common Sandpiper; Hodgson's Hawk Cuckoo; Oriental and Little Cuckoo; Collared Scops Owl; Brown Hawk Owl; Ruddy Kingfisher; Fairy Pitta; Common House Martin; Japanese Robin; White's Thrush; Stub-tailed Bush Warbler; Blue-and-White, Narcissus, and Japanese Paradise Flycatcher.

Winter: Little and Slavonian Grebe; Mandarin Duck; Eurasian Wigeon; Mallard; Spot-billed Duck; Northern Pintail; Northern Shoveler; Common Coot; Olive-backed Pipit; Red-flanked Bluetail; Pale Thrush; Bull-headed Shrike; Hawfinch; Gray and Yellow-throated Bunting.

HOW TO GET THERE

From Kagoshima Airport: 1 hr by car.
Drive east on Rt. 223 to Takaharu and Kobayashi. Rt. 223 passes the lake. For those traveling by train, go from Kagoshima Station to Takaharu Station and take a bus to Haraigawa or to Mi-ike itself. The former are more frequent. Or take a taxi from the station (about 20 min). Ebino-kogen and Kirishimayama can be reached by traveling due south from Ebino or by turning left (north) off Rt. 223 before Mi-ike. Alternatively, take a train to Kobayashi Station and then a Miyazaki Kotsu bus to Ebino-kogen (1 hr).

Accommodation: There is a camp site with bungalows on the shore of Mi-ike ☎(09844)2-4038, and numerous hot spring hotels along Rt. 223, or stay at the nearby Ohjibaru Recreation Center ☎(0984)42-3393, where there are excellent self-catering chalets. At Ebino Plateau, stay at Ebino-kogen Hotel ☎(0984)33-1155.

53. The Southern Ferry Routes 南フェリー航路

Best birding months: April–Oct.

The Nansei Shoto, or southwestern islands of Japan, have several tropical seabird colonies; unfortunately most are on inaccessible off-shore islets. The commercial ferries that connect all the major islands thus provide the best opportunity to see a wide variety of these species including petrels, shearwaters, boobies, terns, and noddies that cannot be seen elsewhere in the country except from the ferry to Ogasawara (10). Ferries are available from Kagoshima in Kyushu to Amami Oshima, Okinawa, Miyakojima, and Ishigakijima, and from Ishigakijima across to Iriomotejima. A weekly boat from Okinawa via Ishigakijima to Keelung in northeast Taiwan is also interesting for seabirds. Although generally not as productive as the northern ferry routes, especially in winter, in sum-mer they provide opportunities to see very different species. The further south you go, particularly in the Yaeyama Shoto, the greater your chance of seeing Bridled and Sooty Tern and Brown Noddy. Short-tailed Albatross are now suspected of having recolonized the Senkaku Islands, west of the Nansei Shoto, so there is the possibility that you might see one.

The ferry from Amami Oshima to Okinawa leaves in the morning and calls in at Okinoerabujima and Yoronjima, arriving at Okinawa after dark. The ferry from Okinawa to Ishigakijima leaves in the evening and

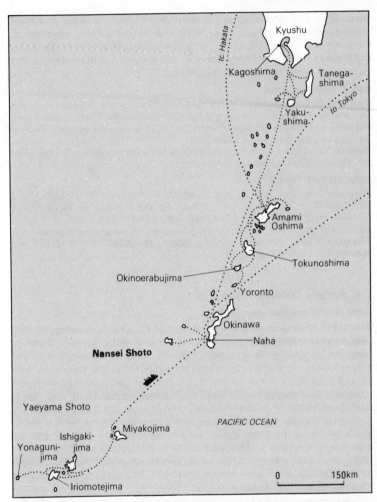

calls in at Miyakojima early in the morning; the section from Miyakojima to Ishigakijima takes about 5 hr, all in daylight and is probably the most interesting section of all. From Ishigakijima boats run regularly to Iriomotejima. Take one of the slower boats (2 hr) since you can go out on deck and watch. This is the best section for the southern terns. The shearwater and skua migrations occur from March to June and from September to November, while terns and Bulwer's Petrel are most in evidence during the summer. If time is a limiting factor, consider flying to Okinawa, taking the ferry down to Ishigakijima, to Iriomotejima and back, then flying back from Ishigakijima.

BIRDS AND SEASONS

Spring to Autumn: Bulwer's Petrel; Streaked, Flesh-footed, Wedge-tailed, and Short-tailed Shearwater; Swinhoe's Petrel; Brown Booby; Eastern Reef Egret; Pomarine and Long-tailed Skua; Greater Crested, Black-naped, Roseate, Bridled, Sooty, and Little Tern; Brown Noddy.

Rarities: Short-tailed Albatross; Audubon's Shearwater; Masked Booby (near the Yaeyama Shoto); Red-tailed Tropicbird.

HOW TO GET THERE

Ferry schedules vary annually and seasonally so it is essential to check with a travel agent for exact schedules. Except for the Okinawa to Taiwan ferry, however, most operate on a daily basis. All ferries have open tatami-style areas, cabins, and restaurants, except for those between Ishigakijima and Iriomotejima. The biggest ferry company is Ryukyu Kaiun, ☎(03)281-1831 in Tokyo and ☎(0988)68-1126 in Kagoshima.

54. Amami Oshima 奄美大島

Good birding months: Jan.–Dec.

The island of Amami, 400 km southwest of Kyushu, is subtropical, very hilly, heavily forested, and surrounded by coral reefs. Some 710 km² in area, its population is less than 90,000, most of whom live in the capital, Naze. Forestry is an important industry, as are sugarcane and fruit. So far Amami has escaped the holidaymaking hordes from the mainland that throng to Okinawa and islands further south and, apart from busy Naze, is pleasantly rural, with quiet roads and beaches.

Several Nansei Shoto specialties are to be found here, with pride of place going to the Lidth's Jay, which, with Amami Black Rabbit, is endemic to this island. Until recently Amami Woodcock, which is common here, was thought to be restricted to Amami alone, but is now known to live on Tokunoshima, northern Okinawa, and on several smaller islands off Okinawa.

Since Ryukyu Scops Owl, Amami Woodcock, the mammals, and the more interesting of the larger frogs are all nocturnal, it is essential to drive along the forest roads at night to see and hear Amami wildlife at its best. The Supa-rindo, a forest track running through the range of hills stretching virtually the whole length of the island, from Naze to Ukenson, is by far the best. If you are on foot, limit yourself to the first sec-

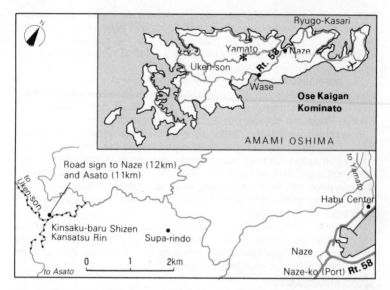

tion known as Kinsaku-baru. Leave Naze heading north along the west side of the harbor, and where the main road bends right, take a narrower road up to the left that climbs past the Habu Center—where locally captured poisonous snakes are pitted against a mongoose. Carry on up a steep hill, then turn left (south) onto a road that passes the city incinerator, conspicuous with its tall chimney, and leads to the main rubbish dump. The track heads south at the turning to the dump. Here you leave the good surface behind and can begin birding, although birding 5–10 km farther south is much better. Carry on along the line of hills, exploring sidetracks wherever these look passable. The track can be very rough in places, so take care especially after rain. You will see the superb tree ferns that tower over the track in places and will see more wildlife along the tracks than if you enter the forest—and be less likely to worry your Japanese friends who fear the poisonous Hime-habu and Habu. Relentless persecution has made them scarce and hard to see but nonetheless poisonous.

Early in the morning you will find Ryukyu Robin and Lidth's Jay very active, and this is a good time to familiarize yourself with the track in readiness for a nocturnal visit. Although Amami Woodcock can be seen crossing the track, more are likely to be seen if you scan, with a powerful flashlight, the open mud banks rising beside the track. This species does not "rode," so do not expect conspicuous crepuscular flights. Ryukyu Scops Owl frequent track-side trees, and before dawn listen for the endemic Amami Thrush (described as a full species in 1986), which, instead of the mournful two-note whistle of White's Thrush, has a Siberian Thrush–like "kiron-tsee" song.

The northeasternmost part of the island is drier and has less natural evergreen broadleaf forest. Instead, it has more Ryukyu Pine, and more sugarcane farms. Here Lidth's Jay are fewer, Black Rabbit are absent, Ryukyu Robin are scarce, but buttonquail are commoner.

In summer, visit Naze harbor to look for Black-naped and Roseate Tern. The latter breed on the small island where the lighthouse is. In spring and autumn, check river mouths for migrant shorebirds and visit the small mud flats at Kominato and Ose Kaigan. Although birdwatching is good all year round, in autumn and winter forest birds are hard to find because they are not singing, and generally more species can be seen from March to May.

The endemic Amami Black Rabbit ventures out onto forest tracks at night, especially where there is overhanging vegetation and it is very likely that you will see several while looking for woodcook. Also look for the scarcer Tree Rat and Amami Spinous Mouse.

BIRDS AND SEASONS
All year: Cinnamon Bittern (in paddies around Kominato); Eastern Reef Egret; Japanese Sparrowhawk; Barred Buttonquail; Amami Woodcock; Japanese Woodpigeon; Red-capped Green Pigeon; Ryukyu Scops Owl; Common Kingfisher; White-backed (distinctive endemic race) and Japanese Pygmy Woodpecker; Pacific Swallow; Ryukyu Minivet; Ryukyu Robin; Amami Thrush; Fan-tailed Warbler; Varied Tit; Lidth's Jay.
Spring & Autumn: Little Ringed, Kentish, Mongolian, Pacific Golden, and Gray Plover; Red-necked Stint; Dunlin; Whimbrel; Wood, Terek, and Common Sandpiper; Gray-tailed Tattler.
Summer: Black-naped and Roseate Tern; Ruddy Kingfisher; Narcissus Flycatcher (rare local race); Japanese Paradise Flycatcher.
Winter: Temminck's Cormorant; Gray-faced Buzzard; Eurasian Kestrel; Eurasian Woodcock; Water Pipit; Yellow Wagtail.

HOW TO GET THERE
From Kagoshima: 1 hr by plane.
There are daily flights from Okinawa, Kagoshima, and Osaka. From Tokyo, fly first to Kagoshima (1 hr 55 min), then to Amami. Cars can be rented either at the airport or in Naze. Two ferry companies operate boats from two different harbors in Kagoshima to Naze in Amami, with the journey taking 11–15 hr. Take a tram from JR Nishi-Kagoshima Station to Izuro (10 min) and walk 5 min to Kagoshima Honko (main habor), or take the tram to Shinko (15 min) for Kagoshima New Harbor. Boats also operate between Amami and Okinawa. For current ferry schedules, check with a travel agent.

Accommodation: Naze has an abundance of accommodation, from youth hostels and minshuku to business and luxury hotels, but I recommend staying in Sango-so ☎ (0997)69-5077 in Wase, a quiet minshuku situated beside the sea. Lidth's Jay are common in the area, and Black-naped and Roseate Tern fish offshore.

55. Yambaru, North Okinawa　ヤンバル（沖縄）

Good birding months: Jan.–Dec.
Best birding months: March–June, Aug.–Oct.

The hilly, forested northern third of Okinawa Island, known as Yambaru, is home to all the island specialties that no visit to Japan is complete without. Foremost among these is the *Yambaru-kuina*, or Okinawa Rail. Rarer than the rail, however, and in considerable danger of extinction through logging of its primary forest nesting areas, is Pryer's Woodpecker.

The forest here is subtropical, composed mostly of broadleaf evergreen trees, with surprisingly low canopy and no emergents. The most outstanding feature of the forests is the tree ferns. The remaining primary forest on the hilltops should be your destination since only here do you have a good chance to see the woodpecker (listen for its sharp, whiplashlike calls and loud drumming). Its habitat is good for all the other island specialties as well.

It is best to explore the forest tracks during the night and certainly around dawn. Amami Woodcock are resident but less common than on Amami (54), Ryukyu Scops Owl can be heard giving their hoarse "u-hu" calls (but note that Oriental Scops Owl pass through in spring and can also be heard calling—they have a three-note whistle), and Okinawa Rail can be found relatively easily, roosting in trees beside the tracks (but you need a powerful torch). There are several interesting tracks, but the best are: Okuni-rindo, a new forest road running north–south along the hilltops; Terakubi-rindo, at the T-junction where it meets Gaji-rindo; and the pipeline road. All are good for woodpecker, rail, and other commoner forest species wherever there are mature trees. The area around Benoki Dam has Okinawa Rail, Ryukyu Scops Owl, Brown Hawk Owl, and Wild Boar. Try also the area around Fungawa Dam early in the morning. The highest density of calling rails is here (listen for their loud "ki-kweer" calls). Some come down to the water's edge around the reservoir, and all the forest species can be seen here, including Pryer's Woodpecker. Birds are most active at dawn; the woodpeckers call and drum more at this time, and after about 07:00 your chances of seeing Ryukyu Robin decrease markedly.

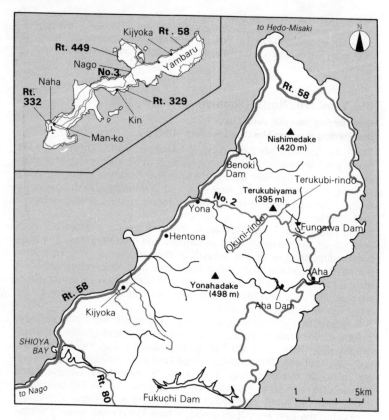

In late September or early October find a hilltop vantage point early in the morning and watch for migrating Chinese Sparrowhawk. Until recently this bird was considered a great rarity in Japan, before it was noticed that birds appeared each autumn on the island. Research has now shown that tens of thousands pass through west Kyushu, Amami, northern Okinawa, and on through the Yaeyama Shoto to Taiwan.

As you drive along the coast north of Nago, watch for Eastern Reef Egret and Blue Rock Thrush along the shore, and in summer Black-naped and Roseate Tern offshore.

Spring from late March to June and autumn from August to October are the best seasons for a combination of endemic and migrant birds.

The typhoon season is from late August to October and can hamper birding. From late December to March is the rainy season in Okinawa, and it can rain up to seventy percent of the time. During this season Pryer's Woodpecker are particularly hard to find.

At night in the forest you are likely to come across fruit bats. You may also encounter Wild Boar, some of the larger frogs, such as Holst's, Ishikawa, or Namiye's Frog (the former gives the deep "won" call and latter the repetitive "gwo-gwo-gwo" commonly heard at dusk), and during the day look for the endemic Ryukyu Tortoise and the endemic salamanders.

BIRDS AND SEASONS

All year: Little Grebe; Eastern Reef Egret; Mandarin Duck; Japanese Sparrowhawk; Okinawa Rail; Amami Woodcock; Japanese Woodpigeon; Red-capped Green Pigeon; Collared and Ryukyu Scops Owl; Brown Hawk Owl; Common Kingfisher; Pryer's and Japanese Pygmy Woodpecker; Pacific Swallow; Ryukyu Minivet; Ryukyu Robin; Blue Rock Thrush; Varied Tit.

Summer: Black-naped and Roseate Tern; Little Cuckoo; Ruddy Kingfisher; Narcissus (rare) and Japanese Paradise Flycatcher.

Autumn: Chinese Sparrowhawk; Gray-faced Buzzard; Common House Martin; Gray-streaked Flycatcher.

Winter: Gray-faced Buzzard; Eurasian Woodcock; Common Sandpiper; Olive-backed Pipit; Gray Wagtail; Red-flanked Bluetail; Pale Thrush; Eurasian Siskin.

HOW TO GET THERE

From Naha: 3–4 hr by car.

Take Rt. 58 from Naha north, first to Nago, then on northward to the bridge at the mouth of Shioya Bay, 21 km further north. From the bridge it is a further 17 km to the main northern cross-island road, prefectural road No. 2, which branches off at Yona village. Turn right here. Road No. 2 winds uphill, crosses the spine of the island, and descends to the east coast at Aha village. About 6 km from the junction with Rt. 58 at Yona, turn right onto Okuni-rindo, a well-made forest track. Continue along the track to well-forested areas for early morning birding. A further 1.6 km up road No. 2, turn left onto Terukubi-rindo, explore the track until the next junction with Sate/Gaji-rindo (after 1 km), at which point turn right, then downhill to the left. Return by the same route. Continuing east along road No. 2, turn left after 1.4 km to explore the pipeline road, and a further 2.1 km along road No. 2 you will cross the bridge at the south end of Fungawa Dam.

By public transport, take a bus to Nago from Naha Bus Center (2 hr), from Nago a Hentona bus (1 hr), and from Hentona a bus to Hedo Misaki (the north cape; can be good for passerines during the migration seasons) and get off at Yona (after 5 min). Walk right, up road No. 2.

Accommodation: In Hentona, stay at Villa Okuma Resort Hotel ☎(0980)41-2123, Minshuku Yutakaya ☎(0980)41-2117, or Hotel Miyashiro ☎(0980)41-2337.

56. Kijyoka, North Okinawa　喜如嘉(沖縄)

Good birding months: Jan.–Dec.
Best birding months: Aug.–April

There are few undeveloped level areas in Okinawa and very few areas of fields, so the paddies at Kin (57) and the *igusa* (rush) fields at Kijyoka are especially attractive to migrant and wintering shorebirds and passerines. Kijyoka has the added attraction that Okinawa Rail can be heard calling from the surrounding hills at night and early in the morning. The fields here are for growing the rushes used, when dried and woven, to cover tatami mats, and during spring and early summer these are very tall and unattractive to shorebirds, though attractive to Cinnamon Bittern and to hordes of dragonflies. The area is best watched by driving slowly along the tracks between the fields. The species recorded here are generally similar to those at Kin, but Kijyoka has the advantage that it can be easily visited after a night or dawn session up in the nearby forest of Yambaru (55).

Don't be surprised by the presence of munias here and at other field sites on Okinawa. The origin of these is in doubt, but the White-rumped Munia at least may be wild colonists from Taiwan.

BIRDS AND SEASONS

All year: Cinnamon Bittern; Japanese Sparrowhawk; Okinawa Rail; White-breasted Waterhen; Watercock (uncommon); Pacific Swallow; Ryukyu Minivet; Fan-tailed Warbler; White-rumped Munia.
Autumn & Winter: Little and Intermediate Egret; Gray-faced Buzzard; Little Ringed and Pacific Golden Plover; Long-toed Stint; Common and Pintail Snipe;

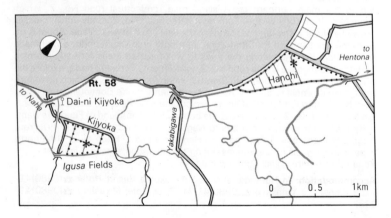

Common Greenshank; Green, Wood, and Common Sandpiper; Yellow and Gray Wagtail.
Rarities: Swinhoe's Snipe; Bluethroat; Tiger Shrike; Little Bunting.

HOW TO GET THERE
Follow the same route as for Yambaru (55), but fork right in Kijyoka village (6 km south of Hentona) to the *igusa* fields. By bus, get off the Nago to Hentona bus at Dai-ni Kijyoka bus stop and walk 10 min to the fields.

Accommodation: See Yambaru (55).

57. Kin, Central Okinawa 金武(沖縄)
Good birding months: Sept.–June
This small area of paddies and the adjacent river on the east side of the island attract a wide variety of migrant and wintering shorebirds and passerines, as this habitat is very scarce. This site should be visited en route to or from Yambaru (55). Several birds rare for Okinawa Prefecture have been found, and as at Kijyoka (56) you can obtain close views of birds here by driving slowly along the tracks between the fields.

BIRDS AND SEASONS
All year: Cinnamon Bittern; Cattle, Eastern Reef, and Little Egret; Japanese Sparrowhawk; White-breasted Waterhen; Common Moorhen; Common Kingfisher; Pacific Swallow; Ryukyu Minivet.
Spring, Autumn, & Winter: Intermediate and Great Egret; Gray-faced Buzzard; Little Ringed and Pacific Golden Plover; Temminck's and Long-toed Stint; Sharptailed Sandpiper; Dunlin; Ruff; Common and Pintail Snipe; Marsh Sandpiper; Common Greenshank; Wood and Common Sandpiper; Gray-tailed Tattler; Redthroated and Water Pipit; Yellow, Gray, and White Wagtail; Siberian Rubythroat; Pale and Dusky Thrush.
Rarities: Chinese Pond Heron; Watercock; Swinhoe's Snipe; Pechora Pipit.

HOW TO GET THERE
From Naha: 2 hr by car.
Drive north from Naha on Rt. 58 up the west coast. Just before Moon Beach, and 36 km north of Naha, turn right onto prefectural road No. 73 and cross over to the east coast. Turn left there onto Rt. 329, which takes you north up the east coast. Continue north, passing Gates 1 and 2 of Camp Hansen. A few hundred meters past Gate 2, turn right at a crossroads (52 km from Naha) and after nearly 1 km, turn left. You will then be entering the area of fields and should drive around the small tracks. If you miss the junction on Rt. 329, you will find yourself crossing a high bridge (Kin Ohashi) with a view down to the paddies and the sea to the east.
　　Alternatively, take a bus from Naha Bus Center to Henoko and get off at Kisem-

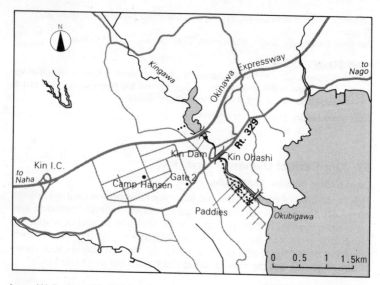

baru. Walk along Rt. 329 for about 300 m, then turn right at the crossroads as above.

To continue to Yambaru, travel north just over 10 km on Rt. 329, turn west onto prefectural road No. 108, then right onto Rt. 58, which will take you to Nago. See Yambaru (55) for further directions.

Accommodation: See Yambaru (55).

58. Man-ko, South Okinawa　漫湖(沖縄)

Good birding months: Jan.–Dec.
Best birding months: Sept.–March

Situated between the main airport and the center of Naha, the capital of Okinawa, the small estuary and tidal mud flats of Man-ko are very accessible, and one of the most interesting sites in Japan for its variety of shorebirds. About 2 km long and less than 1 km wide at its widest point, it is easily viewed from both sides.

In winter several species of duck occur and some shorebirds winter here, for which the Man-ko probably represents their northernmost wintering grounds. From November to February the estuary is the best place in Japan to observe the rare Saunders's Gull. They occur annually in small numbers and I have seen flocks of up to five here.

During the migration season many shorebirds pass through, their numbers and species composition changing daily, making it worth paying several visits to Man-ko. The best time is from September to March, but migrants can also be found here in April and May, and some non-breeding shorebirds stay here throughout the summer, with early returning migrants appearing from July onward. Even in winter the midday temperature is enough to make the birds inactive, so early morning is best, especially if there is a high tide during mid-morning.

BIRDS AND SEASONS
All year: Little and Great Egret; Common Moorhen; Little Ringed, Kentish, and Pacific Golden Plover; Red-necked Stint; Dunlin; Common Sandpiper; Gray-tailed Tattler; Pacific Swallow; Chinese Bulbul; Blue Rock Thrush; Fan-tailed Warbler.
Spring & Autumn: Cattle and Intermediate Egret; Mongolian and Gray Plover; Ruff; Bar-tailed Godwit; Whimbrel; Eurasian and Eastern Curlew; Common Redshank; Common Greenshank; Ruddy Turnstone.

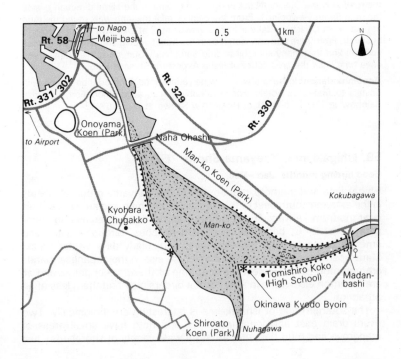

Summer: Intermediate Egret; Wood Sandpiper; Little Tern.
Winter: Gray Heron; Common Teal; Common Black-headed Gull; Mallard; Spot-billed Duck; Northern Pintail; Northern Shoveler; Tufted Duck; Gray-faced Buzzard; Eurasian Kestrel; Peregrine; Mongolian and Gray Plover; Common Snipe; Bar-tailed Godwit; Whimbrel; Eurasian Curlew; Common Redshank; Common Teal; Common Greenshank; Ruddy Turnstone; Pale and Dusky Thrush.
Rarities: Eastern White Stork; White and Black-faced Spoonbill; Common Shelduck; Spoon-billed Sandpiper; Nordmann's Greenshank; Saunders's Gull.

HOW TO GET THERE

From Naha Airport: 15 min by car or taxi.
Taxis are cheaper on Okinawa than on the larger Japanese islands and are a very convenient way of visiting Man-ko. Alternatively, take any bus going from town to the airport or vice versa and get off at Koen-mae bus stop near the United Seamen's Service. Walk back in the direction of town and take a right between a garage and a fried chicken shop. There is a large concrete shrine gate (*torii*) here. This road passes Naha Youth Hostel on the left, then a large athletic stadium on the right. Join a footpath along the river here and walk to the right. You will cross the road at Naha Ohashi (Naha Bridge) continuing in the same direction beside the mud flat to viewpoint 1. From there either take the long walk round the mud flat via Naha Ohashi or take a taxi to viewpoint 2 at Okinawa Kyodo Byoin (a hospital). From here you can watch both the Kokubagawa and Nuhagawa rivers and will find that many shorebirds, and Saunders's Gull, pass this point. If you have time, visit the area south of Naha Airport for Chinese Bulbul.

Accommodation: In Naha there is a wide variety of accommodation, from youth hostels to first-class hotels. For reasonably priced accommodation, try Hotel Rainbow ☎(0988)66-5401 or Hotel New Sanwa ☎(0986)67-4346.

59. Ishigakijima, Yaeyama Shoto 石垣島
Good birding months: Jan.–Dec.

Ishigakijima and Iriomotejima are part of the Yaeyama group of islands in the extreme southwest of the Nansei Shoto chain and are only a short boat trip from Taiwan. These subtropical islands, with an average temperature of 24°C, beautiful coral sand beaches, turquoise seas, and emerald green forests, are attractive, particularly as a winter break. Many species of birds that occur nowhere else in the Japanese islands are common here. However, since none of these are endemic and all are common elsewhere in Asia, global birders may find them less of an attraction.

The southern half of Ishigakijima is interesting ornithologically. Two rivers drain east and west into bays and both have small areas of mangrove and mud flats that attract a wide variety of shorebirds. Just

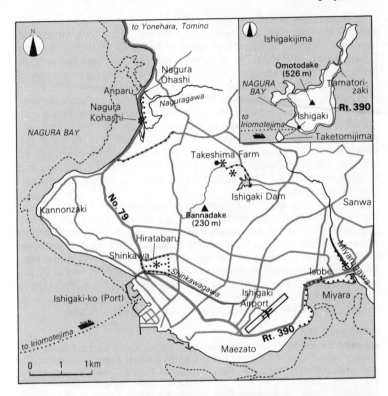

out of Ishigaki City to the northwest is a small area of rice fields to the north of Shinkawa known as Hiratabaru, which is worth a visit at any season to look for Cinnamon Bittern, egrets, and shorebirds. It is easily reached on foot from town. Take prefectural road No. 79 out of town to the west. Just on the outskirts the road crosses a bridge over a small river. At this point you will see the rice fields off to your right. Explore the small roads around the fields.

The area called Anparu, around the mouth of the Naguragawa with its mangrove and mud flats, is well worth visiting and can be seen from the Nagura Ohashi and Nagura Kohashi bridges on No. 79, about 7 km northwest of Ishigaki City. This area is good for shorebirds from October to March. Also check the marshes and paddies just inland for herons, egrets, and crakes.

On the eastern side of the island visit the mouth of the Todorokigawa, about 7 km northeast of Ishigaki City. Fork left about 1 km before the river and explore the lanes and fields in this area for winter starling flocks, pipits, and wagtails. Wherever you find wet paddies or rush fields, watch for Watercock, which you may also hear giving its rapid booming "ogh-ogh-ogh" calls.

In summer, visit the northern cape and look across to Daichi Banarejima, or visit Tamatorizaki in the northeast to look for breeding Black-naped and Roseate Tern. Explore the road that crosses the island near the southern end, visiting Takashima No-en, a small farm, to watch the Emerald Dove that come out to be fed at the house there (4 km east of No. 79); watch for Crested Serpent Eagle over the forest in this area and visit the mouth of the Miyaragawa on the east side to look for the resident Malayan Night Heron.

The short ferry trip to Taketomijima is worthwhile in summer. Leave the ferry and turn right (most visitors go straight on or left, to the popular south side of the island). Follow the beach for a few hundred meters to some offshore rocks where there are Black-naped and a few Bridled Tern in summer, as well as Eastern Reef Egret and shorebirds. The ferry trip across to Iriomotejima should not be missed, and at least a day or two should be spent there. For those interested in adding rarities to their Japanese list, a visit (by boat or plane) should be made to Yonagunijima—the westernmost island of the group—in March.

BIRDS AND SEASONS

All year: Cinnamon Bittern; Malayan Night Heron; Cattle Egret; Eastern Reef Egret; Purple Heron; Spot-billed Duck; Crested Serpent Eagle; Japanese Sparrowhawk; Barred Buttonquail; Slaty-legged and Ruddy Crake; White-breasted Waterhen; Common Moorhen; Watercock; Little Ringed, Kentish, and Mongolian Plover; Red-necked Stint; Dunlin; Whimbrel; Common Greenshank; Wood, Terek, and Common Sandpiper; Gray-tailed Tattler; Ruddy Turnstone; Emerald Dove; Red-capped Green Pigeon; Ryukyu Scops Owl; Pacific Swallow; Ryukyu Minivet; Chinese Bulbul; Fan-tailed Warbler.

Summer: Intermediate Egret; Caspian, Greater Crested, Black-naped, Roseate, and Little Tern; Ruddy Kingfisher; Japanese Paradise Flycatcher.

Spring, Autumn, & Winter: Black-crowned Night Heron; Striated Heron; Little and Great Egret; Gray Heron; Common Teal; Gray-faced Buzzard; Osprey; Large Sand, Pacific Golden, and Gray Plover; Long-toed Stint; Common Snipe; Spotted Redshank; Red-throated and Water Pipit; Yellow and Gray Wagtail; Pale Thrush; Brown Shrike.

Rarities: Eastern White Stork; Oriental Ibis; Ruddy Shelduck; Oriental Pratincole; Saunders's Gull; Red Turtle Dove; Silky, Chinese, and Common Starling; Crested Myna.

HOW TO GET THERE

From Okinawa: 1 hr by plane.

There are regular daily flights from Okinawa to Ishigakijima. A ferry leaves Naha each evening arriving at Miyakojima early next morning and at Ishigakijima in the early afternoon.

Cars can be rented at the airport, and bicycles and small motorcycles from shops near the harbor. The latter are quite adequate for exploring southern Ishigakijima.

Accommodation: A variety of minshuku and hotel accommodation is available in Ishigaki City, but try Business Hotel Nansei near the harbor ☎(09808)2-2422, Minshuku Ishigakijima in the center of town ☎(09808)2-6066, or Minshuku Toyokawa-so, just beyond Anparu ☎(09808)2-1739.

60. Iriomotejima, Yaeyama Shoto　西表島

Good birding months: Jan.–Dec.
Best birding months: Nov.–March

More than eighty percent of this 284-km^2 forested island belongs to the Iriomotejima National Park, home to the endemic Iriomote Wild Cat. Much of the island retains its primary subtropical forest, the most extensive in Nansei Shoto, and there are still areas of mangrove, and attractive beaches and bays. Iriomotejima lies 450 km southwest of Okinawa, and is 30 km from east to west, 20 km from north to south, and the highest point is about 470 m. Birding is best from November to March, when most species can be seen, and snorkeling is also very good. Funaura is a good base for birders, walkers, and swimmers. There are not so many specific points to visit here as on Ishigakijima, but try the areas along the coast road around Sonai, Ohara, Otomi, and Komi villages; birds are easier to find here than further inland. Crested Serpent Eagle hunt from roadside poles, White-breasted Waterhen are abundant in the rice fields, as are Chinese Bulbul around sugarcane and pineapple plantations.

One of the better mangrove areas is the mouth of the Ura-uchigawa, west of Funaura. From just above the road bridge it is possible to take a boat ride 30 min upriver, then walk for 40 min to the Mariyudo and Kampira waterfalls. A forest trail continues from the falls right across the island, but it takes a full day to reach Ohara. It is a pleasant walk but is no better for birds than close to the road, although you are more likely to hear Emerald Dove and have a chance of seeing Wild Boar. A single road runs up the east coast and along the north coast of the island, from Ohara in the southeast, via Funaura to Shirahama in the northwest. The

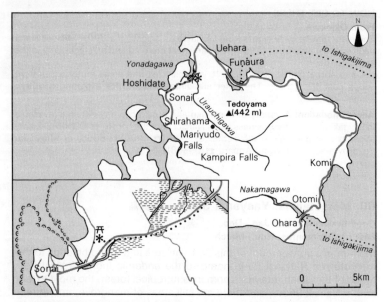

ideal way to explore Iriomotejima is to rent a car or motorcycle in Ohara
(check the Nakamagawa mangroves just north of the village for night
herons) or Funaura, then drive slowly, checking all the paddy areas and
the forest edge. Scan ahead along the roadsides for buttonquails under
overhanging vegetation. River mouths and mangroves attract egrets
and shorebirds, while the paddies are where you will find more
shorebirds, Cinnamon Bittern, and Watercock.

In the Hoshidate area west of Funaura, there are Malayan Night
Heron. These are crepuscular and can be very secretive, so watch the
wet paddies at dawn and dusk. After crossing the Ura-uchigawa, look
for a right fork that heads into Sonai village, just after the garage on the
right, turn right down a narrow track that crosses a small area of fields
to a shrine across on the hillside. If you arrive early, explore the village,
which has some beautiful old Yaeyama-style houses, with outer walls
of coral blocks and tiled roofs.

The boat journey between Ishigakijima and Iriomotejima can be quite
productive for seabirds, although most species breed on small islets off
western Iriomotejima that cannot be reached by the public. You should
see Brown Booby, one or more species of tern, and possibly shearwaters and petrels.

Japan's first Grass Owl, Gray Bushchat, and Long-tailed Shrike were found on Iriomotejima.

BIRDS AND SEASONS

All year: Brown Booby; Cinnamon Bittern; Malayan Night Heron; Eastern Reef Egret; Purple Heron; Spot-billed Duck; Crested Serpent Eagle; Japanese Sparrowhawk; Barred Buttonquail; Slaty-legged and Ruddy Crake; White-breasted Waterhen; Common Moorhen; Watercock; Little Ringed, Kentish, and Mongolian Plover; Common Greenshank; Gray-tailed Tattler; Japanese Woodpigeon; Emerald Dove; Red-capped Green Pigeon; Ryukyu Scops Owl; Pacific Swallow; Chinese Bulbul; Ryukyu Minivet; Fan-tailed Warbler; Narcissus Flycatcher.

Summer: Bulwer's Petrel; Streaked Shearwater; Black-naped, Roseate, Bridled, and Sooty Tern; Ruddy Kingfisher; Japanese Paradise Flycatcher.

Spring, Autumn, & Winter: Cattle, Little, and Great Egret; Eastern Marsh Harrier; Gray-faced Buzzard; Eurasian Kestrel; Common Snipe; Whimbrel; Spotted Redshank; Olive-backed, Red-throated and Water Pipit; Yellow Wagtail; Ryukyu Robin; Brown, Pale, and Dusky Thrush.

Rarities: Great Bittern; Japanese Night Heron; Eastern White Stork; Black-capped Kingfisher; Hoopoe.

HOW TO GET THERE

From Ishigakijima: 1 or 2 hr by sea.
Boats, hovercraft, and hydrofoils are available from Ishigaki harbor to Ohara, Funaura, or Shirahama, but the slower boats are better for seawatching.

Accommodation: There are several minshuku, pensions, and two youth hostels at Funaura, between Funaura and the Urauchigawa is Minshuku Akebonokan ☎(09808)5-6151, and, in Uehara, Minshuku Kiyomiso ☎(09808)5-6251.

A Checklist of the Birds of Japan

Since the publication of the list of Japanese birds in the *Field Guide to the Birds of Japan* (WBSJ and Kodansha International, 1982), which was itself based on the *Checklist of Japanese Birds* (Ornithological Society of Japan, 1974), many additional species have been observed or taxonomic changes have become more generally accepted. In my own *The Birds of Japan: A Checklist*, I have tried to keep abreast of Japan's growing bird list, and in this I am, as ever, extremely grateful to Koichiro Sonobe of the WBSJ for his help. In this list I have extended the second edition of my checklist (1986) and revised the nomenclature, bringing it up to date as of July 1987.

This checklist follows essentially the order and names used by Voous in his *List of Recent Holarctic Bird Species* (British Ornithologists' Union, 1980). Where different English names are more commonly used in Japan I have chosen them, particularly where these are shorter. In some cases the names used here differ from those used in the *Field Guide to the Birds of Japan*. Where this involves the use of accepted alternate names for a given species, I have included both unless they are so similar as not to cause confusion. Some species names were, however, misapplied in the *Field Guide*, such as Great Skua, instead of South Polar Skua, or subspecies names referring to Nearctic populations were used instead of those more appropriate for the Palearctic, such as Whistling Swan instead of Bewick's Swan. In these cases I have given the *Field Guide* names in square brackets, the same as for extinct species, after the currently accepted name. Parentheses are used to denote parts of names that are dropped by many birders. Thus Leach's Storm Petrel is now generally known as Leach's Petrel, and so appears as Leach's (Storm) Petrel. The main body of the list contains all of those species regarded as wild or well established in Japan. More exotic introduced species and escapees are included after the main list following the order and names used by Clements in his *Birds of the World: A Checklist* (1981), and are based on published material in *The Breeding Bird Survey in Japan* (WBSJ, 1980), *Seibutsu daizukan: Chorui* (Kuroda, ed., 1984), and *Japanese Bird Banding in Recent Years (1961-1983)* (Bird Migration Research Center, Yamashina Institute for Ornithology, 1985), and in *Yacho* magazine. I have included the romanized version of the Japanese names for each species in order to facilitate communication with Japanese birdwatchers.

The status of each species is classified under one of the following categories:

A. Species recorded in the wild within the last fifty years (i.e., since 1937)

A1. Species added to the Japanese list since the publication of the *Field Guide* in 1982, and species not included in the *Field Guide*.

B. Species recorded in the wild, but not for more than fifty years.

C. Species occurring in the wild with self-sustaining populations, but which were originally introduced or which are presumed to have been introduced.

D. Species occurring now in the wild, but which are maintained only by regular reintroductions or escapees.

#. Species endemic to Japan, including those which are endemic breeders but which winter outside Japan.

[ ]. Extinct species.

ENGLISH NAME	SCIENTIFIC NAME	JAPANESE NAME	

GAVIIFORMES

GAVIIDAE

☐ Red-throated Diver or Red-throated Loon	*Gavia stellata*	Abi	A
☐ Black-throated Diver or Arctic Loon	*Gavia arctica*	Ohamu	A
☐ Pacific Diver or Pacific Loon	*Gavia pacifica*	Shiroeri-ohamu	A
☐ White-billed Diver or Yellow-billed Loon	*Gavia adamsii*	Hashijiro-abi	A

PODICIPEDIDAE

☐ Little Grebe	*Tachybaptus ruficollis*	Kaitsuburi	A
☐ Great Crested Grebe	*Podiceps cristatus*	Kanmuri-kaitsuburi	A
☐ Red-necked Grebe	*Podiceps grisegena*	Akaeri-kaitsuburi	A
☐ Slavonian or Horned Grebe	*Podiceps auritus*	Mimi-kaitsuburi	A
☐ Black-necked or Eared Grebe	*Podiceps nigricollis*	Hajiro-kaitsuburi	A

PROCELLARIIFORMES

DIOMEDEIIDAE

☐ Black-footed Albatross	*Diomedea nigripes*	Kuroashi-ahodori	A
☐ Laysan Albatross	*Diomedea immutabilis*	Ko-ahodori	A
☐ Short-tailed Albatross	*Diomedea albatrus*	Ahodori	A#
☐ Wandering Albatross	*Diomedea exulans*	Watari-ahodori	A

PROCELLARIIDAE

☐ Northern Fulmar	*Fulmarus glacialis*	Furuma-kamome	A
☐ Solander's Petrel	*Pterodroma solandri*	Hajiro-mizunagidori	A1
☐ Kermadec Petrel	*Pterodroma neglecta*	Kawari-shirohara-mizunagidori	A
☐ White-necked Petrel	*Pterodroma externa*	O-shirohara-mizunagidori	A
☐ Hawaiian or Dark-rumped Petrel	*Pterodroma phaeopygia*	Hawai-shirohara-mizunagidori	A
☐ Bonin Petrel	*Pterodroma hypoleuca*	Shirohara-mizunagidori	A
☐ Black-winged Petrel	*Pterodroma nigripennis*	Haguro-shirohara-mizunagidori	A
☐ Stejneger's Petrel	*Pterodroma longirostris*	Hime-shirohara-mizunagidori	A
☐ Bulwer's Petrel	*Bulweria bulwerii*	Anadori	A
☐ Streaked Shearwater	*Calonectris leucomelas*	O-mizunagidori	A

☐ Flesh-footed or Pale-footed Shearwater	*Puffinus carneipes*	Akaashi-mizunagidori	A
☐ Wedge-tailed Shearwater	*Puffinus pacificus*	Onaga-mizunagidori	A
☐ New Zealand or Buller's Shearwater	*Puffinus bulleri*	Minami-onaga-mizunagidori	A
☐ Sooty Shearwater	*Puffinus griseus*	Haiiro-mizunagidori	A
☐ Short-tailed or Slender-billed Shearwater	*Puffinus tenuirostris*	Hashiboso-mizunagidori	A
☐ Christmas Island Shearwater	*Puffinus nativitatis*	Ko-mizunagidori	A
☐ Audubon's Shearwater	*Puffinus lherminieri*	Seguro-mizunagidori	A

HYDROBATIDAE

☐ Wilson's (Storm) Petrel	*Oceanites oceanicus*	Ashinaga-umitsubame	A
☐ Fork-tailed (Storm) Petrel	*Oceanodroma furcata*	Haiiro-umitsubame	A
☐ Leach's (Storm) Petrel	*Oceanodroma leucorhoa*	Koshijiro-umitsubame	A
☐ Swinhoe's (Storm) Petrel	*Oceanodroma monorhis*	Hime-kuro-umitsubame	A
☐ Band-rumped (Storm) or Madeiran Petrel	*Oceanodroma castro*	Kuro-koshijiro-umitsubame	A
☐ Matsudaira's (Storm) Petrel	*Oceanodroma matsu-dairae*	Kuro-umitsubame	A#
☐ Tristram's (Storm) Petrel [Sooty Storm Petrel]	*Oceanodroma tristrami*	Osuton-umitsubame	A

PELECANIFORMES

PHAETHONTIDAE

☐ Red-tailed Tropicbird	*Phaethon rubricauda*	Akao-nettaicho	A
☐ White-tailed Tropicbird	*Phaethon lepturus*	Shirao-nettaicho	A

SULIDAE

☐ Red-footed Booby	*Sula sula*	Akaashi-katsuodori	A
☐ Masked or Blue-faced Booby	*Sula dactylatra*	Aotsura-katsuodori	A
☐ Brown Booby	*Sula leucogaster*	Katsuodori	A

PHALACROCORACIDAE

☐ Great Cormorant	*Phalacrocorax carbo*	Kawa-u	A
☐ Temminck's or Japanese Cormorant	*Phalacrocorax capillatus*	Umi-u	A

☐ Pelagic Cormorant   *Phalacrocorax pelagicus*   Hime-u   A
☐ Red-faced Cormorant   *Phalacrocorax urile*   Chishima-ugarasu   A

PELECANIDAE
☐ Spot-billed Pelican   *Pelecanus philippensis*   Hairo-perikan   A

FREGATIDAE
☐ Great Frigatebird   *Fregatta minor*   O-gunkandori   A
☐ Lesser Frigatebird   *Fregatta ariel*   Ko-gunkandori   A

CICONIIFORMES

ARDEIDAE

☐ Great or Eurasian Bittern	*Botaurus stellaris*	Sankano-goi	A
☐ Yellow Bittern or Chinese Little Bittern	*Ixobrychus sinensis*	Yoshi-goi	A
☐ Schrenck's (Little) Bittern	*Ixobrychus eurhythmus*	O-yoshi-goi	A
☐ Cinnamon Bittern	*Ixobrychus cinnamomeus*	Ryukyu-yoshi-goi	A
☐ Black Bittern	*Ixobrychus flavicollis*	Takasago-kuro-sagi	A
☐ Japanese Night Heron	*Gorsachius goisagi*	Mizo-goi	A#
☐ Malayan Night Heron	*Gorsachius melanolophus*	Zuguro-mizo-goi	A
☐ Black-crowned Night Heron	*Nycticorax nycticorax*	Goi-sagi	A
☐ Rufous Night Heron	*Nycticorax caledonicus*	Hashibuto-goi	B
☐ Striated or Green-backed Heron	*Butorides striatus*	Sasa-goi	A
☐ Chinese Pond Heron	*Ardeola bacchus*	Akagashira-sagi	A
☐ Cattle Egret	*Bubulcus ibis*	Ama-sagi	A
☐ Swinhoe's or Chinese Egret	*Egretta eulophotes*	Kara-shira-sagi	A
☐ Eastern Reef Egret or Eastern Reef Heron	*Egretta sacra*	Kuro-sagi	A
☐ Little Egret	*Egretta garzetta*	Ko-sagi	A
☐ Intermediate, Plumed or Yellow-billed Egret	*Egretta intermedia*	Chu-sagi	A
☐ Great Egret	*Egretta alba*	Dai-sagi	A
☐ Gray Heron	*Ardea cinerea*	Ao-sagi	A
☐ Purple Heron	*Ardea purpurea*	Murasaki-sagi	A

CICONIIDAE
☐ Black Stork   *Ciconia nigra*   Nabe-ko   A
☐ Eastern White Stork   *Ciconia boyciana*   Konotori   A

THRESKIORNITHIDAE

☐ Japanese Crested Ibis	*Nipponia nippon*	Toki	A
☐ Oriental or Black-headed Ibis	*Threskiornis melanocephalus*	Kuro-toki	A
☐ White Spoonbill	*Platalea leucorodia*	Herasagi	A
☐ Black-faced Spoonbill	*Platalea minor*	Kurotsura-herasagi	A

ANATIDAE

☐ Mute Swan	*Cygnus olor*	Kobu-hakucho	A/C
☐ Bewick's or Tundra Swan [Whistling Swan]	*Cygnus columbianus*	Ko-hakucho	A
☐ Whooper Swan	*Cygnus cygnus*	O-hakucho	A
☐ Swan or Chinese Goose	*Anser cygnoides*	Sakatsura-gan	A
☐ Bean Goose	*Anser fabalis*	Hishikui	A
☐ Greater White-fronted Goose	*Anser albifrons*	Ma-gan	A
☐ Lesser White-fronted Goose	*Anser erythropus*	Karigane	A
☐ Graylag Goose	*Anser anser*	Haiiro-gan	A
☐ Snow Goose	*Anser caerulescens*	Haku-gan	A
☐ Emperor Goose	*Anser canagicus*	Mikado-gan	A
☐ Canada Goose	*Branta canadensis*	Shijukara-gan	A
☐ Brent Goose or Brant	*Branta bernicla*	Koku-gan	A
☐ Lesser Tree Duck, Lesser or Indian Whistling Duck	*Dendrocygna javanica*	Ryukyu-gamo	B
☐ Ruddy Shelduck	*Tadorna ferruginea*	Aka-tsukushi-gamo	A
☐ Crested Shelduck	*Tadorna cristata*	Kanmuri-tsukushi-gamo	B
☐ Common Shelduck	*Tadorna tadorna*	Tsukushi-gamo	A
☐ Mandarin Duck	*Aix galericulata*	Oshidori	A
☐ Eurasian Wigeon	*Anas penelope*	Hidori-gamo	A
☐ American Wigeon	*Anas americana*	Amerika-hidori	A
☐ Falcated Teal or Falcated Duck	*Anas falcata*	Yoshi-gamo	A
☐ Gadwall	*Anas strepera*	Okayoshi-gamo	A
☐ Baikal Teal	*Anas formosa*	Tomoe-gamo	A
☐ Common Teal [Green-winged Teal]	*Anas crecca*	Ko-gamo	A
☐ Mallard	*Anas platyrhynchos*	Ma-gamo	A
☐ Spot-billed Duck	*Anas poecilorhyncha*	Karu-gamo	A
☐ Northern or Common Pintail	*Anas acuta*	Onaga-gamo	A
☐ Garganey	*Anas querquedula*	Shimaaji	A

☐ Northern Shoveler	*Anas clypeata*	Hashibiro-gamo	A
☐ Red-crested Pochard	*Netta rufina*	Akahashi-hajiro	A
☐ Canvasback	*Aythya valisineria*	O-hoshi-hajiro	A
☐ Common Pochard	*Aythya ferina*	Hoshi-hajiro	A
☐ Ring-necked Duck	*Aythya collaris*	Kubiwa-kinkuro	A
☐ Baer's Pochard	*Aythya baeri*	Aka-hajiro	A
☐ Ferruginous Duck or White-eyed Pochard	*Aythya nyroca*	Mejiro-gamo	A
☐ Tufted Duck	*Aythya fuligula*	Kinkuro-hajiro	A
☐ Greater Scaup	*Aythya marila*	Suzu-gamo	A
☐ Lesser Scaup	*Aythya affinis*	Ko-suzugamo	A1
☐ King Eider	*Somateria spectabilis*	Kewata-gamo	A
☐ Steller's Eider	*Polysticta stelleri*	Ko-kewata-gamo	A
☐ Harlequin Duck	*Histrionicus histrionicus*	Shinori-gamo	A
☐ Long-tailed Duck or Oldsquaw	*Clangula hyemalis*	Kori-gamo	A
☐ Common or Black Scoter	*Melanitta nigra*	Kuro-gamo	A
☐ Surf Scoter	*Melanitta perspicillata*	Aranami-kinkuro	A
☐ Velvet or White-winged Scoter	*Melanitta fusca*	Birodo-kinkuro	A
☐ Common Goldeneye	*Bucephala clangula*	Hojiro-gamo	A
☐ Bufflehead	*Bucephala albeola*	Hime-hajiro	A
☐ Smew	*Mergus albellus*	Miko-aisa	A
☐ Red-breasted Merganser	*Mergus serrator*	Umi-aisa	A
☐ Chinese or Scaly-sided Merganser	*Mergus squamatus*	Korai-aisa	A1
☐ Goosander or Common Merganser	*Mergus merganser*	Kawa-aisa	A

ACCIPITRIFORMES

ACCIPITRIDAE

☐ Crested Honey Buzzard	*Pernis ptilorhynchus*	Hachikuma	A
☐ Black Kite	*Milvus migrans*	Tobi	A
☐ White-tailed Eagle	*Haliaeetus albicilla*	Ojiro-washi	A
☐ Steller's Sea Eagle	*Haliaeetus pelagicus*	O-washi	A
☐ Cinereous or Eurasian Black Vulture	*Aegypius monachus*	Kuro-hagewashi	A
☐ Crested Serpent Eagle	*Spilornis cheela*	Kanmuri-washi	A
☐ Eastern Marsh Harrier	*Circus spilonotus*	Chuhi	A

☐ Hen or Northern Harrier	*Circus cyaneus*	Haiiro-chuhi	A
☐ Pallid Harrier	*Circus macrourus*	Munajiro-chuhi	A1
☐ Pied Harrier	*Circus melanoleucus*	Madara-chuhi	A
☐ Northern Goshawk	*Accipiter gentilis*	O-taka	A
☐ Japanese (Lesser) Sparrowhawk	*Accipiter gularis*	Tsumi	A
☐ Northern or European Sparrowhawk	*Accipiter nisus*	Hai-taka	A
☐ Chinese Sparrowhawk or Chinese Goshawk	*Accipiter soloensis*	Akahara-daka	A
☐ Gray-faced Buzzard (Eagle)	*Butastur indicus*	Sashiba	A
☐ Common Buzzard	*Buteo buteo*	Nosuri	A
☐ Upland Buzzard	*Buteo hemilasius*	O-nosuri	A
☐ Rough-legged Buzzard or Rough-legged Hawk	*Buteo lagopus*	Keashi-nosuri	A
☐ Greater Spotted Eagle	*Aquila clanga*	Karafuto-washi	A
☐ Imperial Eagle	*Aquila heliaca*	Katashiro-washi	A
☐ Golden Eagle	*Aquila chrysaetos*	Inu-washi	A
☐ Hodgson's or Mountain Hawk Eagle	*Spizaetus nipalensis*	Kuma-taka	A

PANDIONIDAE

☐ Osprey	*Pandion haliaetus*	Misago	A

FALCONIFORMES

FALCONIDAE

☐ Lesser Kestrel	*Falco naumanni*	Hime-chogenbo	A
☐ Eurasian Kestrel	*Falco tinnunculus*	Chogenbo	A
☐ Amur (Red-footed) Falcon	*Falco amurensis*	Akaashi-chogenbo	A
☐ Merlin	*Falco columbarius*	Ko-chogenbo	A
☐ Northern Hobby	*Falco subbuteo*	Chigo-hayabusa	A
☐ Gyrfalcon	*Falco rusticolus*	Shiro-hayabusa	A
☐ Peregrine or Peregrine Falcon	*Falco peregrinus*	Hayabusa	A

GALLIFORMES

TETRAONIDAE

☐ Hazel Grouse	*Bonasa bonasia*	Ezo-raicho	A
☐ Rock Ptarmigan	*Lagopus mutus*	Raicho	A

☐ Japanese Quail [Common Quail]	*Coturnix japonica*	Uzura	A1
☐ Chinese Bamboo Partridge	*Bambusicola thoracica*	Kojukei	C
☐ Copper Pheasant	*Syrmaticus soemmeringii*	Yamadori	A#
☐ Common or Ring-necked Pheasant	*Phasianus colchicus*	Korai-kiji	C
☐ Green Pheasant	*Phasianus versicolor*	Kiji	A1#
☐ Barred Buttonquail	*Turnix suscitator*	Mifu-uzura	A

RALLIDAE

☐ Slaty-legged Crake or Philippine Banded Crake	*Rallina eurizonoides*	O-kuina	A
☐ Water Rail	*Rallus aquaticus*	Kuina	A
☐ Okinawa Rail	*Rallus okinawae*	Yambaru-kuina	A#
☐ Baillon's Crake	*Porzana pusilla*	Hime-kuina	A
☐ Ashy or White-browed Crake	*Porzana cinerea*	Mamijiro-kuina	B
☐ Ruddy or Ruddy-breasted Crake	*Porzana fusca*	Hi-kuina	A
☐ Swinhoe's Yellow Rail	*Coturnicops exquisita*	Shima-kuina	A
☐ White-breasted Waterhen	*Amaurornis phoenicurus*	Shirohara-kuina	A
☐ Common Moorhen or Common Gallinule	*Gallinula chloropus*	Ban	A
☐ Watercock	*Gallicrex cinerea*	Tsuru-kuina	A
☐ Common or Eurasian Coot	*Fulica atra*	O-ban	A

GRUIDAE

☐ Common Crane	*Grus grus*	Kuro-zuru	A
☐ Hooded Crane	*Grus monachus*	Nabe-zuru	A
☐ Sandhill Crane	*Grus canadensis*	Kanada-zuru	A
☐ White-naped Crane	*Grus vipio*	Mana-zuru	A
☐ Japanese or Red-crowned Crane	*Grus japonensis*	Tancho	A
☐ Siberian White Crane	*Grus leucogeranus*	Sodeguro-zuru	A
☐ Demoiselle Crane	*Anthropoides virgo*	Aneha-zuru	A

OTIDAE

☐ Little Bustard	*Tetrax tetrax*	Hime-nogan	A
☐ Great Bustard	*Otis tarda*	Nogan	A

CHARADRIIFORMES

JACANIDAE
| ☐ Pheasant-tailed Jacana | *Hydrophasianus chirurgus* | Renkaku | A |

ROSTRATULIDAE
| ☐ Greater Painted Snipe | *Rostratula benghalensis* | Tama-shigi | A |

HAEMATOPIDAE
| ☐ Common Oyster-catcher | *Haematopus ostralegus* | Miyakodori | A |

RECURVIROSTRIDAE
| ☐ Black-winged Stilt | *Himantopus himantopus* | Seitaka-shigi | A |
| ☐ Pied Avocet | *Recurvirostra avosetta* | Sorihashi-seitaka-shigi | A |

GLAREOLIDAE
| ☐ Oriental or Indian Pratincole | *Glareola maldivarum* | Tsubame-chidori | A |

CHARADRIIDAE
☐ Little Ringed Plover	*Charadrius dubius*	Ko-chidori	A
☐ Common Ringed Plover	*Charadrius hiaticula*	Hajiro-ko-chidori	A
☐ Long-billed (Ringed) Plover	*Charadrius placidus*	Ikaru-chidori	A
☐ Kentish or Snowy Plover	*Charadrius alexandrinus*	Shiro-chidori	A
☐ Mongolian Plover or Lesser Sand Plover	*Charadrius mongolus*	Medai-chidori	A
☐ Large or Greater Sand Plover	*Charadrius leschenaultii*	O-medai-chidori	A
☐ Oriental Plover [Caspian Plover]	*Charadrius veredus*	O-chidori	A
☐ Eurasian Dotterel	*Charadrius morinellus*	Kobashi-chidori	A
☐ Pacific Golden Plover	*Pluvialis fulva*	Munaguro	A
☐ Gray or Black-bellied Plover	*Pluvialis squatarola*	Daizen	A
☐ Gray-headed Lapwing	*Microsarcops cinereus*	Keri	A
☐ Northern Lapwing	*Vanellus vanellus*	Tageri	A
☐ Great Knot	*Calidris tenuirostris*	Oba-shigi	A
☐ Red Knot	*Calidris canutus*	Ko-oba-shigi	A
☐ Sanderling	*Calidris alba*	Miyubi-shigi	A
☐ Western Sandpiper	*Calidris mauri*	Hime-hama-shigi	A
☐ Red-necked Stint or Rufous-necked Sand-piper	*Calidris ruficollis*	Tonen	A
☐ Little Stint	*Calidris minuta*	Yoroppa-tonen	A
☐ Temminck's Stint	*Calidris temminckii*	Ojiro-tonen	A

☐ Long-toed Stint	*Calidris subminuta*	Hibari-shigi	A
☐ Least Sandpiper	*Calidris minutilla*	Amerika-hibari-shigi	A
☐ Baird's Sandpiper	*Calidris bairdii*	Hime-uzura-shigi	A
☐ Pectoral Sandpiper	*Calidris melanotos*	Amerika-uzura-shigi	A
☐ Sharp-tailed Sand-piper	*Calidris acuminata*	Uzura-shigi	A
☐ Curlew Sandpiper	*Calidris ferruginea*	Saruhama-shigi	A
☐ Rock Sandpiper	*Calidris ptilocnemis*	Chishima-shigi	A
☐ Dunlin	*Calidris alpina*	Hama-shigi	A
☐ Spoon-billed Sand-piper	*Eurynorhynchos pygmeus*	Hera-shigi	A
☐ Broad-billed Sand-piper	*Limicola falcinellus*	Kiriai	A
☐ Stilt Sandpiper	*Micropalama himantopus*	Ashinaga-shigi	A
☐ Buff-breasted Sand-piper	*Tryngites subruficollis*	Komon-shigi	A
☐ Ruff	*Philomachus pugnax*	Erimaki-shigi	A
(GALLINAGININAE)			
☐ Jack Snipe	*Lymnocryptes minimus*	Ko-shigi	A
☐ Common Snipe	*Gallinago gallinago*	Ta-shigi	A
☐ Pintail Snipe	*Gallinago stenura*	Hario-shigi	A
☐ Swinhoe's Snipe	*Gallinago megala*	Chuji-shigi	A
☐ Latham's or Japanese Snipe	*Gallinago hardwickii*	Oji-shigi	A#
☐ Solitary Snipe	*Gallinago solitaria*	Ao-shigi	A
☐ Short-billed Dowitcher	*Limnodromus griseus*	Amerika-ohashi-shigi	A1
☐ Long-billed Dowitcher	*Limnodromus scolopaceus*	Ohashi-shigi	A
☐ Asian or Asiatic Dowitcher	*Limnodromus semipalmatus*	Shiberia-ohashi-shigi	A
(SCOLOPACINAE)			
☐ Eurasian Woodcock	*Scolopax rusticola*	Yama-shigi	A
☐ Amami Woodcock	*Scolopax mira*	Amami-yama-shigi	A#
(TRINGINAE)			
☐ Black-tailed Godwit	*Limosa limosa*	Oguro-shigi	A
☐ Bar-tailed Godwit	*Limosa lapponica*	O-sorihashi-shigi	A
☐ Little Curlew or Little Whimbrel	*Numenius minutus*	Koshaku-shigi	A
☐ Whimbrel	*Numenius phaeopus*	Chushaku-shigi	A
☐ Bristle-thighed Curlew	*Numenius tahitiensis*	Harimomo-chushaku	A
☐ Slender-billed Curlew	*Numenius tenuirostris*	Shirohara-chushaku-shigi	B

☐ Eurasian Curlew	*Numenius arquata*	Daishaku-shigi	A
☐ Eastern, Far Eastern or Australian Curlew	*Numenius madagascariensis*	Horoku-shigi	A
☐ Spotted Redshank	*Tringa erythropus*	Tsuru-shigi	A
☐ Common Redshank	*Tringa totanus*	Akaashi-shigi	A
☐ Marsh Sandpiper	*Tringa stagnatilis*	Ko-aoashi-shigi	A
☐ Common Greenshank	*Tringa nebularia*	Aoashi-shigi	A
☐ Nordmann's or Spotted Greenshank	*Tringa guttifer*	Karafuto-aoashi-shigi	A
☐ Greater Yellowlegs	*Tringa melanoleuca*	O-kiashi-shigi	A
☐ Lesser Yellowlegs	*Tringa flavipes*	Ko-kiashi-shigi	A
☐ Green Sandpiper	*Tringa ochropus*	Kusa-shigi	A
☐ Wood Sandpiper	*Tringa glareola*	Takabu-shigi	A
☐ Terek Sandpiper	*Xenus cinereus*	Sorihashi-shigi	A
☐ Common Sandpiper	*Actitis hypoleucos*	Iso-shigi	A
☐ Gray-tailed or Polynesian Tattler	*Heteroscelus brevipes*	Kiashi-shigi	A
☐ Wandering Tattler	*Heteroscelus incana*	Meriken-kiashi-shigi	A

(ARENARIINAE)

☐ Ruddy Turnstone	*Arenaria interpres*	Kyojo-shigi	A

(PHALAROPODINAE)

☐ Wilson's Phalarope	*Phalaropus tricolor*	Amerika-hireashi-shigi	A1
☐ Red-necked or Northern Phalarope	*Phalaropus lobatus*	Akaeri-hireashi-shigi	A
☐ Gray or Red Phalarope	*Phalaropus fulicarius*	Haiiro-hireashi-shigi	A

STERCORARIIDAE

☐ Pomarine Skua or Pomarine Jaeger	*Stercorarius pomarinus*	Tozokukamome	A
☐ Arctic Skua or Parasitic Jaeger	*Stercorarius parasiticus*	Kuro-tozokukamome	A
☐ Long-tailed Skua or Long-tailed Jaeger	*Stercorarius longicaudus*	Shirohara-tozokukamome	A
☐ South Polar Skua [Great Skua]	*Stercorarius maccormicki*	O-tozokukamome	A

LARIDAE

☐ Great Black-headed Gull	*Larus ichthyaetus*	O-zuguro-kamome	A
☐ Franklin's Gull	*Larus pipixcan*	Amerika-zuguro-kamome	A1
☐ Little Gull	*Larus minutus*	Hime-kamome	A
☐ Sabine's Gull	*Larus sabini*	Kubiwa-kamome	A
☐ Saunders's Gull	*Larus saundersi*	Zuguro-kamome	A

☐ Common Black-headed Gull	*Larus ridibundus*	Yuri-kamome	A
☐ Slender-billed Gull	*Larus genei*	Hashiboso-kamome	A1
☐ Bonaparte's Gull	*Larus philadelphia*	Bonaparuto-kamome	A1
☐ Black-tailed Gull	*Larus crassirostris*	Umineko	A
☐ Ring-billed Gull	*Larus delawarensis*	Kurowa-kamome	A1
☐ Common or Mew Gull	*Larus canus*	Kamome	A
☐ Herring Gull	*Larus argentatus*	Seguro-kamome	A
☐ Slaty-backed Gull	*Larus schistisagus*	O-seguro-kamome	A
☐ Glaucous-winged Gull	*Larus glaucescens*	Washi-kamome	A
☐ Glaucous Gull	*Larus hyperboreus*	Shiro-kamome	A
☐ Iceland Gull	*Larus glaucoides*	Aisurando-kamome	A1
☐ Ross's Gull	*Rhodostethia rosea*	Hime-kubiwa-kamome	A
☐ Black-legged Kittiwake	*Rissa tridactyla*	Mitsuyubi-kamome	A
☐ Red-legged Kittiwake	*Rissa brevirostris*	Akaashi-mitsuyubi-kamome	A
☐ Ivory Gull	*Pagophila eburnea*	Zoge-kamome	A

STERNIDAE

☐ Gull-billed Tern	*Gelochelidon nilotica*	Hashibuto-ajisashi	A
☐ Caspian Tern	*Sterna caspia*	Oni-ajisashi	A
☐ Greater Crested Tern	*Sterna bergii*	O-ajisashi	A
☐ Black-naped Tern	*Sterna sumatrana*	Eriguro-ajisashi	A
☐ Roseate Tern	*Sterna dougallii*	Beni-ajisashi	A
☐ Common Tern	*Sterna hirundo*	Ajisashi	A
☐ Aleutian Tern	*Sterna aleutica*	Koshijiro-ajisashi	A
☐ Spectacled or Gray-backed Tern	*Sterna lunata*	Nanyo-mamijiro-ajisashi	A
☐ Bridled Tern	*Sterna anaethetus*	Mamijiro-ajisashi	A
☐ Sooty Tern	*Sterna fuscata*	Seguro-ajisashi	A
☐ Little Tern	*Sterna albifrons*	Ko-ajisashi	A
☐ Whiskered Tern	*Chlidonias hybridus*	Kurohara-ajisashi	A
☐ Black Tern	*Chlidonias niger*	Hashiguro-kurohara-ajisashi	A
☐ White-winged (Black) Tern	*Chlidonias leucopterus*	Hajiro-kurohara-ajisashi	A
☐ Blue or Blue-gray Noddy	*Procelsterna ceruleus*	Haiiro-ajisashi	B
☐ Black or White-capped Noddy	*Anous tenuirostris*	Hime-kuro-ajisashi	A
☐ Brown or Common Noddy	*Anous stolidus*	Kuro-ajisashi	A
☐ Fairy Tern or White Noddy	*Gygis alba*	Shiro-ajisashi	A

ALCIDIAE

☐ Common Guillemot, Common or Thin-billed Murre	*Uria aalge*	Umigarasu	A
☐ Brunnich's Guillemot or Thick-billed Murre	*Uria lomvia*	Hashibuto-umigarasu	A
☐ Pigeon Guillemot	*Cepphus columba*	Umibato	A
☐ Spectacled Guillemot	*Cepphus carbo*	Keimafuri	A
☐ Marbled Murrelet	*Brachyramphus marmoratus*	Madara-umisuzume	A
☐ Ancient Murrelet	*Synthliboramphus antiquus*	Umisuzume	A
☐ Japanese Murrelet	*Synthliboramphus wumizusume*	Kanmuri-umisuzume	A
☐ Crested Auklet	*Aethia cristatella*	Etorofu-umisuzume	A
☐ Whiskered Auklet	*Aethia pygmaea*	Shirahige-umisuzume	A
☐ Least Auklet	*Aethia pusilla*	Ko-umisuzume	A
☐ Parakeet Auklet	*Aethia psittacula*	Umiomu	A
☐ Rhinoceros Auklet	*Cerorhinca monocerata*	Utou	A
☐ Horned Puffin	*Fratercula corniculata*	Tsunomedori	A
☐ Tufted Puffin	*Lunda cirrhata*	Etopirika	A

PTEROCLIDAE

☐ Pallas's Sandgrouse	*Syrrhaptes paradoxus*	Sakei	A

COLUMBIFORMES

COLUMBIDAE

☐ Rock Dove or Feral Pigeon	*Columba livia*	Dobato	C
☐ Stock Dove	*Columba oenas*	Hime-mori-bato	A1
☐ Japanese Wood-pigeon	*Columba janthina*	Karasu-bato	A
[Bonin Woodpigeon	*Columba versicolor*	Ogasawara-karasu-bato	B#]
[Ryukyu Woodpigeon	*Columba jouyi*	Ryukyu-karasu-bato	B#]
☐ Collared Dove	*Streptopelia decaocto*	Shirako-bato	C
☐ Red Turtle Dove	*Streptopelia tranquebarica*	Beni-bato	A
☐ Rufous or Oriental Turtle Dove	*Streptopelia orientalis*	Kiji-bato	A
☐ Emerald Dove	*Chalcophaps indica*	Kin-bato	A
☐ Japanese Green or White-bellied Pigeon	*Treron sieboldii*	Ao-bato	A
☐ Red-capped, For-mosan or Whistling Green Pigeon	*Treron formosae*	Zuaka-ao-bato	A

CUCULIDAE

☐ Hodgson's or (Horsfield's) Hawk Cuckoo	*Cuculus fugax*	Juichi	A
☐ Indian Cuckoo	*Cuculus micropterus*	Seguro-kakko	A
☐ Common Cuckoo	*Cuculus canorus*	Kakko	A
☐ Oriental Cuckoo	*Cuculus saturatus*	Tsutsudori	A
☐ Little Cuckoo	*Cuculus poliocephalus*	Hototogisu	A
☐ Chestnut-winged Cuckoo	*Clamator coromandus*	Kanmuri-kakko	A

STRIGIFORMES

STRIGIDAE

☐ Collared Scops Owl	*Otus bakkamoena*	O-konoha-zuku	A
☐ Oriental Scops Owl [Scops Owl]	*Otus sunia*	Konoha-zuku	A1
☐ Ryukyu Scops Owl [Scops Owl]	*Otus elegans*	Ryukyu-konoha-zuku	A1
☐ Northern Eagle Owl	*Bubo bubo*	Washi-mimizuku	A
☐ Blakiston's Fish Owl	*Ketupa blakistoni*	Shima-fukuro	A
☐ Snowy Owl	*Nyctea scandiaca*	Shiro-fukuro	A
☐ Brown Hawk Owl	*Ninox scutulata*	Aoba-zuku	A
☐ Ural Owl	*Strix uralensis*	Fukuro	A
☐ Long-eared Owl	*Asio otus*	Torafu-zuku	A
☐ Short-eared Owl	*Asio flammeus*	Komimi-zuku	A
☐ Tengmalm's or Boreal Owl	*Aegolius funereus*	Kinme-fukuro	A
☐ Grass Owl	*Tyto capensis*	Minami-menfukuro	A

CAPRIMULGIFORMES

CAPRIMULGIDAE

☐ Jungle or Gray Nightjar	*Caprimulgus indicus*	Yotaka	A

APODIFORMES

APODIDAE

☐ White-throated Needletail	*Hirundapus caudacutus*	Hario-amatsubame	A
☐ Fork-tailed, White-rumped or Pacific Swift	*Apus pacificus*	Amatsubame	A
☐ Little or House Swift	*Apus affinis*	Hime-amatsubame	A

CORACIIFORMES

ALCEDINIDAE
☐ Ruddy Kingfisher	*Halcyon coromanda*	Aka-shobin	A
☐ Black-capped Kingfisher	*Halcyon pileata*	Yama-shobin	A
☐ Collared Kingfisher	*Halcyon chloris*	Nanyo-shobin	A
[Miyako Kingfisher	*Halcyon miyakoensis*	Miyako-shobin	B#]
☐ Common Kingfisher	*Alcedo atthis*	Kawasemi	A
☐ Crested or Greater Pied Kingfisher	*Ceryle lugubris*	Yamasemi	A

MEROPIDAE
☐ Rainbow or Australian Bee-eater	*Merops ornatus*	Hachikui	B

CORACIIDAE
☐ Dollarbird	*Eurystomus orientalis*	Bupposo	A

UPUPIDAE
☐ Hoopoe	*Upupa epops*	Yatsugashira	A

PICIFORMES

PICIDAE
☐ Eurasian Wryneck	*Jynx torquilla*	Arisui	A
☐ Gray-headed Woodpecker	*Picus canus*	Yama-gera	A
☐ Japanese Green Woodpecker	*Picus awokera*	Ao-gera	A#
☐ Pryer's Woodpecker	*Sapheopipo noguchii*	Noguchi-gera	A#
☐ Black Woodpecker	*Dryocopus martius*	Kuma-gera	A
☐ White-bellied (Black) Woodpecker	*Dryocopus javensis*	Kitataki	B
☐ Great Spotted Woodpecker	*Dendrocopos major*	Aka-gera	A
☐ White-backed Woodpecker	*Dendrocopos leucotos*	O-aka-gera	A
☐ Lesser Spotted Woodpecker	*Dendrocopos minor*	Ko-aka-gera	A
☐ Japanese Pygmy Woodpecker	*Dendrocopos kizuki*	Ko-gera	A
☐ Three-toed Woodpecker	*Picoides tridactylus*	Miyubi-gera	A

PASSERIFORMES

PITTIDAE
☐ Hooded Pitta	*Pitta sordida*	Zuguro-yairocho	A1
☐ Fairy Pitta	*Pitta nympha*	Yairocho	A

ALAUDIDAE

☐ Bimaculated Lark	*Melanocorypha bimaculata*	Kubiwa-kotenshi	A
☐ Greater Short-toed Lark	*Calandrella cinerea*	Hime-kotenshi	A
☐ Lesser Short-toed Lark	*Calandrella rufescens*	Ko-hibari	A
☐ Common or Eurasian Skylark	*Alauda arvensis*	Hibari	A
☐ Shore or Horned Lark	*Eremophila alpestris*	Hama-hibari	A

HIRUNDINIDAE

☐ Sand Martin or Bank Swallow	*Riparia riparia*	Shodo-tsubame	A
☐ Barn Swallow	*Hirundo rustica*	Tsubame	A
☐ Pacific Swallow	*Hirundo tahitica*	Ryukyu-tsubame	A
☐ Red-rumped Swallow	*Hirundo daurica*	Koshiaka-tsubame	A
☐ Common House Martin	*Delichon urbica*	Iwa-tsubame	A

MOTACILLIDAE

☐ Richard's Pipit	*Anthus novaeseelandiae*	Mamijiro-tahibari	A
☐ Blyth's Pipit	*Anthus godlewskii*	Ko-mamijiro-tahibari	A
☐ Olive-backed Pipit or Olive Tree Pipit	*Anthus hodgsoni*	Binzui	A
☐ Tree Pipit	*Anthus trivialis*	Yoroppa-binzui	A
☐ Pechora Pipit	*Anthus gustavi*	Sejiro-tahibari	A
☐ Red-throated Pipit	*Anthus cervinus*	Muneaka-tahibari	A
☐ Water Pipit	*Anthus spinoletta*	Tahibari	A
☐ Forest Wagtail	*Dendronanthus indicus*	Iwami-sekirei	A
☐ Yellow Wagtail	*Motacilla flava*	Tsumenaga-sekirei	A
☐ Citrine or Yellow-hooded Wagtail	*Motacilla citreola*	Kigashira-sekirei	A
☐ Gray Wagtail	*Motacilla cinerea*	Ki-sekirei	A
☐ White Wagtail	*Motacilla alba*	Hojiro or Taiwan-haku-sekirei	A
☐ Black-backed Wagtail [White Wagtail]	*Motacilla lugens*	Haku-sekirei	A1
☐ Japanese Wagtail	*Motacilla grandis*	Seguro-sekirei	A#

CAMPEPHAGIDAE

☐ Ashy Minivet	*Pericrocotus divaricatus*	Sanshokui	A
☐ Ryukyu Minivet [Ashy Minivet]	*Pericrocotus tegimae*	Ryukyu-sanshokui	A1#
☐ Black-winged Cuckoo Shrike	*Coracina melaschista*	Asakura-sanshokui	A

PYCNONOTIDAE

☐ Chinese or Light-vented Bulbul	*Pycnonotus sinensis*	Shirogashira	A
☐ Brown-eared Bulbul	*Hypsipetes amaurotis*	Hiyodori	A

BOMBYCILLIDAE

☐ Japanese Waxwing	*Bombycilla japonica*	Hi-renjaku	A
☐ Bohemian Waxwing	*Bombycilla garrulus*	Ki-renjaku	A

CINCLIDAE

☐ Brown Dipper	*Cinclus pallasii*	Kawagarasu	A

TROGLODYTIDAE

☐ Northern or Winter Wren	*Troglodytes troglodytes*	Misosazai	A

PRUNELLIDAE

☐ Japanese Accentor	*Prunella rubida*	Kayakuguri	A#
☐ Siberian Accentor	*Prunella montanella*	Yama-hibari	A
☐ Alpine Accentor	*Prunella collaris*	Iwa-hibari	A

TURDIDAE (TURDINAE)

☐ Japanese Robin	*Erithacus akahige*	Komadori	A
☐ Ryukyu Robin	*Erithacus komadori*	Akahige	A#
☐ Rufous-tailed or Swinhoe's Red-tailed Robin	*Luscinia sibilans*	Shima-goma	A
☐ Siberian Rubythroat	*Luscinia calliope*	No-goma	A
☐ Bluethroat	*Luscinia svecica*	Ogawa-komadori	A
☐ Siberian Blue Robin	*Luscinia cyane*	Ko-ruri	A
☐ Red-flanked Bluetail, Siberian Bluechat or Orange-flanked Bush Robin	*Tarsiger cyanurus*	Ruri-bitaki	A
☐ Black Redstart	*Phoenicurus ochruros*	Kuro-jo-bitaki	A1
☐ Daurian Redstart	*Phoenicurus auroreus*	Jo-bitaki	A
☐ Stonechat	*Saxicola torquata*	No-bitaki	A
☐ Gray Bushchat	*Saxicola ferrea*	Yamazaki-hitaki	A
☐ Isabelline Wheatear	*Oenanthe isabellina*	Inaba-hitaki	B
☐ Northern or Common Wheatear	*Oenanthe oenanthe*	Hashiguro-hitaki	A
☐ Pied Wheatear	*Oenanthe pleschanka*	Seguro-sabaku-hitaki	A
☐ Desert Wheatear	*Oenanthe deserti*	Sabaku-hitaki	A
☐ Common Rock Thrush	*Monticola saxatilis*	Koshijiro-isohiyo	A1
☐ Blue Rock Thrush	*Monticola solitarius*	Iso-hiyodori	A
☐ White-throated or White-breasted Rock Thrush	*Monticola gularis*	Hime-isohiyo	A

☐ White's or Tiger Thrush	*Zoothera dauma*	Tora-tsugumi	A
☐ Amami Thrush	*Zoothera amami*	O-tora-tsugumi	A1#
☐ Siberian Thrush	*Zoothera sibirica*	Mamijiro	A
[Kittlitz's or Bonin Islands Thrush	*Cichlopasser terrestris*	Ogasawara-gabicho	B#]
☐ Gray or Japanese Thrush	*Turdus cardis*	Kuro-tsugumi	A
☐ Common Blackbird	*Turdus merula*	Kuro-utadori	A
☐ Brown or Brown-headed Thrush	*Turdus chrysolaus*	Akahara	A
☐ Izu Islands or Seven Islands Thrush	*Turdus celaenops*	Akakokko	A#
☐ Gray-backed Thrush	*Turdus hortulorum*	Kara-akahara	A
☐ Pale Thrush	*Turdus pallidus*	Shirohara	A
☐ Eye-browed or Gray-headed Thrush	*Turdus obscurus*	Mamichajinai	A
☐ Dusky Thrush	*Turdus naumanni*	Tsugumi	A
☐ Dark-throated or Black-throated Thrush	*Turdus ruficollis*	Nodoguro-tsugumi	A
☐ Fieldfare	*Turdus pilaris*	Nohara-tsugumi	A
☐ Redwing	*Turdus iliacus*	Wakiaka-tsugumi	A
☐ Mistle Thrush	*Turdus viscivorus*	Yadorigi-tsugumi	A1

SYLVIIDAE (SYLVIINAE)

☐ Stub-tailed or Short-tailed Bush Warbler	*Cettia squameiceps*	Yabusame	A
☐ Japanese Bush Warbler	*Cettia diphone*	Uguisu	A
☐ Fan-tailed Warbler or Zitting Cisticola	*Cisticola juncidis*	Sekka	A
☐ Pallas's (Grasshopper) Warbler	*Locustella certhiola*	Shiberia-sennyu	A1
☐ Middendorff's (Grasshopper) Warbler	*Locustella ochotensis*	Shima-sennyu	A
☐ Lanceolated (Grasshopper) Warbler	*Locustella lanceolata*	Makino-sennyu	A
☐ Gray's Grasshopper Warbler	*Locustella fasciolata*	Ezo-sennyu	A
☐ Japanese Marsh Warbler	*Megalurus pryeri*	O-sekka	A
☐ Black-browed Reed Warbler	*Acrocephalus bistrigiceps*	Ko-yoshikiri	A

☐ Oriental (Great) Reed Warbler	*Acrocephalus orientalis*	O-yoshikiri	A
☐ Thick-billed (Reed) Warbler	*Acrocephalus aedon*	Hashibuto-o-yoshikiri	B
☐ Eastern Crowned Warbler [Crowned Willow Warbler]	*Phylloscopus coronatus*	Sendai-mushikui	A
☐ Pale-legged (Leaf) Warbler	*Phylloscopus tenellipes*	Ezo-mushikui	A
☐ Ijima's Warbler	*Phylloscopus ijimae*	Ijima-mushikui	A#
☐ Arctic Warbler	*Phylloscopus borealis*	Meboso-mushikui	A
☐ Pallas's (Leaf) or Lemon-rumped Warbler	*Phylloscopus proregulus*	Karafuto-mushikui	A
☐ Yellow-browed or Inornate Warbler	*Phylloscopus inornatus*	Kimayu-mushikui	A
☐ Dusky Warbler	*Phylloscopus fuscatus*	Muji-sekka	A1
☐ Wood Warbler	*Phylloscopus sibilatrix*	Mori-mushikui	A1
☐ Willow Warbler	*Phylloscopus trochilus*	Kita-yanagi-mushikui	A1
☐ Goldcrest	*Regulus regulus*	Kikuitadaki	A

MUSCICAPIDAE

☐ Blue-and-White Flycatcher	*Cyanoptila cyanomelana*	O-ruri	A
☐ Ferruginous Flycatcher	*Muscicapa ferruginea*	Miyama-bitaki	A
☐ Sooty or Dark-sided Flycatcher	*Muscicapa sibirica*	Same-bitaki	A
☐ Gray-streaked Flycatcher	*Muscicapa griseisticta*	Ezo-bitaki	A
☐ Asian Brown Flycatcher	*Muscicapa latirostris*	Ko-same-bitaki	A
☐ Red-breasted or Red-throated Flycatcher	*Muscicapa parva*	Ojiro-bitaki	A
☐ Mugimaki Flycatcher	*Ficedula mugimaki*	Mugimaki	A
☐ Tricolored or Yellow-rumped Flycatcher	*Ficedula zanthopygia*	Mamijiro-ki-bitaki	A
☐ Narcissus Flycatcher	*Ficedula narcissina*	Ki-bitaki	A

MONARCHIDAE

☐ Japanese or Black Paradise Flycatcher	*Terpsiphone atrocaudata*	Sankocho	A

TIMALIIDAE

☐ Bearded Tit	*Panurus biarmicus*	Hige-gara	A
☐ Webb's or Vinous-throated Parrotbill	*Paradoxornis webbianus*	Daruma-enaga	A1

AEGITHALIDAE

☐ Long-tailed Tit	*Aegithalos caudatus*	Enaga	A

PARIDAE
☐ Marsh Tit	*Parus palustris*	Hashibuto-gara	A
☐ Willow Tit	*Parus montanus*	Ko-gara	A
☐ Varied Tit	*Parus varius*	Yama-gara	A
☐ Coal Tit	*Parus ater*	Hi-gara	A
☐ Great Tit	*Parus major*	Shiju-kara	A

SITTIDAE
☐ Eurasian Nuthatch	*Sitta europaea*	Goju-kara	A

CERTHIDAE
☐ Common Treecreeper [Brown Creeper]	*Certhia familiaris*	Kibashiri	A

REMIZIDAE
☐ Penduline Tit	*Remiz pendulinus*	Tsurisu-gara	A

ZOSTEROPIDAE
☐ Chestnut-flanked White-eye	*Zosterops erythropleura*	Chosen-mejiro	A
☐ Japanese White-eye	*Zosterops japonica*	Mejiro	A

MELIPHAGIDAE
☐ Bonin Islands Honeyeater	*Apalapteron familiare*	Meguro	A#

DICRURIDAE
☐ Black Drongo	*Dicrurus macrocercus*	Ochu	A

ORIOLIDAE
☐ Black-naped Oriole	*Oriolus chinensis*	Korai-uguisu	A

ARTAMIDAE
☐ White-breasted Wood Swallow	*Artamus leucorhynchus*	Mori-tsubame	A

LANIIDAE
☐ Tiger or Thick-billed Shrike	*Lanius tigrinus*	Chigo-mozu	A
☐ Bull-headed Shrike	*Lanius bucephalus*	Mozu	A
☐ Brown Shrike	*Lanius cristatus*	Aka-mozu	A
☐ Long-tailed or Rufous-backed Shrike	*Lanius schach*	Takasago-mozu	A1
☐ Great Gray or Northern Shrike	*Lanius excubitor*	O-mozu	A
☐ Chinese (Great) Gray Shrike	*Lanius sphenocercus*	O-kara-mozu	A

CORVIDAE
☐ Eurasian Jay	*Garrulus glandarius*	Kakesu	A
☐ Lidth's Jay	*Garrulus lidthi*	Ruri-kakesu	A#
☐ Azure-winged Magpie	*Cyanopica cyana*	Onaga	A
☐ Black-billed Magpie	*Pica pica*	Kasasagi	C
☐ Eurasian Nutcracker	*Nucifraga caryocatactes*	Hoshi-garasu	A

☐ Common Jackdaw	*Corvus monedula*	Nishi-kokumaru-garasu	A1
☐ Daurian Jackdaw	*Corvus dauricus*	Kokumaru-garasu	A1
☐ Rook	*Corvus frugilegus*	Miyama-garasu	A
☐ Carrion Crow	*Corvus corone*	Hashiboso-garasu	A
☐ Jungle or Large-billed Crow	*Corvus macrorhynchos*	Hashibuto-garasu	A
☐ Northern Raven	*Corvus corax*	Watari-garasu	A

STURNIDAE

☐ Silky or Red-billed Starling	*Sturnus sericeus*	Gin-mukudori	A
☐ Daurian Starling or Myna, or Purple-backed Starling	*Sturnus sturninus*	Shiberia-mukudori	A
☐ Red-cheeked Starling or Myna, or Chestnut-cheeked Starling	*Sturnus philippensis*	Ko-mukudori	A#
☐ Chinese or White-shouldered Starling, or Gray-backed Myna	*Sturnus sinensis*	Kara-mukudori	A
☐ Common Starling	*Sturnus vulgaris*	Hoshi-mukudori	A
☐ Gray or White-cheeked Starling	*Sturnus cineraceus*	Mukudori	A
☐ Crested Myna	*Acridotheres cristatellus*	Hakkacho	A/C

PASSERIDAE

| ☐ Russet Sparrow | *Passer rutilans* | Nyunai-suzume | A |
| ☐ Eurasian Tree Sparrow | *Passer montanus* | Suzume | A |

FRINGILLIDAE

☐ Brambling	*Fringilla montifringilla*	Atori	A
☐ Oriental or Gray-capped Greenfinch	*Carduelis sinica*	Kawara-hiwa	A
☐ Eurasian Siskin	*Carduelis spinus*	Ma-hiwa	A
☐ Common Redpoll	*Carduelis flammea*	Beni-hiwa	A
☐ Arctic or Hoary Redpoll	*Carduelis hornemanni*	Ko-beni-hiwa	A
☐ Two-barred or White-winged Crossbill	*Loxia leucoptera*	Naki-isuka	A
☐ Red Crossbill	*Loxia curvirostra*	Isuka	A
☐ Rosy Finch	*Leucosticte arctoa*	Hagi-mashiko	A
☐ Common Rosefinch	*Carpodacus erythrinus*	Aka-mashiko	A
☐ Pallas's Rosefinch	*Carpodacus roseus*	O-mashiko	A
☐ Pine Grosbeak	*Pinicola enucleator*	Ginzan-mashiko	A
[Bonin Islands Grosbeak	*Chaunoproctus ferreorostris*	Ogasawara-mashiko	B#]

☐ Long-tailed Rosefinch	*Uragus sibiricus*	Beni-mashiko	A
☐ Common or Eurasian Bullfinch	*Pyrrhula pyrrhula*	Uso	A
☐ Chinese or Yellow-billed Grosbeak	*Eophona migratoria*	Ku-ikaru	A
☐ Japanese Grosbeak	*Eophona personata*	Ikaru	A
☐ Hawfinch	*Coccothraustes coccothraustes*	Shime	A

EMBERIZIDAE (EMBERIZINAE)

☐ Savannah Sparrow	*Ammodramus sand-wichensis*	Sabanna-shitodo	A
☐ Fox Sparrow	*Zonotrichia iliaca*	Gomafu-suzume	A
☐ White-crowned Sparrow	*Zonotrichia leucophrys*	Miyama-shitodo	A
☐ Golden-crowned Sparrow	*Zonotrichia atricapilla*	Kigashira-shitodo	A
☐ Lapland Bunting or Lapland Longspur	*Calcarius lapponicus*	Tsumenaga-hojiro	A
☐ Snow Bunting	*Plectrophenax nivalis*	Yuki-hojiro	A
☐ Gray Bunting	*Emberiza variabilis*	Kuroji	A
☐ Black-faced Bunting	*Emberiza spodocephala*	Aoji	A
☐ Japanese Yellow Bunting	*Emberiza sulphurata*	Nojiko	A#
☐ Pine Bunting	*Emberiza leucocephala*	Shiraga-hojiro	A
☐ Yellowhammer	*Emberiza citrinella*	Ki-aoji	A
☐ Meadow or Siberian Meadow Bunting	*Emberiza cioides*	Hojiro	A
☐ Gray-headed or Chestnut-eared Bunting	*Emberiza fucata*	Hoaka	A
☐ Yellow-throated Bunting	*Emberiza elegans*	Miyama-hojiro	A
☐ Yellow-browed Bunting	*Emberiza chrysophrys*	Kimayu-hojiro	A
☐ Tristram's Bunting	*Emberiza tristrami*	Shirohara-hojiro	A
☐ Rustic Bunting	*Emberiza rustica*	Kashiradaka	A
☐ Little Bunting	*Emberiza pusilla*	Ko-hoaka	A
☐ Chestnut Bunting	*Emberiza rutila*	Shima-nojiko	A
☐ Yellow-breasted Bunting	*Emberiza aureola*	Shima-aoji	A
☐ Ortolan Bunting	*Emberiza hortulana*	Zuao-hojiro	A1
☐ Common Reed Bunting	*Emberiza schoeniclus*	O-jurin	A
☐ Pallas's Reed Bunting	*Emberiza pallasi*	Shiberia-jurin	A

☐ Japanese Reed Bunting	*Emberiza yessoensis*	Ko-jurin	A
☐ Black-headed Bunting	*Emberiza melanocephala*	Zuguro-chakincho	A

Appendix 1.

Feral species and those with populations maintained by regular re-introductions or escapees.

☐ Budgerigar	*Melopsittacus undulatus*	Sekisei-inko	C/D
☐ Ring-necked or Rose-ringed Parakeet	*Psittacula krameri*	Wakake-honsei-inko	C
☐ Red Avadavat	*Amandava amandava*	Beni-suzume	C
☐ White-rumped Munia	*Lonchura striata*	Koshijiro-kinpara	A/C
☐ Scaly-breasted Munia	*Lonchura punctulata*	Amihara	C
☐ Chestnut Munia	*Lonchura malacca*	Kinpara/Ginpara	C/D
☐ White-headed Munia	*Lonchura maja*	Hekicho	C
☐ Java Sparrow	*Padda oryzivora*	Buncho	C
☐ Yellow-crowned Bishop	*Euplectes afer*	Ogoncho	C
☐ Bank Myna	*Acridotheres ginginianus*	Kihohohakka	C

Appendix 2.

Category E. Exotic escapees some of which have bred.
E1. Escapees that could feasibly reach Japan as wild birds and thus may eventually be included in category A.
E2. Escapees that are extremely unlikely ever to reach Japan as wild birds.

☐ Eurasian White Pelican	*Pelecanus onocrotalus*	Momo-iro-perikan	E1
☐ Northern Bobwhite	*Colinus virginianus*	Korin-uzura	E2
☐ Reeve's Pheasant	*Syrmaticus reevesii*	Onaga-kiji	E2
☐ Barbary Dove or Ringed Turtle Dove	*Streptopelia roseogrisea*	Juzukake-bato	E2
☐ Zebra Dove	*Geopelia striata*	Choshyo-bato	E2
☐ Black-chinned Fruit Dove	*Ptilinopus leclancheri*	Nodoguro-hime-aobato	E2
☐ Alexandrine Parakeet	*Psittacula eupatria*	O-honsei-inko	E2

☐ Plum or Blossom-headed Parakeet	*Psittacula cyanocephala*	Kosei-inko	E2
☐ Mustached or Red-breasted Parakeet	*Psittacula alexandri*	Daruma-inko	E2
☐ Monk Parakeet	*Myiopsitta monachus*	Okina-inko	E2
☐ Red-billed Leiothrix	*Leiothrix lutea*	Soushicho	E2
☐ Green-backed Tit	*Parus monticolus*	Kibara-shijukara	E1
☐ Red-headed Bunting	*Emberiza bruniceps*	Chyakincho	E1
☐ Red-crested Cardinal	*Paroaria coronata*	Kokancho	E2
☐ European Goldfinch	*Carduelis carduelis*	Goshiki-hiwa	E1
☐ Orange-cheeked Waxbill	*Estrilda melpoda*	Hokocho	E2
☐ Black-rumped Waxbill	*Estrilda troglodytes*	Kaedecho	E2
☐ White-throated Munia	*Lonchura malabarica*	Ginbashi	E2
☐ Masked Weaver	*Ploceus intermedius*	Men-hataoridori	E2
☐ Red Bishop	*Euplectes orix*	Kinrancho	E2
☐ Green Indigo-bird	*Vidua chalybeata*	Shikoncho	E2
☐ Pin-tailed Whydah	*Vidua macroura*	Tennincho	E2
☐ Paradise Whydah	*Vidua paradisea*	Houojaku	E2
☐ Asian Pied Starling	*Sturnus contra*	Hojiro-mukudori	E1
☐ Common Myna	*Acridotheres tristis*	Indohakka	E2
☐ Taiwan Blue Magpie	*Urocissa caerulea*	Sanjaku	E2

List of Mammals Mentioned in the Text

ENGLISH NAME	SCIENTIFIC NAME	JAPANESE NAME
Ryukyu Fruit Bat	*Pteropus dasymallus*	O-komori
Japanese Macaque	*Macaca fuscata*	Nihonzaru
[Wolf	*Canis lupus*	Nihon-o-kami]
Racoon Dog	*Nycteuretes procyonoides*	Tanuki
Red Fox	*Vulpes vulpes*	Kitsune
Brown Bear	*Ursus arctos*	Higuma
Asiatic Black Bear	*Selenarctos thibetanus*	Tsukinowaguma
[?Sea Otter	*Enhydra lutris*	Rakko]
Otter	*Lutra lutra*	Nihon-kawa-uso

Yellow Marten	*Martes melampus*	Ten
Sable	*Martes zibellina*	Kuro-ten
Badger	*Meles meles*	Ana-guma
*Mink	*Mustela vison*	Minku
*Masked Palm Civet	*Paguma larvata*	Hakubishin
Small-eared cat	*Felis bengalensis*	Tsushima-yamaneko
Iriomote Wild Cat	*Mayailurus iriomotensis*	Iriomote-yamaneko
Northern Fur Seal	*Callorhinus ursinus*	Ottosei
Steller's Sea Lion	*Eumetopias jubata*	Todo
Ribbon Seal	*Phoca fasciata*	Kurakake-azarashi
Harbor Seal	*Phoca vitulina*	Gomafu-azarashi
Kurile Seal	*Phoca kurilensis*	Zenigata-azarashi
Pacific White-sided Dolphin	*Lagenorhynchus obliquidens*	Kama-iruka
Wild Boar	*Sus scrofa*	Inoshishi
Sika Deer	*Cervus nippon*	Shika
Japanese Serow	*Capricornis crispus*	Kamoshika
*Formosan Tree-squirrel	*Callosciurus caniceps*	Taiwan-risu
Giant Flying Squirrel	*Petaurista leucogenys*	Musasabi
Flying Squirrel	*Pteromys volans*	Momonga
Japanese Squirrel	*Sciurus lis*	Nihon-risu
Red Squirrel	*Sciurus vulgaris*	Ezo-risu
Asiatic Chipmunk	*Tamias sibiricus*	Shima-risu
*Muskrat	*Ondatra zibethicus*	Masukuratto
Tree Rat	*Rattus legatus*	Kenaga-nezumi
Amami Spinous Mouse	*Tokudaia osimensis*	Amami-togenezumi
Japanese Dormouse	*Glirulus japonicus*	Yamane
*Nutria	*Myocastor coypus*	Nutoria
Asiatic Pika	*Ochotona hyperborea*	Naki-usagi
Japanese Hare	*Lepus brachyurus*	No-usagi
Arctic Hare	*Lepus timidus*	Yuki-usagi
Amami Black Rabbit	*Pentelagus furnessi*	Amami-no-kuro-usagi

Bibliography

Anon. *Okinawa by Road: A Traveller's Guide to the Island*. Tokyo: Kume, 1985.

Bassin, G. *The Tokyo Transit Book*. Tokyo: The Japan Times, 1983.

Bisignani, J. D. *The Japan Handbook*. Tokyo: The Japan Times, 1983.

Brazil, M. A. "Bird-watching Year in Hokkaido," in *Birding* 18 (2) (1986): 91–97.

—— . "Mixed Fortunes for the Japanese Crane," in *Wildlife* 25 (19) (1983): 369–71.

—— . "Owl of the Setting Sun (Blakiston's Fish Owl)," in *BBC Wildlife* 3 (3) (1985): 110–15.

—— . "Sea-Eagle Sunrise (Steller's Sea Eagle)," in *BBC Wildlife* 4 (12) (1986): 588–92.

—— . *The Birds of Japan: A Checklist*. 2nd edition, 1986.

—— . "The Endemic Birds of the Nansei Shoto," in *World Wildlife Fund Japan: Conservation of the Nansei Shoto, Part 2* (1985), 11–35.

Britton, D., and Hayashida, T. *The Japanese Crane: Bird of Happiness*. Tokyo and New York: Kodansha International, 1981.

Clements, J. *Birds of the World: A Checklist*. New York: Facts on File, 1981.

Environment Agency. *The Birds and Terrestrial Mammals of Japan*. Tokyo: Environment Agency, 1976.

Fodor's Japan, 1986. New York: McKay, 1986.

Hotta, A., with Ishiguro, Y. *A Guide to Japanese Hot Springs*. Tokyo and New York: Kodansha International, 1986.

Imaizumi, Y. *Colored Illustrations of the Mammals of Japan* (in Japanese). Osaka: Hoikusha, 1960.

Kodansha Encyclopedia of Japan. Tokyo: Kodansha, 1983.

Kuroda, N. (ed.). *Seibutsu daizukan: Chorui* (Wildlife Guide: Birds). Tokyo: Sekai Bunkasha, 1984.

Maeda, S. *The Nippon Alps: Kamikochi*. Tokyo: Graphic-sha, 1984.

Mapple–Nippon 1:250,000. Tokyo: Shobunsha, 1985.

Matsuda, T., and Fujimaki, Y. *Hokkaido tancho gaido* (Birdwatching Guide to Hokkaido). Sapporo: Hokkaido Shinbunsha, 1984.

Matsui, M. *Nihon no dobutsu* (Japanese Animals). Tokyo: Shogakkan, 1976.

McQueen, I. *Japan: A Travel Survival Kit*. Victoria, Australia: Lonely Planet Press, 1986.

Minato, M. (ed.). *Japan and Its Nature*. Tokyo: Heibonsha, 1977

Noh, T., and Kimura, J. C. (eds.). *Japan: A Regional Geography of an Island Nation.* Tokyo: Teikoku-shoin, 1983.

Okinawa Yacho Kenkyukai. *Okinawa-ken no yacho* (The Birds of Okinawa). Tomigusuku-son, Okinawa: Okinawa Yacho Kenkyukai, 1986.

Ornithological Society of Japan. *Checklist of Japanese Birds.* Tokyo: Gakken, 1974.

Reischauer, E. O. *The Japanese.* Tokyo and Rutland, Vermont: Charles E. Tuttle, 1978.

Takedatsu, M., and Ogawa, I. 1981. *Hokkaido no tori* (Popular Birds of Hokkaido). Sapporo: Hokkaido University Press, 1981.

Tsujii, T., Fujita, I., and Ogawa, I. *Hokkaido shizen gaido* (Nature Guide to Hokkaido). Sapporo: Hokkaido Shinbunsha, 1982.

Voous, K. H. *List of Recent Holarctic Birds Species.* London: British Ornithologists' Union, 1980.

Wild Bird Society of Japan. *Chorui hanshoku chizu chosa, 1978* (The Breeding Bird Survey in Japan, 1978). Tokyo: WBSJ, 1980.

——— . *A Field Guide to the Birds of Japan.* Tokyo and New York: WBSJ and Kodansha International, 1982.

——— . *Concise Guide to Waterbirds* and *Concise Guide to Land Birds* (in Japanese). Tokyo: WBSJ, 1983.

——— . *Nihon no tancho- chi 777.* Vol. 1: *Hokkaido to Tohoku;* Vol. 2: *Kanto to Chubu;* Vol. 3: *Kinki Isei.* (Birdwatching Guide to Japan Vols. 1, 2, and 3; in Japanese). Tokyo: WBSJ, 1984.

Wild Bird Society of Japan, Sapporo Chapter. *Sapporo no badowochingu gaido* (Birdwatching in Sapporo). Sapporo: WBSJ, 1983.

Weatherly, J. K. *Japan Unescorted.* Tokyo and New York: Kodansha International and Japan Air Lines, 1986.

Yamashina, Y. *Birds in Japan: A Field Guide.* Tokyo: Shubun International, 1982.

Yamashina Institute for Ornithology. *Nihon no kyorui hyoshiki chosa (1961–83)* (Japanese Bird Banding in Recent Years [1961–83]). Abiko: Bird Migration Research Center, Yamashina Institute for Ornithology, 1985.

Index to Bird Species and Sites

An asterisk indicates that the name was misapplied in the first edition of the *Field Guide to the Birds of Japan*.
Parentheses are used around parts of names that are now commonly dropped by many birders.